A History to Remember

A History to Remember

TCU in Purple, White, and Black

Frederick W. Gooding Jr.

Sylviane Ngandu-Kalenga Greensword

Marcellis R. Perkins

TCU Press

Fort Worth, Texas

TCU 150 1873–2023

Library of Congress Cataloging-in-Publication Data

Names: Gooding, Frederick W., Jr., author. | Greensword, Sylviane Ngandu-Kalenga, 1982- author. | Perkins, Marcellis, 1996- author.
Title: A history to remember : TCU in purple, white, and Black / Frederick W. Gooding Jr., Sylviane Ngandu-Kalenga Greensword, Marcellis Perkins.
Description: Fort Worth, Texas : TCU Press, [2023] | Includes bibliographical references. | Summary: "This book chronicles, contextualizes and organizes the underexplored history of African American memory at TCU. This work makes a new contribution by focusing specifically upon the understudied role of Blacks generally within TCU lore, whether it be through the student, staff, faculty, administrator or alumni perspective. Anyone interested in race relations, memory and North Texas history will find both the text and its layered analytical approach appealing. Readers can immediately relate to the historical and social significance of African Americans based upon the following distinct points: 1) the collective African American presence has steadily grown in significance and size, 2) chronicling the African American experience at TCU provides an opportunity to analyze and assess whether TCU is fulfilling its Vision in Action, and 3) charting TCU's growth in diversity reverberates greatly locally and regionally given TCU's established position in North Texas and its overall potential for influence"– Provided by publisher.
Identifiers: LCCN 2022046782 | ISBN 9780875658452 (hardback)
Subjects: LCSH: Texas Christian University–Students–History. | College integration–Texas–Fort Worth–History. | African American students–Education (Higher)–Texas–Fort Worth–History. | College students, Black–Education (Higher)–Texas–Fort Worth–History.
Classification: LCC LD5311.T382 G66 2023 | DDC 378.764/5315–dc23/eng/20220928
LC record available at https://lccn.loc.gov/2022046782

TCU Press

TCU Box 298300
Fort Worth, Texas 76129

Design by Bill Brammer

To my son, Frederick W. Gooding III, who, too,
will forever be a part of TCU Black history.

—FREDERICK W. GOODING JR.

To my parents, Professor Pius Ngandu Nkashama
and Maman "Godée" Godeliève Kalenga, who taught me
the importance of history and storytelling.

—SYLVIANE NGANDU-KALENGA GREENSWORD

To my family: You were with me every step of the journey.
There will never be enough words to express my thank you.

—MARCELLIS R. PERKINS

Why We Capitalize *Black*

The spelling of *Black* with a capital B denotes that we are talking about more than just a color, but a set of lived experiences shared among those who identify as Black American in this country. Although this can be true for people with white skin as well, we do not capitalize the w, as that form has long been used by white supremacy groups. Plus, Black is often used as an identifying adjective when most aspects of mainstream culture were not only white-dominated, but considered the default for normal. The distinctiveness of the Black experience is in part forged by the exclusion from normative white experience and culture. Finally, we wish to recognize that while many Black Americans may share commonalities across their varied life experiences, not all Black individuals located in the United States of America necessarily originally hail from America. This designation thereby allows for recognition of the diversity of the diaspora that stretches outward from the continent of Africa into all parts of the globe, including the Caribbean.*

*See generally, Keishel Williams, "For Some Children of Immigrants, 'African American' Doesn't Fit Their Unique, Black Experiences in the US," *Yahoo!* News, July 16, 2021, https://news.yahoo.com/children-immigrants-african-american-doesnt-191638747.html.

Land Acknowledgment

As a university, we acknowledge the many benefits we have of being in this place. It is a space we share with all living beings, human and nonhuman. It is an ancient space where others have lived before us. The monument created jointly by TCU and the Wichita and Affiliated Tribes reminds us of our benefits, responsibilities, and relationships. We pause to reflect on its words:

This ancient land, for all our relations.

We respectfully acknowledge all Native American peoples who have lived on this land since time immemorial. TCU especially acknowledges and pays respect to the Wichita and Affiliated Tribes, upon whose historical homeland our university is located.

A Word about the N-word

Within this text, the reader will readily find not only several references to the n-word, but will find it spelled out in its full form (i.e., n-i-g-g-e-r). We wish to apprise the reader ahead of time that while our current society may frown upon its public use for numerous reasons that continue to be debated, what we do know is that it was employed with all of its pejorative implications during the thick of the Jim Crow era on TCU's campus, at the very minimum via TCU publications like the student newspaper the *Skiff* and the *TCU Horned Frog* yearbook. If and when the reader discovers the n-word, it will only be because we as the authors and editors decided against censoring the hard truths of the past. The word was indeed used by TCU students. The word was indeed used by Texas residents. The word was indeed used by many American citizens during that time. Thus, for us to reprint the original text of an authentic source and alter the appearance of this word is to inject our current perspective on that of the past. To avoid this conflict, we simply will allow the past to speak for itself. We will then allow the reader to draw their own conclusions.

FOREWORD

Reflection, Recovery, and Remembrance as a Path to Racial Healing

In 1869, just four years after the end of the Civil War, Addison and Randolph Clark began envisioning the establishment of a coeducational school in rural northeast Texas where students could earn degrees and cultivate character. That higher education institution would eventually be known as Texas Christian University (TCU). On the current "Mission & History" page of TCU's website, the Clark brothers are lauded as "Fort Worth-based minister-teachers."[1] One must click the "Diversity, Equity & Inclusion" (DEI) tab to find the more complex history of the institution's founders: the Clark brothers, members of a slaveholding family and veterans of the Confederate army, created a college for young *white* men and women in 1873.[2]

TCU's DEI webpage also offers insights into the institution's Black history through the "Race and Reconciliation Initiative Names Chair; Hosts First Town Hall" link where in the "First Year Survey Report," one can learn of the Black wage workers who were employed at the institution by the early 1900s, of the early twentieth-century initiatives that allowed limited enrollment of Black students in special programs, and of the trustees' 1964 decision to desegregate the institution.[3] The Race and Reconciliation Initiative was established in 2020, the same year that the murders of African Americans, including Ahmaud Arbery in Georgia, Breonna Taylor in Kentucky, and George Floyd in Minnesota, sparked global protests and calls for accountability and justice. As TCU began examining its history of racism, enslavement, and the Confederacy, a global pandemic was killing millions of people and shutting down nearly everything everywhere, a conflux of recurring racism and significant suffering that offered the public time to reflect and then remember or recover the things they or others had wanted them to forget or never know. In that historic moment of reflection and resolve, TCU's administration publicly acknowledged that the institution's narrative is incomplete, and that racial healing is essential for the development of an inclusive campus community.

This volume of essays invites readers into that historical space of incompleteness through a meticulous documentation of TCU's evolution from a small Reconstruction-era conservative Christian coed school for white students, supported by the labor of Black wage workers, to a twenty-first century predominately white higher education institution committed to reconciliation and racial healing. It centers the Black experience in this approach in a state where the history of Black people is often hidden—such as the recently recovered Sugar Land 95 burial ground where convicted laborers leased to work for the state on a plantation were interred in unmarked graves.[4] Contributions to this volume are recovering Black TCU history in a state where the stories of Black life can be distorted—such as the characterization of enslaved Africans forcibly transported to America in the belly of slave ships as "immigrants" and "workers" in a textbook used in the Texas school system.[5] Before racial healing can occur, however, the institution must engage in truth-telling that includes an acknowledgment of the psychological, socioeconomic, and spiritual impact of practices and policies that have caused harm to Black Americans at TCU, in the local community, and in the nation throughout history.

Through an engagement in the public accounting of its complex history, TCU joins a global network of higher education institutions that are recovering, remembering, and recreating narratives informed by multiperspectivity. This methodology is grounded in the belief that history is most effectively learned through an embrace of a multivocal approach that values voices that have been overlooked or marginalized in traditional narratives. Listening to the voices that emerge in *A History to Remember: TCU in Purple, White, and Black* shifts the experiences of Black people in the institution's history from the shadows to the forefront. In so doing, it makes the path to reconciliation and racial healing possible.

— RHONDDA ROBINSON THOMAS

Calhoun Lemon Professor of Literature
Clemson University

Author of *Call My Name, Clemson: Documenting the Black Experience in an American University Community*

Notes

1. "Our History Starts with a Family," Mission & History, Texas Christian University, accessed September 18, 2022, https://www.tcu.edu/about/mission-history.php.

2. "Race & Reconciliation First Year Survey Report, April 21, 2021," Race & Reconciliation Initiative, Texas Christian University, accessed September 18, 2022, https://www.tcu.edu/race-reconciliation-initiative/files/rri-first-year-survey-report.pdf.

3. "Race & Reconciliation First Year Survey Report, April 21, 2021."

4. "The Sugar Land 95," Convict Leasing and Labor Project, accessed September 18, 2022, https://www.cllptx.org/sugarland95.

5. Michael Schaub, "Texas textbook calling slaves 'immigrants' to be changed, after mom's complaint," *Los Angeles Times*, October 5, 2015, accessed September 18, 2022, https://www.latimes.com/books/jacketcopy/la-et-jc-texas-textbook-calls-slaves-immigrants-20151005-story.html.

Acknowledgments

I am firstly thankful to my colleague Dan Williams who first expressed belief in this project. Thank you Teresa Dahlberg for your research support as well. While we three coauthors composed our own text from our own research, we also benefitted from the archival research of other colleagues, most especially those who worked under the direction of TCU's Race & Reconciliation Initiative. All of these individuals are listed in our Appendix and are greatly appreciated. Further, this book would not be possible without the kind and consistent contributions from Mary Couts Burnett Library staff, and it is necessary to single out Mary Saffell as the library team member to whom we are most indebted. Finally, I am proud and appreciative of the combined efforts of my co-collaborators, Sylviane Greensword and Marcellis "Mr. Marvelous" Perkins—their synergy, enthusiasm, and passion for creating a space and place to talk about TCU and the Black experience warms me still.

—FREDERICK W. GOODING JR.

Introduction

Why Do We Call Graduation "Commencement"?

At many institutions of higher learning across the nation, when students have finished their academic obligations and prepare to be publicly recognized for their diligent study, quite often such graduation ceremonies will employ the word "commencement" to best describe the event. The irony of course being that, far from commencing or starting again, the student is primed and ready to celebrate the conclusion of their studious role and expects to be relieved of their attendant scholarly obligations (i.e., coursework and exams). In actuality, the word "commencement" signifies the beginning of a new chapter within the student's life, one that includes reconciling a new relationship with an institution that never really ends in the purest sense—the student and the school will be forever linked moving forward (most especially if the student moves on to accomplish anything noteworthy). Thus, while the student celebrates the end of coursework and exams, their relationship with their alma mater in so many ways is only just beginning.

How appropriate for us to contemplate the beginning of a new relationship literally at your, the reader's, fingertips! While this book physically represents the end of research, writing, and scholarly collaboration for a particular and finite book project, in actuality it is only the beginning of an important conversation that will only continue to develop, evolve, and expand over time.

In other words, this book was never designed to be exhaustive. Instead, it represents a historical accounting of the collective Black American experience as filtered through the more specific lens of Texas Christian University (TCU).

TCU is a university like so many others—it has its dedicated campus, thriving student population, and growing reputation to constantly manage. Thus, there is nothing singularly unique about TCU insofar as it is an institution dedicated to the principle of education like so many others. Yet, what is distinctive is that TCU has its own particular, specialized, and nuanced history behind how it seeks to fulfill its dedication to education as guided by the motto, *Disciplina est Facultas*, or "Learning is Power."

While TCU's history as an institution begins in 1873, essentially right when the Civil War's failed Reconstruction period was drawing to a close (i.e., 1865–1877), its location in the relatively isolated northern region of Texas was an important factor that helped shape the early growth and independent development of TCU. There were few options for higher education in North Texas when TCU opened, and to date, TCU easily stands as the largest institution of higher education within the Fort Worth metropolitan area. While TCU does have peer and aspirant institutions, as a private university it was relatively free to grow at its own pace, as opposed to a University of Texas, which observes a different relationship with the public as the state university system's flagship.

This pace of growth, especially as it relates to Black Americans, is what interests us here. Thus, while this book

Above
TCU's school motto is reflected by the iconic and beloved Frog Fountain, which has become an enduring symbol of growth and change. *Courtesy of TCU Photo Collection.*

necessarily invokes TCU history, the book does not center the higher-education institution of TCU as the "protagonist." But rather, what we seek to do in this book is provide a bit more historical context for how Black Americans specifically experienced TCU over time in light of larger societal changes and specific policy changes at TCU. This book does not serve as a compendium for every single Black name ever affiliated with TCU—nor should it have to do so. By simply looking at TCU through the perspective of the Black experience, we wish to spotlight the interiority[1] of this specific experience.

Leveraging numerous data sources—including two key, student-driven source documents in the TCU *Horned Frog* yearbook and the school newspaper the *Skiff*—the student voices themselves help paint the picture that as a private, Predominately White Institution (PWI)[2] in North Texas, TCU at times struggled with a lack of education in, exposure to, and experience with Black culture—although we do not suggest that TCU as an institution has remained racially recalcitrant over the years. Segregation was the norm everywhere all the way through the 1960s, with such practices not just limited to Texas nor just to the South; TCU unfortunately also fell prey to such anti-blackness.

It is indisputable that efforts have been made to improve race relations on campus. In fact in fall 2018, "TCU became the first university in the country to have pillars created to represent the National Panhellenic Council (NPHC)," with NPHC membership featuring nine historically Black American founded fraternities and sororities.[3] However, while it would be easy to satisfy apologists and point to recently instituted policies or several physical campus changes as "proof" that TCU has always harbored good intentions when it comes to contemporary race relations, that would not be quite accurate. There are indeed some embarrassing and dark chapters within TCU's past when it comes to race relations, but we explore aspects of this history (though not all) only to help contextualize our overarching focus, which is the Black experience. By centering the Black experience in this historical accounting, we offer yet another tool with which one can qualitatively measure TCU's growth—or change over time—outside of traditional metrics of student body size, size of endowment, size of grant dollars awarded to faculty, and so on.

From a strictly quantitative perspective, we do know that TCU is ranked within the top one hundred colleges and universities (according to *U.S. News and World Report*),[4] and that its tuition is, shall we say, *not insignificant*.[5] We also know that TCU as a PWI simply has had limited Black input or influence up until this point in time. With this book, we aim to flesh out the contours of this influence. By studying TCU's past relationship with Black Americans, we raise tough questions about the prospects of Black presence within TCU's future: will such presence on campus merely be tepidly tolerated,[6] or will it be enthusiastically encouraged?

In the process, we plan to share what we learned about some trailblazing, sacrificial, and dedicated individuals who helped TCU grow through both individual and collective efforts. Moreover, this book is not just about Black students, alumni, staff, and faculty making headway and achievements within a racial vacuum simply for the sake of it, but rather, this is a story of continued struggle against larger societal forces that presented friction along the way. The university thus plays a key role in reflecting the story of continued struggle that we share here. In sharing this story, do note that events closest in time to our publication date are relatively "new," do not benefit from multiple insights, perspective, and cross-references that might help us make sense of their relative importance; consequently they receive less attention from us within these pages. Yet, at every step of the way, we wish to analyze and learn how and why some patterns appear so stubbornly persistent when it comes to race relations with Black Americans, despite the actions and changes of an institution willing to change. Hence, we plan to study not just change over time, but also *consistency over time*. In other words, we wish to take full stock of what has changed and what has not as we collectively consider new areas for additional growth.

A Bit about TCU

Texas Christian University. Whether it be three words, or three letters (i.e., TCU), within the North Texas community and increasingly beyond, the colors purple and white carry currency, significance, and meaning to many. TCU has changed in size, structure, and scholarly offerings over the years since its founding in 1873. From the expansion of its physical footprint to the explosion of its athletic popularity to the burgeoning growth of its Honors College (and attendant academic reputation), its Nursing and Medical School expansions, and its business school's nationwide recognition, TCU has only continued to grow in prominence ever since its humble beginnings with only a handful of students in Thorp Spring, Texas.

Technically, the educational institution that would later become TCU started in Fort Worth, but was not always situated within Fort Worth. What began as an effort to make classical, character-building education more accessible in North Texas[7] was a relatively humble effort by the Clark brothers Addison and Randolph to educate just thirteen students in 1869 at the Male and Female Seminary of Fort Worth.

Exponential growth demanded that less than five years later, in 1873, they move to a larger facility in Thorp Spring, Texas, to best accommodate their 450 students under a new charter as Add-Ran Male and Female College. Located in Hood County, Thorp Spring is roughly forty miles southwest of Fort Worth, where it "had been a camping place and council ground for the Comanches before the whites took their hunting grounds."[8] To their relief, the Brothers Clark found refuge in the sleepy town of Thorp Spring in efforts to escape non-Christian influences (i.e., drinking, smoking, gambling, and the like) observed near "Hell's Half Acre," the nickname earned by Fort Worth's "boisterous" red-light district, where the dynamics of a free-wheeling rancher culture intersected with the parasitic diversions accompanying the new Texas and Pacific Railway depot.[9]

The Clarks initially received the endorsement of the Disciples of Christ church, but they still controlled and operated the school during the formative stages. After striking a deal of endowment support with the Disciples of Christ to ensure its long-term future, yet another charter was commissioned in 1889, thereby rebranding the institution as Add-Ran Christian University.[10] After drafting the new 1889 charter, the Brothers Clark gave the institution entirely over to the Disciples of Christ.[11] The institution moved again to Waco, Texas, in 1895, where it began to morph in form and function, taking on intercollegiate sports and a mascot (i.e., the fierce and fearsome horned frog) and changing its name to Texas Christian University in 1902. TCU moved back to Fort Worth from Waco in 1910 after a devastating fire.

Just as fire can have fertilizing qualities,[12] TCU has only continued to grow well after the Waco fire, even earning the tongue-in-cheek nickname, "Texas Construction University,"[13] based upon the feverish rate of new buildings erected as the university continues to expand its trademark gold-brick footprint. In addition to its widening physical footprint from the initial gift of fifty acres by the city of Fort Worth,[14] TCU has

Above
TCU cofounder, Addison Clark.
Courtesy of TCU Photo Collection.

Above
TCU cofounder, Randolph Clark.
Courtesy of TCU Photo Collection.

only continued to grow in its size and national reputation as a mid-sized liberal arts institution. While ever-anxious administrators are likely to disagree with the following statement, given its relative value to other institutions ahead of it within national rankings, TCU's $2 billion-plus dollar endowment positions it quite well for long-term sustainability.[15]

Despite its humble beginnings of only thirteen students, as of fall 2019 TCU boasted a total undergraduate and graduate student population of 11,024 students with 698 full-time faculty. While classified as a PWI, or Predominately White Institution, TCU's official website labeled *Quick Facts* touts that "1 in 4 are students of color."[16] What started off as a completely all-white school has morphed over time into an institution more reflective of the modern era.

Yet such growth is by no means complete—growing pains are bound to continue as members of the TCU community wrestle with ideas about how it can continue to prosper and develop in a healthy manner. As of fall 2021, TCU was host to a student body that was listed as 65.5% White, 15.8% Hispanic/Latino, 4.7% International (not specified), 2.8% Asian (not specified), 0.3% American Indian/Alaska Native, and roughly 5.2% Black.[17] Nonetheless, of this total Black population, the local newspaper, the *Fort Worth Star-Telegram*, reported in 2018 that over one-third of all undergraduate Black males were classified as scholarship athletes,[18] suggesting that still more work can be done to truly diversify the student body—most especially when it comes to including members of the Black "middle class experience"—a problem facing many institutions of similar ilk.[19]

After all, when a four-year commitment will cost paying families upwards of a quarter-million dollars for an undergraduate education, without significant scholarship aid TCU remains a financial possibility for only so many families. Arguably, affluent families need education too, and there is no shame—only honor—in pursuing a high-quality education. Yet the reality is such that the two intersecting identities of class and race doubtless play a factor in how TCU looks, feels, and operates. In fact, TCU does not look the way it does by accident! Both Southern Methodist University (#23) and TCU (#35) were among the thirty-eight schools across the country that had more students from families of the nation's top 1 percent earners than from the bottom 60 percent, according to a 2017 *New York Times* article.[20] Thus, if Black Americans have traditionally had limited access to TCU or to the socioeconomic channels that funnel into TCU, then in terms of pure quantitative analysis, the TCU Black American experience itself may be limited.

For approximately three-fifths, or nearly 60 percent of TCU's 150-year history, Black students were not fully enrolled or recognized as students. This absence creates a considerable gap. Yet Black people still made contact with the campus and touched various parts of the early university's operation. Hence, the purpose of this book is to provide a proper platform whereby the collective Black experience at TCU can not only be documented, but also shared. Undoubtedly, TCU founders Addison and Randolph Clark deserve credit for opening up their educational institution to both women and men from the very inception. Surprisingly, there was a time and space when the seemingly obvious decision to open up an institution of higher learning to half the population was considered "forward thinking," and TCU was one of the few institutions west of the Mississippi to do such a thing.[21]

However, nearly a century would pass after TCU's founding (i.e., ninety-one years) before TCU hosted its first cohort of full-time, fully enrolled Black American students in credit-bearing classes in 1964. Once Black Americans touched upon the campus academically, athletically, artistically, and administratively, the institution simply has not been the same. TCU has evolved as a direct result—for the better—and it is time to properly document this fascinating change over time.

A Bit about Black Americans

Memories are deceptively complex in that they can exist in two spheres: 1) objectively as an event transpired or as a person lived, 2) subjectively as one chooses how to remember the person or event. Take for example, a parent has a child who has their first birthday. The child being born on say, September 14, is an objective, observable phenomena. Birth certificate records either can confirm or deny the occurrence of the nativity which resulted in the addition of another person on the planet. However, how the parent remembers the birthday is another matter entirely.

TCU, incidentally, celebrates the culmination of 150 birthdays during the 2023 calendar year with its sesquicentennial celebration. How and what TCU chooses to celebrate and emphasize is what remains to be seen. With ample material to choose from over a century and a half period, deciding what is representative and how to share it are not simple questions.

Hence our contribution here: we seek to add to the conversation by endeavoring to flesh out yet another perspective—a Black perspective—with which to tell the TCU story.

A word here on the value of memory is important because nostalgia can be a powerful drug that is not objective in the least. Meaning that when people reminisce, they may only remember parts of a story, parts that may be selective based upon the individual's preferences. And the sum of so many moments big and small over a four-year period is so great that it is not unusual for alumni to distill their TCU experience into to a few key memories that stand out as the steady passage of time softens our grip on detail. Many alumni may "only recall" great memories of their experience and may not remember or focus upon the negative aspects—especially those negative aspects that mostly concerned other people. Hence it may be difficult to engender sympathy for racial tensions experienced by younger Black Americans currently on campus among older white alumni who can remember nothing but a "good experience" while at TCU. Further, it may be difficult to process the idea that while one was having "a great experience" at TCU that others experienced discomfort—or even trauma.[22] We acknowledge that it is possible for both stories to coexist *and be true* at the same time; there is no one singular story.

Hence, when we talk about telling TCU's story in purple, white, and Black, it is also important to parse out the complexity of the Black American experience. "Black American" is a term commonly used within formal writings to describe individuals whose ancestors hail from the Black diaspora, or movement of bodies from the originating point of the continent of Africa. Rather than be more country specific (i.e., Italian American or German American), Black American is a designation that encompasses an entire continental mass. Because of the enormity of the continent of Africa, calling someone Black American may also be an awfully polite way of indicating that the individual has non-white skin. Yet "Africa" is vague in pinpointing positionality. North Africa encompasses a vastly different region and mix of countries and cultures distinct from West Africa, whereas West Africa is regionally distinct from East Africa, and so forth. So "African American" is an identifying term largely used for those of the African diaspora who live in the United States of America.

For our purposes with this book, while vague, Black American ironically is a broader, more inclusive, and more accurate term to describe an increasingly international population on TCU's campus. Thus, one can be from the twin island republic of Trinidad & Tobago, be of the Black diaspora, and yet not be African American, per se. Trinidad, for example, is its own sovereign nation separate from the United States of America. It has its own culturally specific markers of national flag, national bird, national anthem, etcetera. Yet Trinidad is not unique, as there are several Caribbean nations and, in the African continent, over fifty countries. In other words, three students from Ghana, Nigeria, and Tunisia would all be considered Black Americans and not African Americans, with the latter term used almost exclusively for people of the Black diaspora born in America.

Finally, the encompassing term "Black" allows for us to unify a group based upon shared experiences, as international locality has ironically been used by whites to artificially create confusing barriers and hierarchies of value. It is perversely ironic to note, however, that people who "appeared Black" were not subjected to anti-Blackness if they were able to prove that they were not originally from the United States. For instance, in 1948 the National Committee on Segregation in the Nation's Capital issued a report that addressed the confusing dance of American race relations when it reported that "four Negro students from the British West Indies sat at a downtown lunch counter. The waitress informed them they would have to stand to receive service. But when they produced their British diplomatic passes, she apologized, remarking she didn't realize they were 'not niggers.'"[23]

This vulgar anecdote reminds us that often in the United States of America during the height of Jim Crow segregation, being Black was not as problematic as being both Black *and* American, especially if asserting or claiming the benefits of full American citizenship. It follows that although we use the term "Black" to be inclusive of several related, but distinct cultural experiences, the use of the word "integration" throughout this text almost always specifically refers to *Black American* integration on TCU's Fort Worth campus. After all, some international non-white students and faculty were part of TCU's campus climate well before Black American integration in the 1960s, with Abdullah Ben Kori's 1905 employment from Syria as an example.[24] However, it appears most anti-integration sentiments discovered in our research were focused upon Black American participation closest to home.

The Road Ahead

Thus as we reflect upon TCU's history in "purple, white, and Black," we start with TCU's inaugural Race and Reconciliation Initiative (RRI) Postdoctoral Fellow, Dr. Sylviane Greensword, who in *Chapter 1: Humble Beginnings*, illustrates how even though not formally enrolled, the Black fingerprint was ever-present in the early architecture and maintenance of the educational enterprise later christened as *TCU*.

Then in *Chapter 2: Breakthroughs*, RRI Graduate Research Assistant, Marcellis Perkins, answers numerous questions regarding the journeys of brave and valiant souls who dared to be among the first within TCU's legacy. Next, TCU's Dr. Ronald E. Moore Endowed Professor of the Humanities, Dr. Frederick Gooding Jr., delves a bit deeper into the choreography that resulted in sustained Black presence on campus in *Chapter 3: University Life*.

Mr. Perkins continues his important profiles of courage by exploring a key source of Black participation within TCU lore in *Chapter 4: Athletics*. Not to be facetious, but one simply wonders how much more different Black presence on campus would feel without the literal infusion of Black bodies into sports. It goes without saying that numerous Black bodies have contributed directly toward elevating the local profile and national brand through athletic competitive success, which still continues to pay dividends for TCU's visibility.

In *Chapter 5: Alumni*, Dr. Greensword, as Lead Researcher of the RRI's Oral History Project, provides readers with an intimate recounting of Black experiences by shining a light on previously unknown and unheralded individuals who, as TCU alumni, have both the standing and authority to share their perspective on what they saw, heard, and felt while students on TCU's campus. Their testimonies evidence TCU's "growing pains" as these former students, by their mere presence, challenged TCU to continue evolving on racial matters. Greensword then holds serve in *Chapter 6: Student Activity & Activism*, where she illustrates how once Black students became part of the tuition-paying population, they almost immediately did what they could to ingratiate themselves to their new environment while simultaneously shouldering the burden of teaching others about their experience—at an institution of higher learning that had been segregated for nearly a century.

Returning in 1910 after the Waco fire, TCU has been located in Fort Worth for over a century. Mr. Perkins explores the extent of TCU's relationship with the outlying and surrounding Black local enclaves in *Chapter 7: Community*. In addition to understanding to what degree TCU has connected successfully with the Black community, this chapter may lend insights into some of the structural barriers in creating a local pool of prospective TCU students. Low Black enrollment numbers (relative to their local population) may indicate that Black high school students just do not consider the largest university closest to them as a viable option. Given the continued underrepresentation of Black students on campus, however, this chapter may point out additional opportunities for growth.

Together, these chapters will guide the reader through a larger, exploratory inquiry about change over time; especially as seen through the prism of Black existence on a campus like TCU, from the postbellum era through the post-World War II stage and into the twenty-first century, with its sesquicentennial celebration. Thus, in *Chapter 8: Ongoing Challenges*, Gooding, as he does in the *Introduction*, will provide a bird's-eye view of some consistent and salient themes that help thread together the conversation about Black presence at TCU, for continued dialogue and conversation. Again, this book is neither dispositive nor definitive, but when it comes to Black American memory at TCU, and how should it be remembered and retold, we offer this book and the content herein simply as another suggested entry point. While the angles are manifold, we believe in time the truth shall be told.

The Story Thus Far

Various studies have endeavored to learn how people remember people, places, and events with results varying based upon individual location, disposition, frame of mind, and amount of activity during the memory's formation.[25] Yet when it comes to what a collective body remembers, or when the pronoun switches from "I," emphasizing the individual (e.g., "I remember") to "we," underscoring the whole (e.g., "We remember"), the memory often also begins to change. Thus, what the collective remembers *and how* the collective presents shared memory compared to how individuals preserve

Above
TCU's pristine Waco campus circa 1908, just two years before the devastating fire prompted its move to Fort Worth, TX. *Courtesy of TCU Photo Collection.*

their memories is another conversation entirely. So how do we remember Black history at TCU?

This work makes a new contribution by focusing upon the generally understudied role of Blacks within the TCU narrative, whether it be through the student, staff, faculty, or alumni perspective. Several books exist addressing aspects of TCU's specific history, with the recently published *Honors at TCU: Celebrating Fifty Years of Achievement* (TCU Press, 2019) likely coming closest to the scope of this proposed book. *Honors at TCU* charts and chronicles the growth and development of the John V. Roach Honors College as it has embraced its mission to help raise the academic profile of the university during its decade of existence.

But likely the first fully regarded history of TCU came through author Colby Hall, with his 1947 rendition of *History of Texas Christian University*. This thorough tome has many redeeming qualities, but seeing how the book was published nearly two decades before the university officially integrated, there is perhaps not much material to glean about the Black American experience at TCU.

The next major TCU historical offering, *Texas Disciples*, features author Colby Hall returning six years later in 1953 to add on to the historical record with a more nuanced portrait of the early history of the Disciples of Christ movement essential to TCU's identity. Of course, founding brother Randolph Clark first published a manuscript entitled *Reminiscences* in 1919—but while this reflection provides the best insight into the early history of the Clark family, it does not chronicle the development of TCU (which was still racially segregated at the time of publication).

Then in 1969, Joseph Lynn Clark published *Thank God We Made It! A Family Affair with Education*, adding on mostly to the Clark family history. Born in 1881, within TCU's early nurturing grounds of Thorp Spring, Joseph Lynn Clark was the nephew of TCU cofounder and Confederate Lieutenant Addison Clark and the son of TCU cofounder Randolph Clark. Joseph Lynn Clark not only ended up being a long-term faculty member at Sam Houston State University (despite obtaining his undergraduate bachelor's degree from TCU), but he also was a cofounder and member of the Texas Commission on Interracial Cooperation.[26]

In early 1974, Jerome A. Moore published a history covering TCU's inaugural century with *Texas Christian University: A Hundred Years of History*. While there was an opportunity for Moore in his book to speak to TCU's transition to integration within the previous years leading up to 1974, he simply chose to focus upon other aspects of TCU's history, given the limited resources likely available to him at that time. In 1986, Leonard Sanders and TCU Press offered *How Fort Worth Became the Texasmost City, 1849-1920*. While it does not provide significant revelations about the TCU Black experience, the book does provide additional historical context for the postbellum, Jim Crow society in which TCU was born.

Thus, thinking critically about TCU's Black history offers a creative but revealing lens toward understanding Black Americans' political and positional relationship within academia generally. By specifically analyzing Black presence at TCU over the years, this ambitious project seeks to make more explicit that which is perhaps hidden in plain view. The specific lens of Black history at TCU begs the question: "What does Black presence reflect and reinforce not only specifically about TCU, but about North Texan race relations generally?"

To engage this overarching query effectively, the book's structure will weave in and out of a historical framework first pioneered by TCU's Race & Reconciliation Initiative entitled *Operation: Triangulation*.[27] In looking at a vast time period spanning a century and a half, there are three key periods

Above
The RRI logo elegantly displays the ongoing, regenerative work of reconciliation by illustrating the iconic Frog Fountain as water plumes forever in motion. *Courtesy of TCU MKC.*

that will, in sum, provide a survey overview of the historical ground that TCU has covered. These three key historical periods, or "windows in time," point to larger themes that can be studied in additional detail, in time. The three periods are: 1) *The Founding Years: TCU, Slavery, and the Confederacy, 1861–1891*, 2) *Transition to Integration, 1941–1971*, and 3) *Recent but Related Histories, 1998–2020*. It is our hope that unifying these three perspectives will provide additional insight into the Black experience that currently plays an indelible part in the larger "TCU Experience." We return to the concept of reconciliation and TCU's efforts in this regard in Chapter 8.

As publicly shared narratives or school lore reflect and reinforce publicly shared sentiment about an institution, it is incumbent upon other members of the community to think critically about all the images created, depicted, celebrated, and lauded as part of TCU iconography. Along these lines, this book investigates the meaning of image, the symbology of inclusion, and the function of public memory in creating a larger TCU narrative that recognizes the Black experience. By leveraging principles of Black interiority,[28] this book explores the academic, athletic, artistic, and cultural impact of a group of people that was not formally included for nearly the first century of TCU's existence. Anyone interested in race relations, memory, and North Texas history will find both the text and its layered analytical approach appealing.

The Way It Was

In considering the Black experience at TCU, it may be no surprise that, as with many higher education institutions, TCU has both shining moments worthy of boastful pride and several dark, embarrassing chapters that should chasten even the most faithful for the road ahead. But as indicated earlier, when considering the query "What does Black presence reflect and reinforce not only specifically about TCU, but about North Texan race relations generally?" material we cover within this book's pages should not necessarily be applied only to TCU, but can be seen as a larger instructive commentary. In other words, an appreciation of the bigger picture will illustrate that to the extent that members of the TCU community abided by, tolerated, remained silent about, or in some cases, flat out explicitly expressed racist activity or sentiments, it was only because TCU was *not* exceptional; TCU was perhaps "normal."

What Do We Mean?

Unfortunately, as amazing as it is alarming, the Jim Crow segregation period that endured for roughly over half a century (i.e. 1896-1954) was considered "normal" in the immediate aftermath of a failed twelve-year Reconstruction. *How Fort Worth Became the Texasmost City* instructs that,[29] if anything, hell had only really begun for African Americans who, after the Era of Enslavement was formally concluded in late 1865, had to endure a volatile and unpredictable world that included, but was not limited to: Black Codes, convict leasing system, and the creation and early rise of the domestic terrorist organization founded by jilted former Confederate soldiers—the Ku Klux Klan (KKK). All the while, Black Americans were often saddled with the most dangerous and dirtiest jobs, were repeatedly subject to the fear of random and rampant lynchings, church bombings, and cross burnings, and were resigned to tolerate gross and unchecked racism, not to mention legally codified segregation.

Therefore, the concept of Black people obtaining an education to actually *be equal*, and not just "be free" from enslavement, was still foreign and controversial: "The establishment of Black education was much more than teaching the ABCs to little children of color. It was a political proposition. Black education helped define and forge the race relations that shaped the entire twentieth century and beyond."[30] In effect, Black education was a political issue that many schools like TCU simply avoided. To the point prior, TCU was enabled by a larger society whereby segregation became codified as a matter of law (as opposed to an informally observed, local custom or tradition) when the United States Supreme Court in 1896 decided in the case *Plessy v. Ferguson* that society should behave in a manner consistent with "separate, but equal."

Racial segregation, quite simply, was the lay of the land.

And segregation was the way it was, whether on TCU's campus or any other throughout the United States. TCU is located within the state of Texas, and Texas is located within the United States of America. Once again, if racism did manifest itself on TCU's campus through the expressions of its tuition-paying students, then such a moral failing falls both at the proverbial feet of TCU of course, but also at the feet of so many families who sent students from all over the country to matriculate through TCU. Thus, any racism that manifests itself at TCU is not TCU's alone. Many share in the need for repair.

But what was even worse was that TCU existed in a world where the Ku Klux Klan was not only paraded down Washington, DC's Pennsylvania Avenue in full view of the US Capitol, but was also featured and feted at the local state fair hosted in nearby Dallas, Texas, in 1923.[31] Due to Texas Senate Bill 3 being passed in 2021, if one is teaching K-12, one must take care not to produce guilt over certain historical topics, including the KKK.[32] It is the collective view of the coauthors that: 1) this book was not created to become part of any formal K-12 educational system, as it is published by TCU Press, and 2) if leveraging religious symbols as messages of fear on unarmed and unsuspecting families (i.e., a "burning cross"), bombing churches, and lynching individuals extrajudicially is wrong, then we believe the KKK is also wrong and feel little guilt if that last sentence produces any consternation. If anything, we feel horrible that fellow Americans were treated so horribly within their own country.

If the KKK was wrong, then racial violence was also wrong. Unfortunately, Tarrant County (i.e., where TCU is located within the city of Fort Worth) was not immune to such domestic terrorism. In December of 1921, Fort Worth resident Mr. Fred Rouse was killed outside of sanctioned legal means (i.e., lynched) just a mere ten-minute drive from TCU's campus. Racial discrimination was quite pervasive at that point in time.[33]

To be clear, KKK presence within Fort Worth was no passing fancy. Thanks in part to D. W. Griffith's *Birth of a Nation* (1915), which stylized hooded members of the Klan as heroes literally riding in on horses to save the damsel in distress (ironically from a "Black male" as portrayed by a white male in blackface), the Klan experienced a second wave resurgence that saw national attendance peak around four million in 1925.[34] Fort Worth was not immune to this fervor, with KKK members having "lit a thirty-five-foot cross on Camp Bowie Boulevard to mark the opening of their grand 'Beno Bazaar,' featuring carnival attractions, vaudeville acts, and other amusements as well as the giveaway of sixteen new Fords."[35] Rumors and whispers even swirled that longtime TCU professor (1899–1921) and short-time mayor of Fort Worth (1921–1924) E. R. Cockrell held Klan affiliations. There is no direct evidence establishing Cockrell's membership with any local KKK chapter, but given the fact that the KKK reached its political zenith around the time that he was in power as mayor, there is a good chance that he may have interacted with other Klan members—whether knowingly or not.[36]

Fortunately, change can indeed occur over time. Thus, an interesting development to keep watch on is how symbols formerly used for hate and division can be transformed to an opposite and even more powerful message of love and healing. A large Ku Klux Klavern, or meeting hall for Ku Klux Klan members, was built and utilized within the city of Fort Worth for official KKK purposes up until the 1920s. The Klavern was later sold to a pecan company and then fell into disrepair. However, as of this printing, TCU dance professor Adam McKinney, through his and his husband's tireless advocacy along with other strong community partners, was able to secure funds sufficient to purchase the building and plan to rename it the Fred Rouse Community Center for Arts and Healing.[37]

Healing is indeed required of many parts of Fort Worth and Tarrant County when it comes to Black citizens generally—from the fact that zip code 76104,[38] or the Stop Six[39] or Como neighborhoods—all relatively near TCU—remain mostly Black American and mostly under-resourced.

Speaking of nearby, Fort Worth's most prominent public pool at Forest Park is only minutes away from TCU's campus, nestled within a bucolic and well-appointed upper-middle-class neighborhood. It was also racially segregated up until the 1970s. Before it was integrated (which would be nearly two decades after the 1954 Supreme Court decision in *Brown v. Board of Education* that allowed for desegregation with "all deliberate speed"), the pool would open the facilities to tax-paying Black residents only on one day of the year—Juneteenth.[40]

Juneteenth, of course, is the local holiday that observes the date when Blacks in Texas finally learned about their freedom with the public announcement of General Order No. 3, on June 19, 1865. This event, traditionally observed by southwestern states, gained national prominence and became a federal holiday on June 19, 2021, thanks in part to nationally recognized efforts by Fort Worth resident Opal Lee. While having no official connection to TCU (although she was selected by the TCU Board of Trustees to receive an honorary doctorate in December 2021), Lee did network within the same Fort Worth community in which TCU is located, and as a solitary, single former educator, galvanized a larger political movement of national import and prominence—something that universities have the power to do as well.

Speaking of power, apparently the Black individuals who used the Forest Park pool on Juneteenth had the power to contaminate the water to the point that public park officials would drain the pool the following day, notwithstanding the disinfectant properties of the chlorine used as a standard tool in public pools since the 1890s.[41] TCU is located a mere mile away from Forest Park pool. While the Forest Park pool desegregated in the 1970s, it was not until the 1990s that the Colonial Country Club—a golf course less than one mile away[42]—would also racially desegregate.

The historically under-resourced and mostly Black Como neighborhood is not only located close to TCU, but likely was the residence of several Black workers who were the "help" at nearby locales that required inexpensive labor. But in efforts to avoid burdening the employers of such labor with shame, a physical wall that "stretched for ten blocks to separate Blacks and whites in Fort Worth" was constructed to enclose this area where Black people were living.[43] While these incidents do not reflect directly upon TCU, they directly reflect the larger environment in which TCU was located; one which observed rigid racial segregation—both physically and psychologically. In Fort Worth and in Texas, such regimented racial relations were reinforced with mores of polite Southern etiquette and were frequently reinforced by expectations of southern hospitality.[44] It would be difficult to defend the idea that TCU was a bubble immune from such racialized thinking and policy that was not only naturalized, but legalized in society. TCU existed when virulent, obvious, and offensive racism was explicit, expressed, and accepted. In other words, to say that TCU was immune would perhaps be the equivalent of asserting that one can jump into a pool and not get wet.

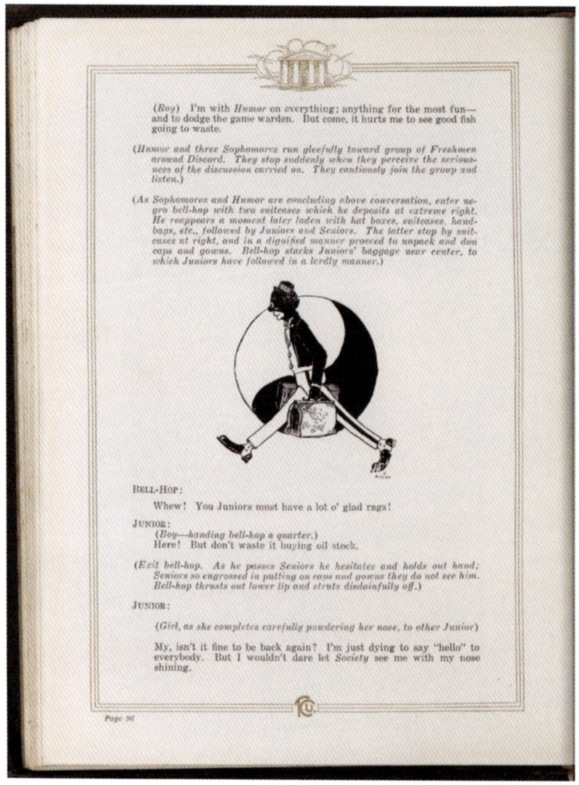

(*Boy*) I'm with *Humor* on everything; anything for the most fun—and to dodge the game warden. But come, it hurts me to see good fish going to waste.

(*Humor and three Sophomores run gleefully toward group of Freshmen around Discord. They stop suddenly when they perceive the seriousness of the discussion carried on. They cautiously join the group and listen.*)

(*As Sophomores and Humor are concluding above conversation, enter negro bell-hop with two suitcases which he deposits at extreme right. He reappears a moment later laden with hat boxes, suitcases, handbags, etc., followed by Juniors and Seniors. The latter stop by suitcases at right, and in a dignified manner proceed to unpack and don caps and gowns. Bell-hop stacks Juniors' baggage near center, to which Juniors have followed in a lordly manner.*)

BELL-HOP:

Whew! You Juniors must have a lot o' glad rags!

JUNIOR:

(*Boy—handing bell-hop a quarter.*)
Here! But don't waste it buying oil stock.

(*Exit bell-hop. As he passes Seniors he hesitates and holds out hand; Seniors so engrossed in putting on caps and gowns they do not see him. Bell-hop thrusts out lower lip and struts disdainfully off.*)

JUNIOR:

(*Girl, as she completes carefully powdering her nose, to other Junior*)

My, isn't it fine to be back again? I'm just dying to say "hello" to everybody. But I wouldn't dare let *Society* see me with my nose shining.

Page 96

Above
The Minstrel bell-hop was one of several "strictly allegorical" characters of a play entitled *A Pageant: In Three Acts* to present "the conservative student opinion" for the college year 1919–1920. *Courtesy of TCU Photo Collection, 1920* Horned Frog.

The Founding Years

What follows in the next pages merely sets the stage for the Black history at TCU we endeavor to explore shortly. Even though Black Americans were not present on campus via the formal, intellectual framework of students or professors, Black people were nonetheless on the campus and minds of TCU students. Black staff or employees provided a number of services directly to campus, spanning cooking to janitorial to landscaping duties. The Black image was also on the white mind as a journey through yearbooks and school newspaper archives will freely attest.[45]

But when we state that the Black image was on the white mind, unfortunately, it was a distorted image. It might be within the reader's jurisdiction to assign fault to the students if what we know to be objectionable *now* was or should have been objectionable *then*. If anything, such racially misguided attitudes may have proliferated only because of an absence of Black students, faculty, and additional staff. Many early inhabitants of that TCU universe before the modern era of integration simply suffered from a lack of *education*, *exposure*, and *experience*—otherwise known affectionately in my TCU John V. Roach Honors College classes as "the 3Es."[46] Without a formal curriculum, or substantive exposure, or meaningful, shared experiences with Black people within the larger community or with Black students, faculty, and staff on campus,

TCU students would necessarily be deficient with respect to navigating race relations.

Thus much of what will be briefly described is merely a means to provide proper historical context and does not represent the views of all TCU students then or to come. These are not our opinions, but rather, we step aside to allow the reader to experience the voices of students themselves directly, as these historical receipts do exist. What follows are bullet points that provide additional context as to how Black people were seen by tuition-paying students who expressed themselves freely through the student newspaper, the *Skiff* or the student yearbook, the *Horned Frog*, during TCU's early years:

■ a 1908 football game recap that described TCU running back Bertram Bloor's prowess as, "Bloor starred. Time after time he hit the line for ten yards and more. He waded thru it like a nigger goes thru a watermelon."[47]

■ a 1911 report on a program of the Shirley Literary Society that referred to a sophomore "who had more announcements than a nigger's dog had fleas."[48]

■ a 1913 letter from a former TCU student living in New York City, complaining about "'thick-lip' Africans sitting 'jam-up' side by side with whites, in every street car."[49]

■ a 1914 "Pep Carnival Funds to Furnish Goode Hall Parlors" article that mentions a circle of customers for the "Hit the Negro Baby" stand[50]—as incredulous as it sounds, this "game," which involved paying patrons throwing balls or eggs at the unprotected heads of Black persons for fun, was a popular amusement for many with recorded instances as early as the 1880s and as late as the 1950s.[51]

■ a 1914 announcement for "Big Circus and Side Shows at the Pep Carnival, Nov. 6, Also Minstrels and Animals": Booth 6 of the carnival was advertised to feature "Negro Minstrels" described as "heavy-weights, spade-footed, kinky-headed, pug-nosed, and as black as the ace of spades."[52]

■ a 1915 op-ed entitled "A Little Ventilation Please" complaining about professors who fail to keep their classrooms properly ventilated: "When several classes meet one right after the other in the same room, and the stale air is not permitted to escape, it smells like a negro hut where about five negroes had slept with everything closed tight all night."[53]

■ in the 1915 *Horned Frog* yearbook on page 101, there is a depiction of several half-naked Black minstrel figures physically spelling out the word "CLUBS" with their bodies at the start of the campus club pictures section inside of the yearbook.[54]

■ a 1918 story about students obtaining chickens for a picnic "'nigger' fashion" (that is, by stealing them).[55]

■ a 1921 poem about a woodpecker which included the lines, "He works like a nigger / To make the hole bigger."[56]

■ a 1923 poem titled "African Golf" about Black men shooting dice, which begins with the lines, "Five coal Black niggers with heavy scowls / All sat together, cheek and jowl."[57]

■ a 1924 survey inquiring, "Can you solve these?" ("shall negroes, Jews and others be admitted on basis of equality into:[58]

1. Class rooms?
2. Eating places?
3. Dormitories?
4. Social affairs?
5. Fraternities?
7. Athletic teams?").

The Importance of Voice

When understanding Black American history, whether national or local in scope, it is also important to comprehend the context surrounding Black voice. History is known as the study of change over time. Thus, in studying the relationship of Black Americans to their own voices within this country, while we know so much about the Black American experience, it is as amazing as it is alarming to consider how much there still is to learn! Principally because the actual, authentic Black American voice is missing in volumes throughout numerous points in our shared history. Western culture prides itself on having a literate culture as a sign and symbol of

BUD-NIPPERS

MEMBERS

Minnie Proctor
Vista Woods
Margaret Gibson
Viola Caldwell
Annie McLendon
Lola McFarland
Mary Hanen
Una Stark
Gladys Huckabee

MEMBERS

Mora Moore
Irene Carson
Lera Brown
Pansy Bozeman
Ellen Hartgrove
Ethel Johnson
Lela Johnson
Lena B. Reeder
Maud Keith

OFFICERS

Amboline Tyson . . . . *President*
Mary Grace Muse . . . . . . *Vice-President*
Ada Veale . . . . *Secretary*

1915

Left and Below
Black minstrel figures spell out the word "Clubs," ironically "including" the Black image when there were no Black students enrolled on campus at time of publication. *Courtesy of TCU Photo Collection*, 1915 *Horned Frog*.

civilization, and was often used as a metric against other cultures who were oral in tradition.[59] It is a cruel irony that Black Americans were sometimes disparaged for not being "more literate," since it is difficult to record one's intimate thoughts and feelings when it was initially illegal for Black Americans to learn how to read and write.[60]

Thus, in simply remembering the history of enslavement and the social strictures that were placed upon public Black intellect (which makes the early achievements of W. E. B. Du-Bois, Ida B. Wells, or Hubert Harrison all the more eye-opening), it was nearly two and a half centuries after their arrival (if we use the date of 1619)[61] before Black Americans could technically be public in their written recognition of their own histories. From a historical perspective, if one wishes to study Black lives before 1865 (the year the era of enslavement was formally concluded by passage and ratification of the Thirteenth Amendment—not the signing of the Emancipation Proclamation),[62] then most of what one will learn will ironically be through mostly white, non-Black voices. Court records. Bills of Sale. Lawsuits over transactional disputes. Diaries—some that range from the philosophical and romantic to the descriptive and pedantic to the cruel and sadistic (e.g., the demented and detailed diary of Thomas Thistlewood).[63] This is what makes the story of Gustavas Vassa all the more significant, as he was one of the first to describe the horror that was the Middle Passage in his own words.[64]

Moving forward through time, it was still incredibly difficult for Black Americans to create a "literate-based" culture in the midst of a Jim Crow society that legally observed segregated schools at least from 1896, when the *Plessy v. Ferguson* decision mandating "separate but equal" came down, to 1954, when *Brown v. Board of Education* mandated school desegregation "with all deliberate speed." Thus, with schools just now opening up to "more equal" opportunity in the mid-1950s, and a consistent lack of structural access to such opportunities and resources, it is not difficult to see how there would be a paucity of works that tell the Black American experience with Black voices. It was not until after the civil rights movement of the 1960s, with the gradual dissemination of school desegregation, that we start to see a larger infusion of Black voices, with Joseph Henry Clark and Darlene Clark Hines being but a few of the few.

Suffice it to say, so much of what we know of the Black American experience, no matter how factually true, still may be missing the Black voice. Thus, what we three authors aim to do through this project is both to illuminate and to elevate Black voices. This history may in fact read differently from other texts, and perhaps that is precisely the point! While not necessarily directly affected by the events, we are *directly connected* to these events as fellow members of the Black American experience, and therefore we may present the information and material in a different way than one with *a priori*, or indirect, observational experience. We wish to illuminate Black voice through Black voice.[65] The fact that we have three proud members of the Black experience serving as coauthors on this collaborative research project only speaks to the importance of continuing to create additional spaces for storytelling.

In referencing our brief literature review earlier, very few works provide a detailed or exclusive focus upon aspects of the Black TCU experience for sustained, concentrated periods. There are only cursory references or brief descriptions. Thus, in approaching this project, we three authors were keenly aware and sensitive about our positionality. We are three Black American scholars of different genders, ages, and ethnicities who have bonded together to illuminate an important story of value, visibility, and voice. In so doing, we are conscious of our collective Black voice, hopeful we will leverage additional angles of analysis and understanding for the premise that there is no singular way to experience TCU. There is no denying that many students who matriculate and graduate from TCU thoroughly enjoy their experience. We wish to explore whether the same can be said for Black TCU students, staff, and faculty—namely, whether members of TCU's Black community feel ownership stakes in calling TCU their own as well. In other words, we have the opportunity to wrestle with whether Black students, staff, and faculty genuinely appreciate and love the TCU experience, or whether Black individuals simply withstand TCU only because they appreciate the awesome opportunities that TCU may provide.

The "father of Harlem radicalism," Hubert Harrison, said that if one truly wants to test the bounds and limits of American democracy, then they should look no further than Black Americans as the "touchstone of the modern democratic idea."[66] Thus with Black TCU students, staff, faculty, and alumni serving as bellwethers, let us check in directly with how TCU is pursuing its *Disciplina est Facultas* motto as it pertains to any and all who dare to wear the purple—and wear it with pride. How Black Americans are treated still serves as a powerful litmus test for how other future TCU citizens will be treated. That is, given the historical weight of systemic discrimination specifically targeted toward Blacks, chances are that if Black Americans are being treated fairly within a particular venue, then others stand a good chance as well. Conversely, inconsistent treatment of Black Americans reminds us of the work that still needs to be done to bridge the gap between theory and practice.

To better gain a handle on TCU memory and specifically what it means for the value and visibility of Black Americans in the many facets of its operation, this book is the product of prodigious research in the archives of many sources, which include but are not limited to the primary source documents of the Chancellor's Papers, minutes from the Board of Trustees, and minutes from Student Government, in addition to secondary sources such as the TCU school newspaper and yearbook (i.e., the *Skiff* and the *Horned Frog*), as well as the local newspaper, the *Fort Worth Star-Telegram*.

This project is the culmination of collaboration by several TCU factions, but above all, TCU faculty and students worked closely to research, organize, and digitize all the available papers relevant to the TCU Black experience. TCU students, staff, and faculty were also quite resourceful in arranging and executing interviews with living alumni and key community figures to flesh out the "circle of life" before and after passing through TCU's campus.[67]

In sum, the future of TCU depends upon the ability of the shared collective to accurately share all aspects of its shared memory, and no longer feel the burden of sequestering the truth out of self-preservation. Indeed, there are some darker chapters of TCU's past that must come to light, but as we shine a candle unto those times, may the story be one of continuous evolution and growth as TCU endeavors to "lead on" by reflecting upon its relative progress. We are proud to add this perspective and lens to the existing TCU narrative, for as an institution of higher learning, it is only appropriate that past, present, and future members of the TCU collective simply learn the truth—a compelling story told in purple, white, and Black.

Chapter 1

Humble Beginnings

Thorp Springs Eternal

The initial site of what would be known as Texas Christian University (TCU) is located by the banks of the Brazos River, formerly Comanche territory in modern-day Hood County. After a series of attacks between Comanche and Texan forces by the Brazos River, local Indian reservations were officially barred in 1859. In the same process, the State of Texas seized control of these tribal lands. Although individual citizens and private companies could purchase portions of the seized land from the State, the Native tradition designated this land as Comanche hunting property, and the conflict between Comanche and white settlers would ensue for decades afterwards. Col. Pleasant Hill Thorp, a blacksmith originally from Virginia, by way of Tennessee, settled in what is now Hood County in 1834, while Texas was still part of the Mexican federation. Thorp fought during the Texas Revolution for the Army of the Republic of Texas. In 1841, he joined Brigadier General Edwin Morehouse's Indian hunting expedition, which led him to discover and covet the land that would become Thorp Spring, in the Brazos River valley, across from Comanche Peak.[1]

There is no indication that Pleasant Thorp fought during the Civil War. Nevertheless, his support for the Confederacy was probable, as his town hosted the Confederate Twentieth Battalion's station. His social statuses included the title of slaveowner. In effect, local historians, including Thorp's descendant Barbara Thorp Wilkins, explain that enslaved labor was instrumental to the building of the town of Thorp Spring, including the colonel's two-and-a-half story limestone edifice that would later host the first TCU/AddRan classes: "Streets were laid out forty feet wide; work was started on the big stone house, with Thorp's few slaves providing most of the labor."[2] Censuses of Burleson and Johnson Counties from 1850 and 1860 indicate that Thorp owned three mulatto boys and one Black woman. It is quite probable that he owned more than the aforementioned individuals, however. The enslaved woman listed on the 1860 census was named Jude. The youngest boy listed was her son, Charley Thorp, who would become a prominent member of the Thorp Spring community and one of TCU's very first *servant-leaders*, or employees.

The Clarks

While Addison and Randolph Clark are credited as the noble cofounders of TCU, their father Joseph A. Clark was the mastermind behind the educational enterprise and was very much involved in the daily operations of the university. Slave schedules and other primary documents indicate that Joseph A. Clark was also a slaveowner. An 1851 census record details that he owned at least one thirteen-year-old boy. An 1856 promissory note also shows that he rented a slave, George, to a man named John Harris.[3] In a correspondence to his sons, Clark

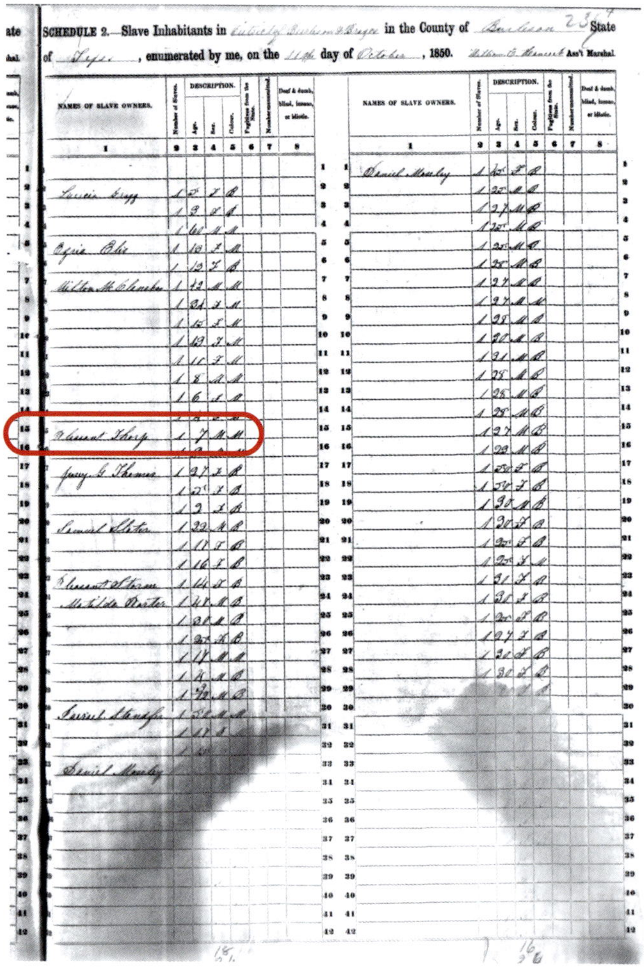

Above
Pleasant Thorp owned two biracial children while residing in Burleson County. *Courtesy of the National Archives in Washington, DC.*

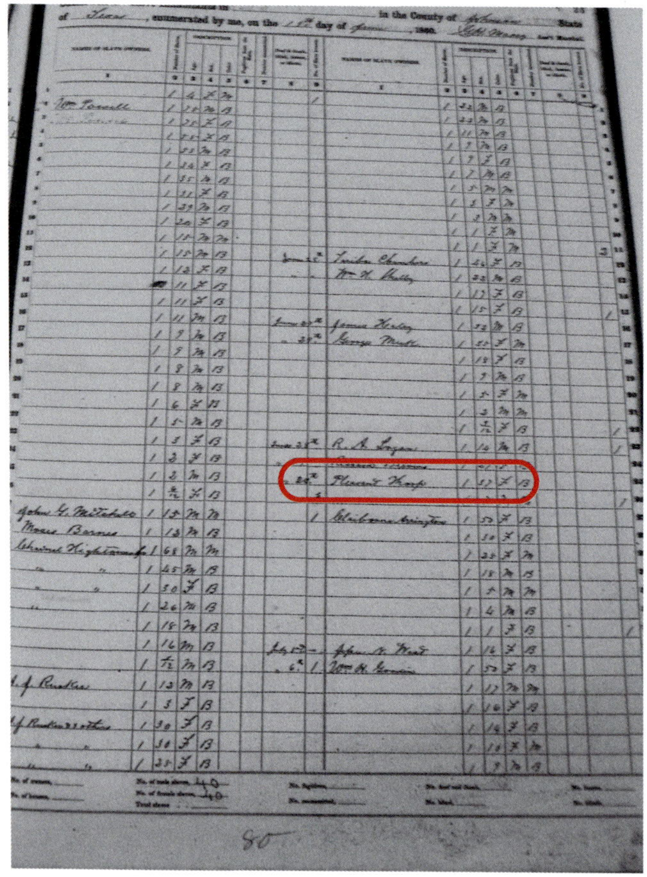

Above
Pleasant Thorp brought Charley and his mother Jude from Burleson County to what would be Thorp Spring. *Courtesy of the National Archives in Washington, DC.*

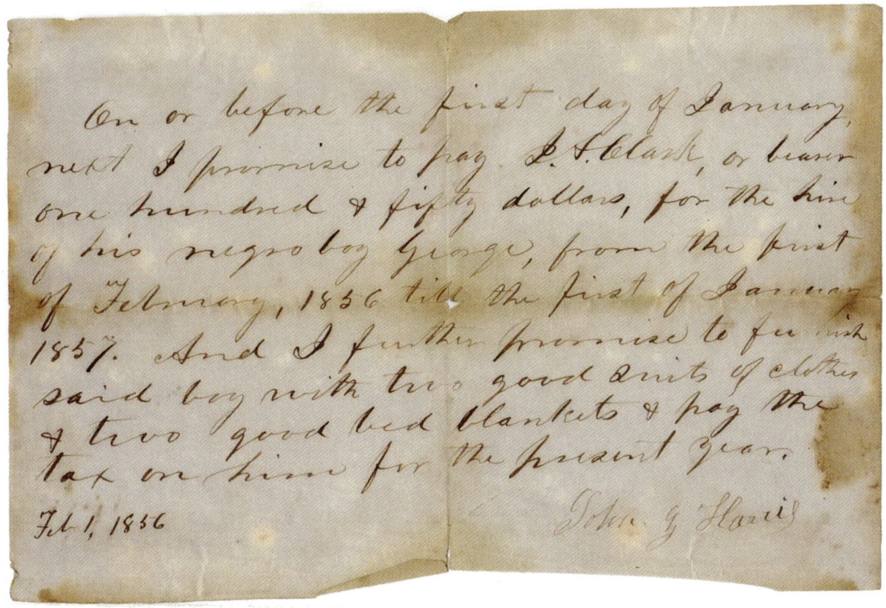

On or before the first day of January
next I promise to pay J. A. Clark, or bearer
one hundred & fifty dollars, for the hire
of his negro boy George, from the first
of February, 1856 till the first of January
1857. And I further promise to furnish
said boy with two good suits of clothes
& two good bed blankets & pay the
tax on him for the present year.
Feb 1, 1856
John G. Harris

On or before the first day of January next I promise to pay J. A. Clark, or bearer one hundred & fifty dollars, for the hire of his negro boy George, from the first of February, 1856 till the first of January 1857. And I further promise to furnish said boy with two good suits of clothes & two good bed blankets & pay the tax on him for the present year.
Feb. 1, 1856
John [middle initial] Harris

Right
Agreement between John Harris and Joseph A. Clark to borrow a slave. *Courtesy of Joseph Lynn Clark Papers, Box 36, Folder 1.*

amusingly described how his son Bud water-tortured a slave named George, because he "would not get out of [his] way."[4]

The relationship between the Brothers Clark and the Confederacy is less ambiguous, however. Addison Clark officially enrolled as a Confederate serviceman in 1862, while Randolph serviced the Confederacy through acts of volunteerism. According to Randolph Clark's 1919 memoir, *Reminiscences*, Addison enrolled reluctantly, as he believed war to be against Christian standards of behavior; he simply sought to defend his home against the invading enemy.[5] Nevertheless, local Fort Worth researcher Ronald Burriss points out: "This explanation for Addison's abandonment of his Christian pacifist principles rings somewhat hollow when one considers that neither Texas nor Grayson County faced any imminent threat of invasion in early 1862 (and Texas was never successfully invaded during the war)."[6] In 1932, Randolph noted that he did not want to be remembered for his affiliation with the Confederacy: "I would like to have that part [. . .] left blank in the last reckoning."[7] Yet Randolph would remain actively involved in Confederate veterans' affairs.

Randolph's father, Joseph A. Clark, did not evidence active support for secession. Nevertheless, his business benefitted from the war and the Confederacy, as the sale of commodities to war areas yielded enough profits for him to purchase a hundred-horse ranch estate. His postwar attitude revealed his sense of racial entitlement.[8] In a 1868 letter to his sons, Joseph shared his view of the aftermath of the Civil War: "Gen. Hancock [. . .] has ordered that all negroes be disarmed. [. . ,] If they get up a general fight in the North—and I think they will—I am in favor of Texas raising the Lone Star, and making an effort for a separated independent government. If they get up a big fight there, Mongrels and Negroes will go by the board here in short order. What a time it will be."[9] In another 1868 letter to Randolph and Addison, father Clark discussed his apprehension over the postbellum presidential election: "If the conservatives of the North submit to

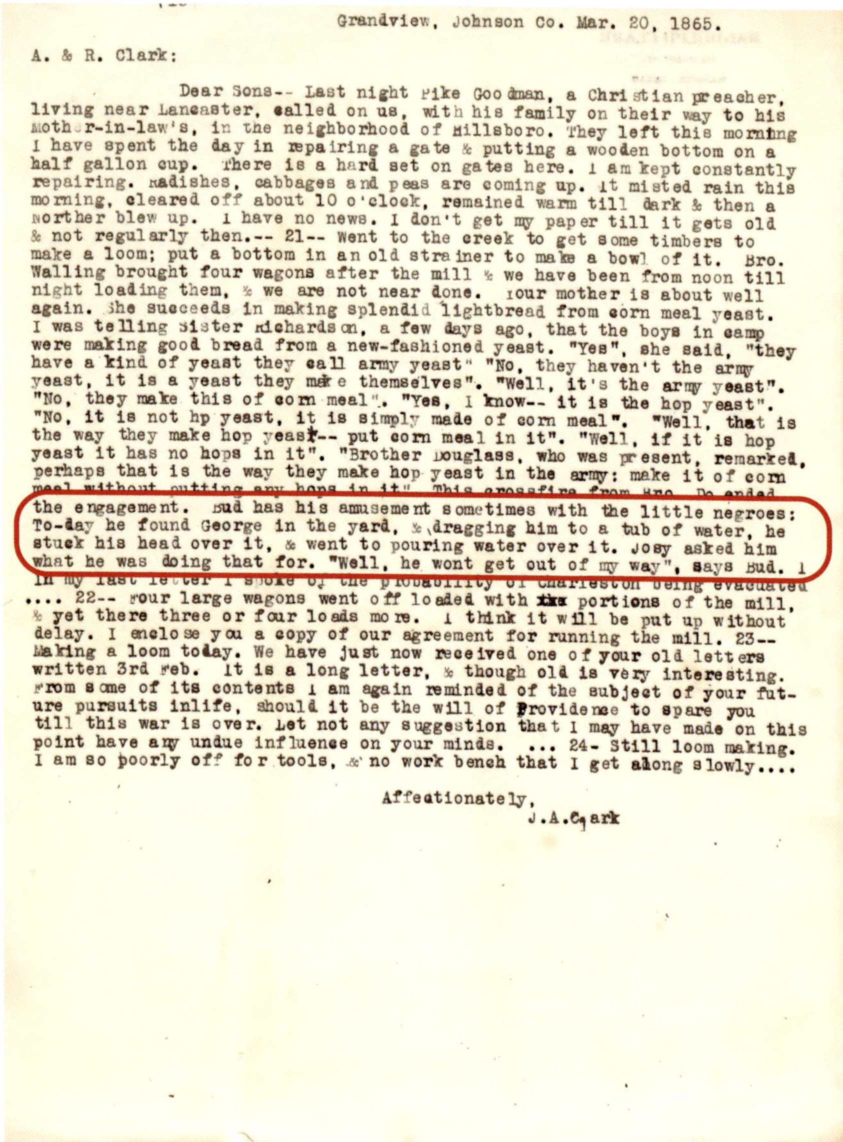

Grandview, Johnson Co. Mar. 20, 1865.

A. & R. Clark:

Dear Sons-- Last night Pike Goodman, a Christian preacher, living near Lancaster, called on us, with his family on their way to his Mother-in-law's, in the neighborhood of Hillsboro. They left this morning I have spent the day in repairing a gate & putting a wooden bottom on a half gallon cup. There is a hard set on gates here. I am kept constantly repairing. Radishes, cabbages and peas are coming up. It misted rain this morning, cleared off about 10 o'clock, remained warm till dark & then a Norther blew up. I have no news. I don't get my paper till it gets old & not regularly then.-- 21-- Went to the creek to get some timbers to make a loom; put a bottom in an old strainer to make a bowl of it. Bro. Walling brought four wagons after the mill & we have been from noon till night loading them, & we are not near done. Your mother is about well again. She succeeds in making splendid lightbread from corn meal yeast. I was telling Sister Richardson, a few days ago, that the boys in camp were making good bread from a new-fashioned yeast. "Yes", she said, "they have a kind of yeast they call army yeast" "No, they haven't the army yeast, it is a yeast they make themselves". "Well, it's the army yeast". "No, they make this of corn meal". "Yes, I know-- it is the hop yeast". "No, it is not hp yeast, it is simply made of corn meal". "Well, that is the way they make hop yeast-- put corn meal in it". "Well, if it is hop yeast it has no hops in it". "Brother Douglass, who was present, remarked, perhaps that is the way they make hop yeast in the army: make it of corn meal without putting any hops in it". This crossfire from Bro. D. ended the engagement. Bud has his amusement sometimes with the little negroes: To-day he found George in the yard, & dragging him to a tub of water, he stuck his head over it, & went to pouring water over it. Josy asked him what he was doing that for. "Well, he wont get out of my way", says Bud. I in my last letter I spoke of the probability of Charleston being evacuated .... 22-- Four large wagons went off loaded with the portions of the mill, & yet there three or four loads more. I think it will be put up without delay. I enclose you a copy of our agreement for running the mill. 23-- Making a loom today. We have just now received one of your old letters written 3rd Feb. It is a long letter, & though old is very interesting. From some of its contents I am again reminded of the subject of your future pursuits inlife, should it be the will of Providence to spare you till this war is over. Let not any suggestion that I may have made on this point have any undue influence on your minds. ... 24- Still loom making. I am so poorly off for tools, & no work bench that I get along slowly....

Affectionately,
J.A.Clark

Above
Joseph A. Clark describes his son's mistreatment of George, an enslaved individual, in a letter addressed to Addison and Randolph. *Courtesy of Joseph Lynn Clark Papers, Box 36, Folder 1.*

this we shall be bound hand and foot and delivered over to the negro and (worse than the negro) white associate. So, in my judgement, there will be either another war or we shall be worse than enslaved."[10] Joseph explained that war would then be inevitable.

Notwithstanding the chaos of Reconstruction, the Clarks adopted teaching careers to restore a sense of order and Christian discipline within the new postwar era.[11] In *History of Texas Christian University: A College of the Cattle Frontier*, past TCU Dean Colby Hall (also former academic dean of Brite and history professor) discusses the priorities of Randolph and Addison Clark as they decided to invest in education: "They had returned from the [Civil] War with the recognition that the Southland had to be rebuilt. As Randolph put it: 'There were opportunities for young men in various fields of labor; there were temptations for gain in lawful and unlawful ways. The need was for men to give unselfish service in rebuilding on better foundations, all the business of the country.'"[12]

Addison and Randolph originally wanted to create a public institution. However, the Ironclad Oath enactment of 1862 prevented supporters of the Confederacy from public service.[13] The brothers thus founded AddRan Male and Female College as a private university in 1873. AddRan was relatively progressive, due to its coed structure. However, admission was not extended to non-whites. While not explicitly stated in admissions materials that TCU was for "whites only," likely there was no need to state the obvious, given the overarching and encompassing nature of Jim Crow segregation that was considered "normal" at that point in time, not just in Texas, but throughout most parts of the country.[14]

Enslavement's Legacy at TCU: The Case of Charley and Kate Thorp

In the early 1850s, Col. Pleasant Thorp arrived in the Granbury area with Charley (who also went by Henry W. Charles "Chas" Thorp) and his mother.[15] An 1860 slave schedule record shows that the colonel had in his possession a thirty-seven-year-old Black woman and a seven-year-old mulatto boy. According to Charley's death certificate, his mother's name was Jude. Both of his parents were from Caldwell, Texas. While Charley's father is listed as "Unknown" in all records, Charley had a close, filial relationship with the colonel.

After the Civil War, Charley, now emancipated, remained in the town of Thorp Spring, as it was not uncommon for formerly enslaved individuals to stay in the immediate vicinity of where they worked and were most familiar. He married and had at least one child in 1880 with Leone Hightower,[16] an emancipated slave and the daughter of Simon Hightower[17]—a prominent persona who founded the renowned Texas freedmen settlement, The Colony.[18] Leone died the same year, at which point Charley returned to his former master's residence as a member of his household, according to an 1880 census where he is listed as a twenty-seven-year-old widower.[19] Despite Charley's inability to read or write,[20] he either demonstrated proficiency or cultivated trust at such a high level that the colonel placed Charley in charge of his own personal affairs.[21]

In a parallel fashion, Kate Lee, who would become Charley's wife, was another emancipated slave with strong connections to TCU. She was born in 1861, as a slave of Roswell Lee, who later became the father-in-law of TCU cofounder Randolph Clark when Clark married Lee's daughter, Ella Lee. Roswell Lee served as a Confederate officer during the Civil War. The Lees also owned Kate's mother, a Black woman, and Kate's brother Louis. Both Kate and Louis are listed as mulatto in census records, which indicates that, as Charley's did, their father may have identified as white. As a child, Kate was described as having "wide eyes, shiny teeth, broad nose, and kinky hair."[22]

After emancipation, Kate and her family remained in close contact with their former enslavers, to the point where Kate's mother requested that Mrs. Susan Lee, Roswell's widow, raise Kate and Louis as her own children, away from uneducated Black children. According to Randolph Clark's son Joseph Lynn Clark, Mrs. Lee became Kate's legal guardian,[23] and in an 1870 census, Kate is listed as a full member of Susan Lee's household. By the age of ten, Kate could read, but not write.[24] Around 1873, Kate, now a quite young and recently divorced mother, accompanied her stepsister Ella Blanche (eight years her elder) and Ella's husband Randolph Clark to Fort Worth, then to Thorp Spring, where she met and married Charley Thorp.[25]

Charley and Kate were highly regarded within the Thorp Spring community. They worked for AddRan Male and Female College for over twenty years, until the campus was moved to Waco in 1895. Charley oversaw numerous housekeeping

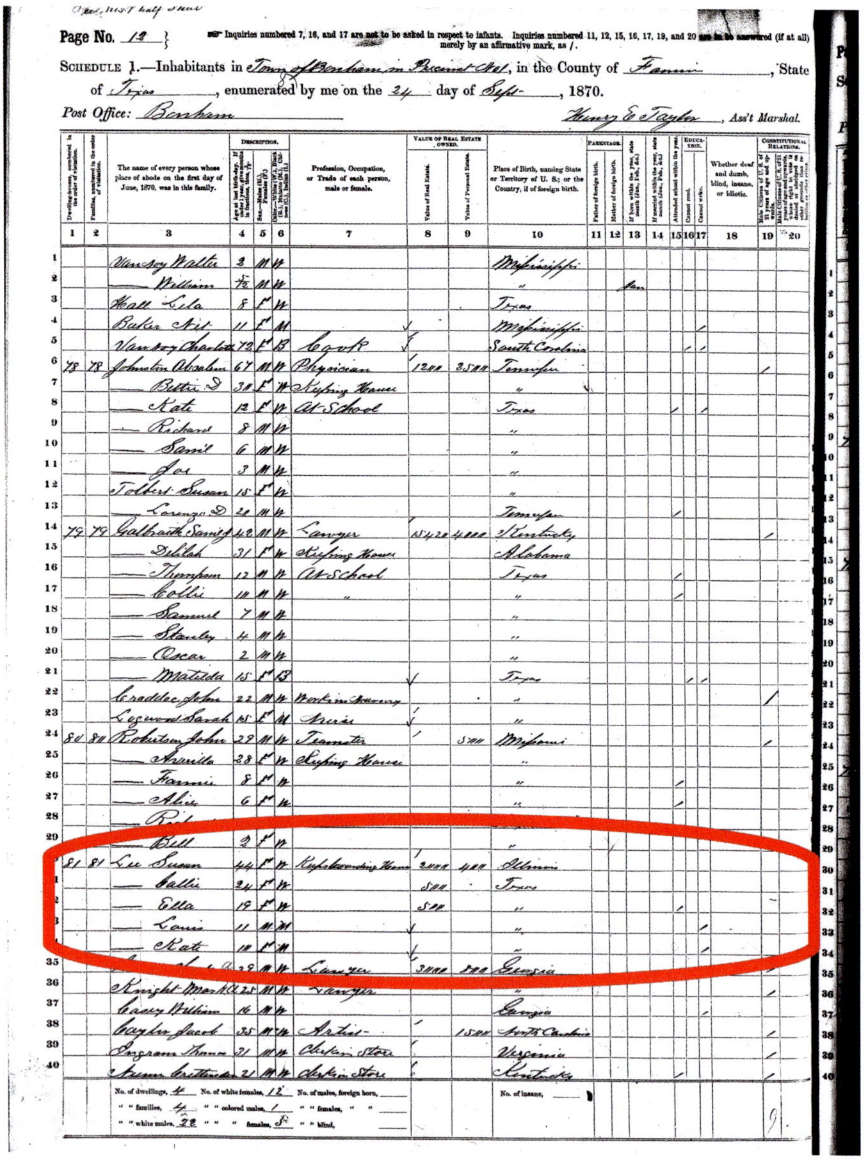

Page No. 12

Inquiries numbered 7, 16, and 17 are not to be asked in respect to infants. Inquiries numbered 11, 12, 15, 16, 17, 19, and 20 are to be answered (if at all) merely by an affirmative mark, as /.

SCHEDULE 1.—Inhabitants in Town of Bonham in Precinct No1, in the County of Fannin, State of Texas, enumerated by me on the 24 day of Sept, 1870.

Post Office: Bonham — Henry E Taylor, Ass't Marshal.

Line	Dwelling	Family	Name	Age	Sex	Color	Occupation	Real Estate	Personal Estate	Place of Birth
1			Vansey? Walter	3	M	W				Mississippi
2			— William	4/12	M	W				"
3			Hall Lila	8	F	W				Texas
4			Baker Kit	11	F	M				Mississippi
5			Vansey Charlotte	72	F	B	Cook			South Carolina
6	78	78	Johnston Absalom	67	M	W	Physician	1200	3500	Tennessee
7			— Bettie D	38	F	W	Keeping House			"
8			— Kate	12	F	W	At School			Texas
9			— Richard	8	M	W				"
10			— Saml	6	M	W				"
11			— Joe	3	M	W				"
12			Tolbert Susan	15	F	W				
13			— Lorenzo D	20	M	W				Tennessee
14	79	79	Galbraith Saml J	40	M	W	Lawyer	15420	4000	Kentucky
15			— Delilah	31	F	W	Keeping House			Alabama
16			— Thompson	12	M	W	At School			Texas
17			— Collie	10	M	W	"			"
18			— Samuel	7	M	W				"
19			— Stanley	4	M	W				"
20			— Oscar	2	M	W				"
21			— Matilda	15	F	B				Texas
22			Craddock John	22	M	W	Work in tannery			"
23			Lazarus? Sarah	45	F	M	Nurse			"
24	80	80	Robertson John	29	M	W	Teamster		500	Missouri
25			— Ariella	28	F	W	Keeping House			"
26			— Fannie	8	F	W				"
27			— Allie	6	F	W				"
28			— R[illegible]							
29			— Bell	2	F	W				"
30	81	81	Lee Susan	44	F	W	Keeping boarding House	2000	400	Illinois
31			— Callie	24	F	W			500	Texas
32			— Ella	19	F	W			500	"
33			— Louis	11	M	M				"
34			— Kate	10	F	M				"
35			[illegible]	29	M	W	Lawyer	3000	800	Georgia
36			Knight Mark A	25	M	W	Lawyer			
37			Casey William	16	M	W				Georgia
38			Taylor Jacob	35	M	W	Artist		1500	North Carolina
39			Ingram Thomas	31	M	W	Clerk in Store			Virginia
40			[illegible] Crittenden	21	M	W	Clerk in Store			Kentucky

No. of dwellings, 4 No. of white females, 12 No. of males, foreign born, — No. of insane, —
" " families, 4 " " colored males, 1 " " females, "
" " white males, 22 " " " females, 8 " " blind,

Above
In 1870, Kate and her brother were under Mrs. Susan Lee's legal guardianship. *Courtesy of National Archives and Records Administration.*

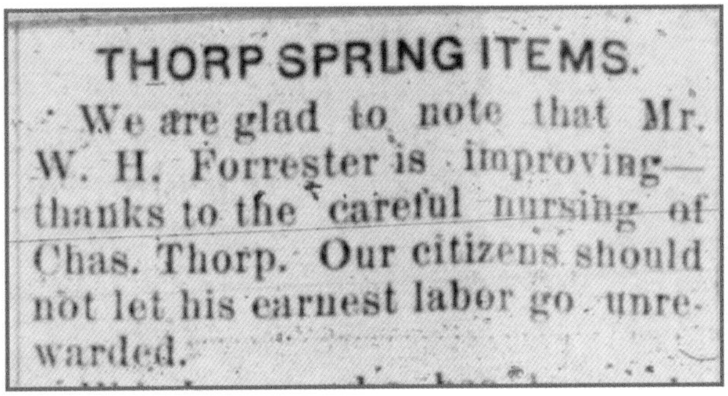

THORP SPRING ITEMS.

We are glad to note that Mr. W. H. Forrester is improving—thanks to the careful nursing of Chas. Thorp. Our citizens should not let his earnest labor go unrewarded.

Above
The *Granbury News*, March 8, 1894.
Courtesy of Granbury Depot.

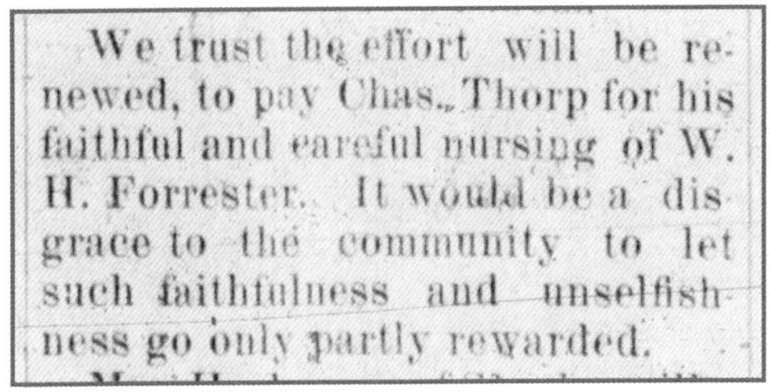

We trust the effort will be renewed, to pay Chas. Thorp for his faithful and careful nursing of W. H. Forrester. It would be a disgrace to the community to let such faithfulness and unselfishness go only partly rewarded.

Above
The *Granbury News*, June 7, 1894.
Courtesy of Granbury Depot.

duties: he was the campus's lead security guard, handyman, and landscaper. What is particularly compelling is that not only did he perform the manual labor, but his insight was valued and consulted as well. For example, Joseph Lynn Clark explains that Charley "advised on improvements."[26] Charley's firefighting role extended to the entire town of Thorp Spring, and he was often celebrated for his selfless attendance to the sick, as illustrated by the 1894 newspaper clippings.[27] Likewise, Kate provided laundry, nursing, and midwife services to AddRan and the town.

Charley also ensured discipline among students, or anyone in the community. He investigated infractions on campus and would later be nicknamed "the FBI."[28] The fact that a Black man would yield such authoritative power is noteworthy. Indeed, even after TCU's official integration nearly a century later in 1964, parents of white students would still frown upon the idea of having a Black person disciplining their children. Mildred Sims, an African-American graduate of the class of 1969, was denied a resident assistant position in her TCU dorm for this very reason.[29]

Charley did not adhere to the pious lifestyle that the Clarks advocated. He was known to be occasionally profane, and he questioned the veracity of Randolph's sermons, despite their close relationship. In Joseph Lynn Clark's family memoir *Thank God We Made It!* Charley is also reported to have openly teased and criticized Randolph's daughter, whom he nicknamed "Sook." Randolph claimed that Charley's acquaintances were not the most reputable: "the associations formed did not inspire him to high aims."[30] This would lead him to often be caught at the wrong place at the wrong time.[31] Nevertheless, Charley was a tax-paying,[32] mostly law-abiding citizen. Ironically, the only major lawsuit in which Charley's good standing was questioned was when his former owner's son, Henry Pleasant Thorp, sued him for debt and foreclosure in 1898.

After Charley's death, Randolph Clark wrote an encomium where he deplored the fact that Charley's lack of education did not do his intellect justice: "With opportunity, he could have been the equal of Booker Washington in education." Charley's giftedness was all the more exceptional in light of the fact that in the nineteenth century, education and schooling were not considered a priority throughout the state of Texas, regardless of race, but the Clarks believed in the power of education to foster social and spiritual well-being, and their enterprise was the result. In fact, Texas was one of the last five states to make school attendance compulsory in 1915.

Charley and Kate purchased 137 acres of land from Col. Thorp in 1894, near the AddRan campus. They lived "East of the old college building in Thorp Spring," and their land, despite being located in a predominantly white area, was known as "the Charley Thorp property." The property remained in the family until 1951.[33]

In the 1910 census records, Kate remained listed as a laundress, and Charley's occupation at the time of his death was "Servant."[34] In 1915, at the surprising age of fifty-five, Kate gave birth to Charley's last known daughter, Christine.

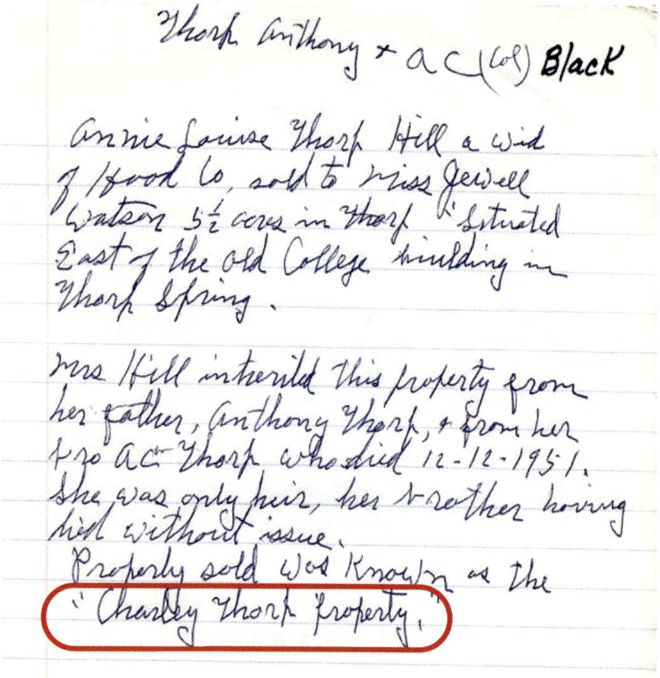

Thorp Anthony + A C (Col) Black

Annie Louise Thorp Hill a wid of Hood Co, sold to Miss Jewell Watson 5½ acres in Thorp "Situated East of the Old College building in Thorp Spring.

Mrs Hill inherited this property from her father, Anthony Thorp, + from her bro A C Thorp who died 12-12-1951. She was only heir, her brother having died without issue.

Property sold was known as the "Charley Thorp property."

Left
Notes from Judge Davis of Hood County, page 6A. *Courtesy of Granbury Depot.*

Note Transcription:

Thorp Anthony + A C (Col) ***Black***

Annie Louise Thorp Hill a wid of Hood Co. sold to Miss Jewell Watson 5 ½ acres in Thorp. Situated East of the Old College building in Thorp Spring.

Mrs. Hill inherited this property from her father, Anthony Thorp, and from her bro A C Thorp who died 12-12-1951. She was only heir, her brother having died without issue.

Property sold was known as the "Charley Thorp Property."

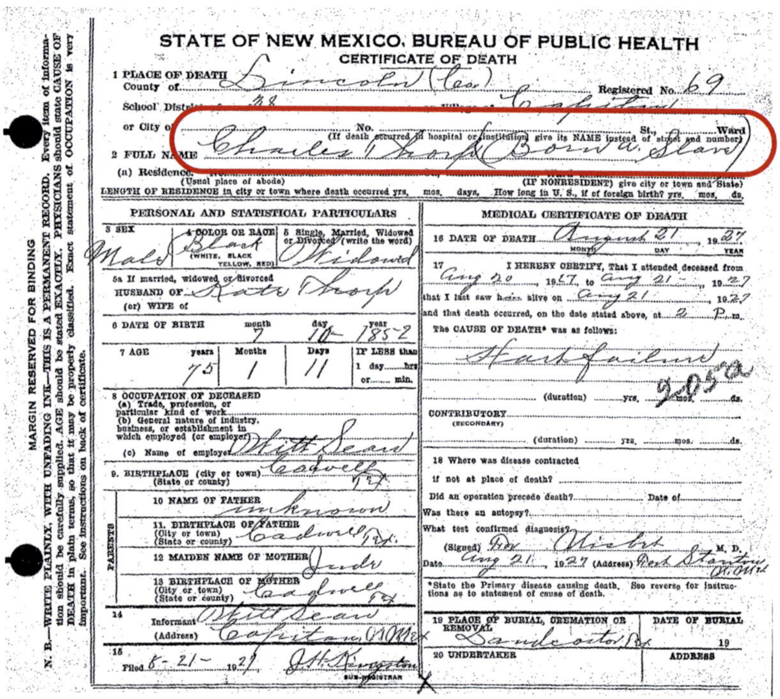

N. B.—WRITE PLAINLY, WITH UNFADING INK—THIS IS A PERMANENT RECORD. Every item of information should be carefully supplied. AGE should be stated EXACTLY. PHYSICIANS should state CAUSE OF DEATH in plain terms, so that it may be properly classified. Exact statement of OCCUPATION is very important. See instructions on back of certificate.

MARGIN RESERVED FOR BINDING

STATE OF NEW MEXICO, BUREAU OF PUBLIC HEALTH
CERTIFICATE OF DEATH

1 PLACE OF DEATH County of Lincoln Co. Registered No. 69
School Dist. 38 Village of Capitan
or City of ... No. ... St., ... Ward (If death occurred in hospital or institution give its NAME instead of street and number)
2 FULL NAME Charles Thorp (Born a Slave)
(a) Residence. (Usual place of abode) (If nonresident) give city or town and State)
LENGTH OF RESIDENCE in city or town where death occurred yrs. mos. days. How long in U. S., if of foreign birth? yrs. mos. ds.

PERSONAL AND STATISTICAL PARTICULARS
3 SEX Male
4 COLOR OR RACE Black
5 Single, Married, Widowed or Divorced (write the word) Widowed
5a If married, widowed or divorced HUSBAND OF (or) WIFE of Kate Thorp
6 DATE OF BIRTH month 7 day 10 year 1852
7 AGE years 75 Months 1 Days 11 IF LESS than 1 day ...hrs. or ... min.
8 OCCUPATION OF DECEASED (a) Trade, profession, or particular kind of work (b) General nature of industry, business, or establishment in which employed (or employer) (c) Name of employer Whitt Sears
9. BIRTHPLACE (city or town) (State or county) Cadwell Tex.
10 NAME OF FATHER unknown
11. BIRTHPLACE OF FATHER (City or town) (State or county) Cadwell Tex.
12 MAIDEN NAME OF MOTHER Jude
13 BIRTHPLACE OF MOTHER (City or town) (State or county) Cadwell Tex.
14 Informant Whitt Sears (Address) Capitan N Mex
15 Filed 8-21-1927 J H Kingston Sub-Registrar

MEDICAL CERTIFICATE OF DEATH
16 DATE OF DEATH August 21 1927
17 I HEREBY CERTIFY, That I attended deceased from Aug 20, 1927, to Aug 21, 1927 that I last saw him alive on Aug 21, 1927 and that death occurred, on the date stated above, at 2 P.m.
The CAUSE OF DEATH* was as follows: Heart failure
(duration) ... yrs. ... mos. ... ds.
CONTRIBUTORY (SECONDARY) (duration) ... yrs. ... mos. ... ds.
18 Where was disease contracted if not at place of death?
Did an operation precede death? ... Date of ...
Was there an autopsy?
What test confirmed diagnosis?
(Signed) Dr. Nisbet, M. D.
Date Aug 21, 1927 (Address) Fort Stanton, N. Mex
*State the Primary disease causing death. See reverse for instructions as to statement of cause of death.
19 PLACE OF BURIAL, CREMATION OR REMOVAL Sandicoto Tex. DATE OF BURIAL 19
20 UNDERTAKER ADDRESS

Left
Charley Thorp's death certificate. *Courtesy of Santa Fe Bureau of Vital Records and Health Statistics.*

Kate died in Dallas shortly after. Charley never remarried; he worked as a live-in servant in the household of Witt Sears's family, another prominent white family in Thorp Spring. He died at the age of seventy-five in New Mexico, in 1927, and Mr. Sears signed his death certificate as the informant.

All in all, unlike numerous previously built southern colleges, AddRan's benefit from and association with slavery was relatively subtle and indirect. Slave labor was utilized to build infrastructures, but these infrastructures were built before they were part of the university. Several founders had fought for and supported the Confederacy. Men like Pleasant Thorp, Joseph A. Clark, and several early faculty members built their fortune using profits from slave labor and conducting business with the Confederacy, but they did so as private citizens, not in the name of the institution.

Similarly, the Thorp Spring locale attracted the children of wealthy plantation owners, who had also built their fortunes (whence tuition paid to AddRan originated) from slave labor. While there is no official paper trail of the connection between TCU and slavery, this connection was common knowledge, as illustrated by a 1923 pageant script in celebration of the university's fifty-year anniversary. This segment of the Golden Jubilee Celebration was contributed by the TCU English Department and presented by the students. Scenes throughout the pageant showcase the founding and progress of TCU during its initial years. More specifically, Episode III of the pageant script depicts Addison and Randolph Clark at a church in Waco. Addison preaches, the church responds, and then people enter the church bearing gifts: a lumberjack, a cattleman, a farmer from the panhandle, and a southern plantation owner with cotton and rice. The plantation owner's lines read, "Far to the south was thy call heard, above the singing voice of the darkies, tending the rice and the cotton, with my harvest I come for thy sustenance."[35]

Early Student Life at AddRan

Race relations on campus

Beside Kate, Charley, and their children, there is strong indication of a Black presence elsewhere in the early AddRan janitorial and landscaping crew. While no official institutional document mentions the presence of Black Americans on the AddRan campus, other primary sources clearly show that several Black people resided and worked on campus and in its vicinity. Nevertheless, relations between Blacks and whites were marked by proxemic restrictions, as social norms discouraged physical closeness with non-whites. The following photograph on page 26 displays students, staff, and their children.[36] One Black woman stands far off, excluded from the group. In an 1890 journal entry, Mattie Harlin, an AddRan student, wrote: "As we were walking back some little niggers come in behind us. We meet some of the boys and they laugh at us for being with the darkeys."[37] Another journal entry reports how Harlin's friend Daisy pushed a Black child who was delivering laundry to the female dormitory.

In contrast, the lionizing of whiteness was indeed manifest among the student population. An 1880 article in the AddRan newspaper the *Student* details the story of "a most heinous crime" involving "a little white boy and two negros in a field" and a "third negro approached the parties with a gun and took deliberate aim at the innocent little white boy and fired."[38] The white boy died and the story says the Black boy was arrested despite claiming it was an accident, which was determined to be false after a police investigation. Without seeking to speculate on the veracity of facts reported in this article, the rhetoric employed to recount this tragic incident clearly demonstrates the extent of the disdain for and demonization of Black children.[39]

In 1891, students organized a performance of Mark Twain's best-selling novel, *Huckleberry Finn*. The performance was dramatized by Thomas Marshall Clark (brother of Randolph and Addison Clark) and Addison Clark Jr. (son of Addison Clark). While the racially charged script can be attributed to Twain's authorship, it is also noteworthy that the Clarks utilized the term "nigger" and other racial slurs quite abundantly not only in the scripts, but also in the scene descriptions. This custom of denigrating Black Americans in student entertainment would ensue for decades onward. For example, a 1919 edition of the *Skiff*[40] reports an event called "KKK Revived" where students parodied a Klan parade for entertainment.[41] While there is not concrete evidence that the event was racially motivated, the students did in fact make light of the fact that the Klan was a terroristic organization. They played this idea up for laughs and the affair was documented as a particularly enjoyable occasion.

In the 1920s, TCU hosted a carnival, and the events were documented in a newspaper article titled "Students and Faculty Hold High Carnival with Red Soda, Freaks, Minstrels,

Above
AddRan College at Thorp Springs, TX, n.d. Box 1/ Mattie Cooper Harlin Collection/ Photograph of AddRan College with Mattie Harlin; arrow indicates unidentified Black female present. *Courtesy of Special Collections, Mary Couts Burnett Library, Texas Christian University.*

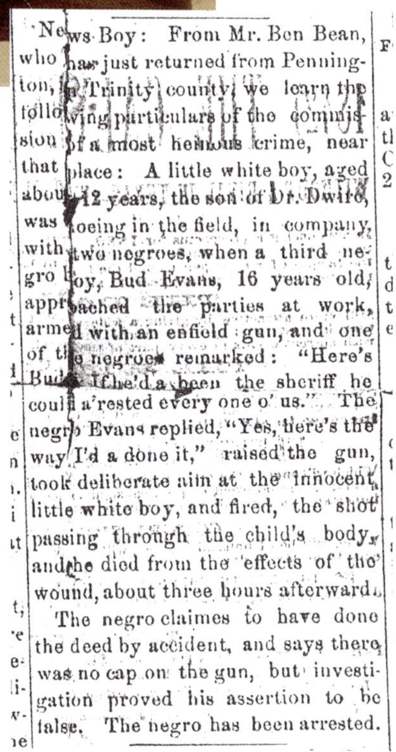

News Boy: From Mr. Ben Bean, who has just returned from Pennington, in Trinity county, we learn the following particulars of the commission of a most heinous crime, near that place: A little white boy, aged about 12 years, the son of Dr. Dwire, was hoeing in the field, in company with two negroes, when a third negro boy, Bud Evans, 16 years old, approached the parties at work, armed with an enfield gun, and one of the negroes remarked: "Here's Bud. If he'd a been the sheriff he could a'rested every one o' us." The negro Evans replied, "Yes, here's the way I'd a done it," raised the gun, took deliberate aim at the innocent little white boy, and fired, the shot passing through the child's body, and he died from the effects of the wound, about three hours afterward.

The negro claimes to have done the deed by accident, and says there was no cap on the gun, but investigation proved his assertion to be false. The negro has been arrested.

Right
The *Student* was a student-edited newspaper at AddRan. The repeated references to the victim as a "little white boy" or "innocent little white boy" vividly contrast with other boys, who are simply called "the negroes"—illustrating the race-based sympathy that AddRan editors sought to elicit in their rendition of the incident. *Courtesy of Granbury Depot.*

and All." Attractions included "a movie, a negro minstrel, and a tight-wire act. There was actually an old plantation minstrel, without which a carnival would be irreparably crippled. Considering the fact that the minstrel was almost entirely extemporaneous, a precedent being established in that it was produced without a single rehearsal, the show 'went over' splendidly."[42] In the larger Fort Worth area, minstrel entertainment programs were also available and appealing to the general population. For instance, an event announced in a newspaper clipping with the headline, "Honest-to-Goodness Minstrel Program of Elks Is Revealed."[43] The article details that the off-campus Fort Worth show featured interlocutor Amon G. Carter, one of TCU's most prominent contributors. The program listed songs such as "Mammy Jinny's Jubilee" and a performance named "Emancipation Day in Alabama" included a selection titled "A Swell Coon" and "Picked on a Nigger."

Black Americans and White Supremacy after Thorp Spring

At the turn of the century, TCU's vision of expansion was no longer fit for the Thorp Spring locale. In order to attract more cosmopolitan students and faculty, the university relocated to Waco, Texas, in 1895, where it remained until 1910, when a fire destroyed the facility and the campus moved back to Fort Worth. In Waco, not only was the institution offered a larger building (a former school) to work with, but there were also multiple railroads leading into the burgeoning city, making it more centrally located and more easily accessible. Several trustees were business leaders in Waco. They also pushed for the potentially more prosperous change of scenery.

A similar employment of Black labor was visible at the university's subsequent locations. For example, Benjamin Jones was a biracial, formerly enslaved man who worked for TCU as a "Farm Laborer" after its relocation to Waco.[44] Additionally, whether in Waco or Fort Worth, a survey of directories (city directories, until the mid-1920s, featured a "C" to indicate that a resident was "Colored" or Black) helps locate several Black American families as residents living within the vicinity of TCU (as was the case for Charley and Kate Thorp and Benjamin Jones)[45] or on the actual campus itself, which seems unlikely unless these were employees of the university. At all three early TCU locations (Thorp Spring, Waco, and Fort Worth), children of white, male faculty benefited from homeschooling, as their mothers and private tutors provided them with instruction. Black "help" often allowed for white mothers to be free to focus upon the business of home education. As an alternative, the Thorp Spring and Waco university systems also operated a primary and preparatory school, which mostly serviced the children of white faculty.[46]

Directory information indicates the presence of Black married couples on university grounds. Photographs and other primary documents of the time also place Black children on university grounds. However, to date there is no discoverable evidence demonstrating that the children of Black domestic and janitorial employees of TCU ever attended school. There was considerable logistical difficulty on this score, wrought by the existing rules of Jim Crow segregation. For example, Kate and Charley's children, who resided close to campus, had limited access to education. The nearest Black schools were located by The Colony, an African American settlement in Granbury formed after emancipation. It was several hours on horseback from TCU. Furthermore, The Colony did not provide education beyond the eighth grade. In order to pursue a high school program, students had to commute from Granbury to Fort Worth, which was probably too far a distance for most of them, given the limited access to transportation. Likewise, TCU's campus in Waco was quite remote and isolated from the rest of the city, and no Black school was established in the university's vicinity. Benjamin Jones's school-aged children could neither read nor write at the time of his employment at TCU. Such an assumption is recurrent in census records, which commonly state that these generations of Black residents had no formal education.

The legacy of slavery at TCU has thus manifested itself through this need or desire to secure the proximity of Black domestic employees at the expense of their and their children's education. Their speedy availability to perform manual tasks previously assigned to enslaved workers is indeed reminiscent of antebellum norms. For instance, in the 1920s, a budget report indicated that some workers resided on campus in a facility called the "Servant House."[47] While no staff was listed in the campus directory until 1948, a 1920 census details that nine Black Americans resided on TCU property. They were listed as "Lodgers" of Philosophy Professor

Errett McDiarmid (head of household), who lived there with his wife and four children. While all but one were reported to be literate, the census report omits the actual level of education for these individuals only. The Servant House remained on campus until the 1930s, according to map and blueprint records.[48]

The lack of access to education for Black employees' children was therefore the direct consequence of three factors: 1) the restrictive system of segregation that forbade Black children access to campus educational resources, 2) the absence of Black schools near campus, 3) and the very fact that these children's parents worked for TCU.

Above
TCU aerial view, 1928; Servant House in red circle. *Courtesy of TCU Digital Repository.*

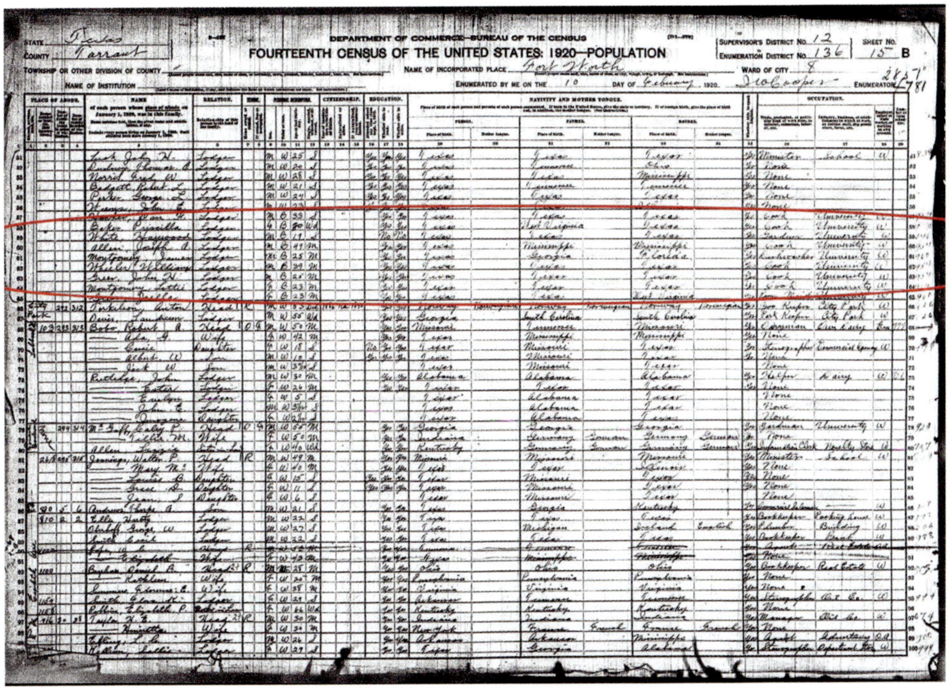

Left
Nine African Americans officially resided on campus in 1920. *Courtesy of Fort Worth Ward 8, Tarrant Texas; Roll T625-1850.*

Below
The servants' house labeled on a 1927 contour map. *Courtesy of TCU Asset Management and Technical Services.*

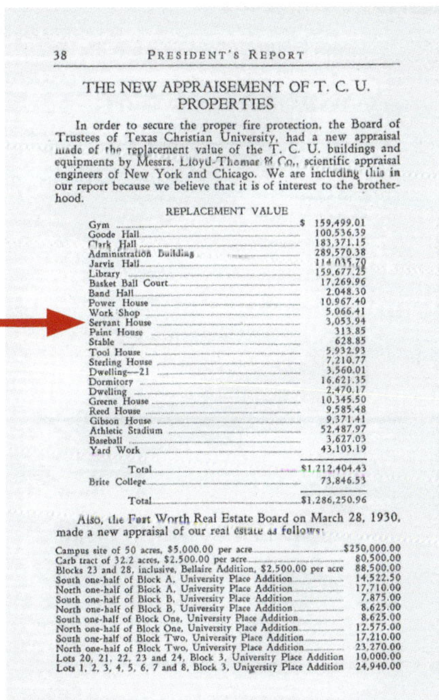

38 PRESIDENT'S REPORT

THE NEW APPRAISEMENT OF T. C. U. PROPERTIES

In order to secure the proper fire protection, the Board of Trustees of Texas Christian University, had a new appraisal made of the replacement value of the T. C. U. buildings and equipments by Messrs. Lloyd-Thomas & Co., scientific appraisal engineers of New York and Chicago. We are including this in our report because we believe that it is of interest to the brotherhood.

REPLACEMENT VALUE

Gym	$ 159,499.01
Goode Hall	100,536.39
Clark Hall	183,371.15
Administration Building	289,570.38
Jarvis Hall	114,035.70
Library	159,677.25
Basket Ball Court	17,269.96
Band Hall	2,048.30
Power House	10,967.40
Work Shop	5,066.41
Servant House	3,053.94
Paint House	313.85
Stable	628.85
Tool House	5,932.93
Sterling House	7,210.77
Dwelling—21	3,560.01
Dormitory	16,621.35
Dwelling	2,470.17
Greene House	10,345.50
Reed House	9,585.48
Gibson House	9,371.41
Athletic Stadium	52,487.97
Baseball	3,627.03
Yard Work	43,103.19
Total	$1,212,404.43
Brite College	73,846.53
Total	$1,286,250.96

Also, the Fort Worth Real Estate Board on March 28, 1930, made a new appraisal of our real estate as follows:

Campus site of 50 acres, $5,000.00 per acre	$250,000.00
Carb tract of 32.2 acres, $2,500.00 per acre	80,500.00
Blocks 23 and 28, inclusive, Bellaire Addition, $2,500.00 per acre	88,500.00
South one-half of Block A, University Place Addition	14,522.50
North one-half of Block A, University Place Addition	17,710.00
South one-half of Block B, University Place Addition	7,875.00
North one-half of Block B, University Place Addition	8,625.00
South one-half of Block One, University Place Addition	8,625.00
North one-half of Block One, University Place Addition	12,575.00
South one-half of Block Two, University Place Addition	17,210.00
North one-half of Block Two, University Place Addition	23,270.00
Lots 20, 21, 22, 23 and 24, Block 3, University Place Addition	10,000.00
Lots 1, 2, 3, 4, 5, 6, 7 and 8, Block 3, University Place Addition	24,940.00

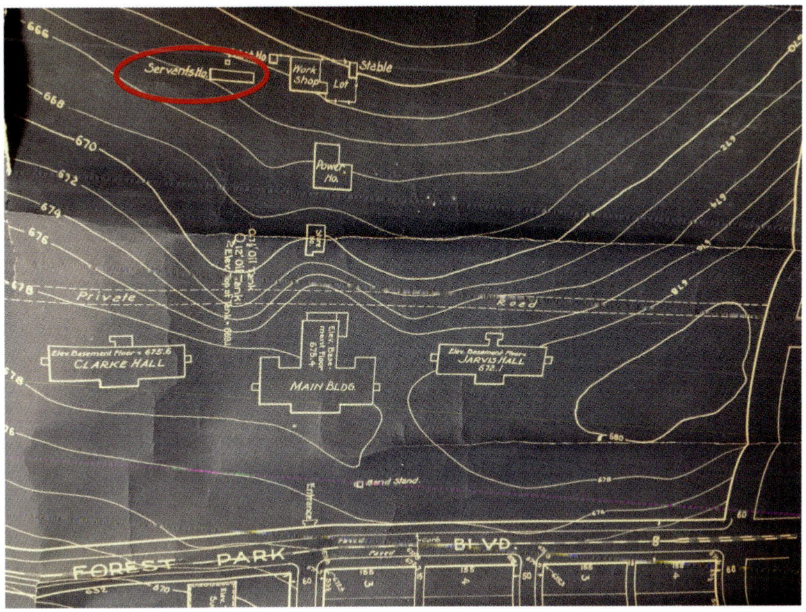

Left
In 1930, the Servant House was still listed as TCU property. *Courtesy of TCU Digital Repository.*

Chapter 2

Breakthroughs

Integrating Integration

When we think of Texas Christian University (TCU) now, what we see is a university coated in its distinctive yellow-brown brick occupying over three hundred acres in one of the largest cities in the country.[1] With a mission to "educate individuals to think and act as ethical leaders and responsible citizens in a global community," the hopeful Clark brothers imprinted their belief that education was foundational to a community and city, and into generations who dared to come to "Hell's Half Acre," or Fort Worth's red light district. Now extending over a large portion of University Drive, the centerpiece of which was a small hopeful idea of a college for two brothers, there stands an institution that has made itself known across Texas and throughout the entire country. As even more buildings have been erected, multitudes of chancellors have made their mark, and scholars have refined their skills, the reputation of TCU has grown prominent.

But to speak of TCU in all of its glory and valor without mentioning the full history is to overlook the *shadows* its ivory towers also created and perpetuated. As institutions began to integrate during the 1960s after the landmark *Brown v. Board of Education* decision,[2] TCU became one of the many institutions that would drag its feet into this new direction. This hesitation should come as no surprise, given the use of blackface, the display of the Confederate flag, and the painfully obvious taunting of Black custodial staff—all by white students in the early yearbooks. Though in favor of integration, then Vice Chancellor James Moudy's (who became chancellor in 1965) apprehension about it and his hesitancy were apparent when he spoke of interracial dating and miscegenation as a social threat.[3] These items do not fully encompass or reflect the mindset of *all* members of the campus community during that time, but this anti-Black rhetoric was the most visible of the perspectives documented in the *Skiff*, yearbooks, and campus speeches. All of which indicates that the culture of TCU had not yet evolved enough to be welcoming to the Black faculty, staff, and students who would also want to come to make their mark on this same campus.

Eventually, the trajectory of integration became unavoidable. Nevertheless, Chancellor Moudy's thoughts and concerns remained the prevalent opinion. In a TCU student-written publication found in *IMAGE*, he was quoted as saying, "Many people feared interracial dating and marriage."[4] Despite his conflicting views on the matter, Moudy still proceeded with integration, with the support of the board of trustees, in 1964. Continuing his thoughts, Moudy stated, "For Christian reasons, it should have been sooner, but for practical reasons, it was not done sooner. The reason we were late doing it was because we were a little fearful of what the parents would think."[5]

The practical concerns were an honest assessment of where TCU was at that time in regard to race. The university was not prepared to integrate Black students on campus, yet

Above
Freshman student Charles Bailey in blackface."Sho is Blue." *Courtesy of the* Horned Frog, *1950.*

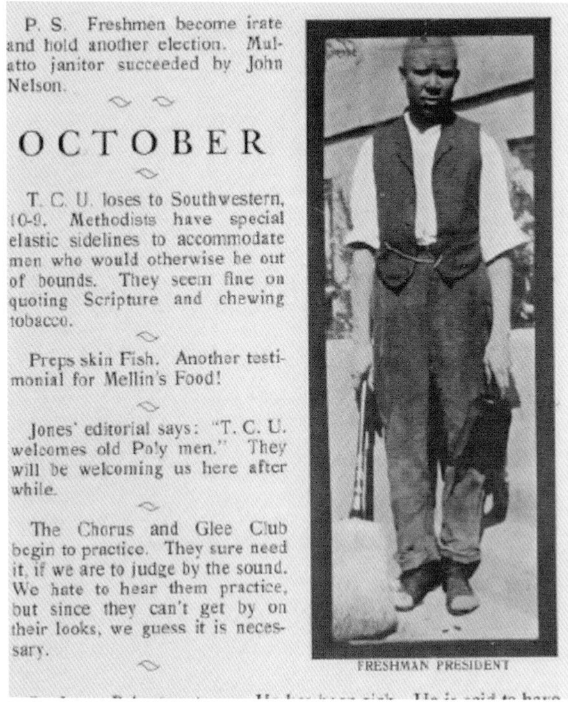

P. S. Freshmen become irate and hold another election. Mulatto janitor succeeded by John Nelson.

OCTOBER

T. C. U. loses to Southwestern, 10-9. Methodists have special elastic sidelines to accommodate men who would otherwise be out of bounds. They seem fine on quoting Scripture and chewing tobacco.

Preps skin Fish. Another testimonial for Mellin's Food!

Jones' editorial says: "T. C. U. welcomes old Poly men." They will be welcoming us here after while.

The Chorus and Glee Club begin to practice. They sure need it, if we are to judge by the sound. We hate to hear them practice, but since they can't get by on their looks, we guess it is necessary.

FRESHMAN PRESIDENT

Above
Upperclassmen prank freshmen by "electing" mulatto janitor as a class president. *Courtesy of the* Horned Frog, *1915.*

Left
Student Sandra Sutherland in blackface. Sutherland was a member of the sorority Alpha Delta Pi and of Mu Phi Upsilon, a national professional music sorority. *Courtesy of the* Horned Frog,*1960.*

Right
Members of Delta Sigma Fraternity dressed in confederate flags. *Courtesy of the* Horned Frog, *1971.*

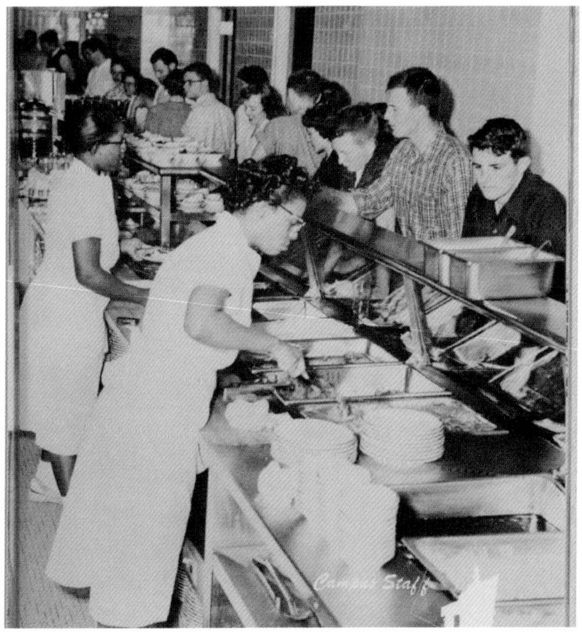

Right
Café staff. *Courtesy of the* Horned Frog, *1960.*

employed Black staff in jobs of service. As early as the 1910s, TCU had begun to recruit and enroll students of international background from places such as Spain, followed by Peru, China, Korea, Mexico, yet would not find Black students permittable to attend.[6] Just shy of being one hundred years old, the university's culture of exclusion had become ingrained in TCU's fabric. Integration not only challenged who TCU had become; it also called into question who it would like to become moving forward. The culture of excellence and "prestige" that TCU had been so proud to claim now had to consider the ways in which this excellence was an illusion with respect to race relations.

New Steps

Once integration began to slowly materialize and Black students began to be able to enroll as undergrad students in 1964, their mere presence would activate a counterculture that would over time build a growing legacy. For some, the purpose of their struggle to find space on this campus only became clear later: they were trailblazing the path for TCU's Black population who would come after. Despite the shadows of exclusion, taunting, and simple, overt racism, the early waves of Black faculty, staff, and students found a way to shine bright enough to light a path for future generations of Black Horned Frogs, who found comfort in their breakthroughs. Whether it was known or not, earlier Black occupants left an imprint on this campus that added to something just as long-standing as the buildings that enclose space.

There is no linear timeline that can fully trace the steps of all of the first Black position holders who created a counterculture here at TCU. Nor enough words to detail how impactful Black people have been as they forged ahead through trial and denial to make their presence known. Their attempts not only challenged an institution to think about its perpetuation of exclusion and systematic racism, but also about the culture it wishes to create for all students in the future.

This is probably why names such as Tyrone Wilson, Lorretta Gamble, Ken Bunting, Carolyn Bailey, Pat Kane, and many more have become overlooked or forgotten. We could argue the question "What is the story that we at TCU tell ourselves about ourselves?" But to be more direct, this is to also ask "Whom have we forgotten about, whose contributions have we excluded from our memories, and what accomplishments did we glance past as insignificant?" Ultimately, when we ask those questions, it should lead us to names and time periods that have in fact contributed to making this campus *more* aligned to what the Clark brothers desired the institution to be, but beyond the racial exclusion that they too had a hand in and which created barriers to equal access and opportunity. But these answers should not be the ending point of our quest within the shadows. It will also be equally important that we ask the more relevant question here, which is "What is the TCU legacy in respect to the breakthroughs that Black people have created?"

They Came, They Saw, They Became

Through intensive research we came across the names of Charley and Kate Thorp, formerly enslaved Black people who were mentioned in the previous chapter. Upon the death of Charley Thorp, Randolph Clark said that Charley "was not allowed to get an education; the associations formed did not inspire him to high aims. Charley was endowed with far more than ordinary intellect. He could have made the equal of Booker Washington, or the successful businessmen of his race, yet he was not allowed to have a vision of that life. . . . Who is responsible for this waste?"[7]

It is possible that this was a rhetorical question, but it would be ironic if the cofounder of an educational institution recognized a Black individual's intellectual potential, while overlooking how they were also personally responsible in the gatekeeping of such educational access. As if the conspirators of Charley's disenfranchisement were invisible or nonexistent. Obviously, it is easier to judge the past through today's lens; however, we can also acknowledge the hypocrisy of such a position in the moment.

Not only should we acknowledge the early Black presences on TCU's campus that played an instrumental role in the university's foundation, but also that these individuals, whose names and stories were not important enough to the institution to officially document and educate, did the invaluable work of cooking, cleaning, and ensuring that the daily operations of the institution remained intact. The story of Charley and Kate is reflective of many of the Black students, faculty, and staff members who would encounter TCU: to come and

Right
The Importance of staff. *Courtesy of the* Horned Frog, *1954.*

When stifling clouds of dust blew into Fort Worth early in the spring of 1954, even the gleaming new Religion Center became coated with West Texas and New Mexico dirt. University janitors swept and scrubbed and mopped. It was hard to keep buildings clean when the dust would not stop blowing.

Often the University community overlooks the importance of school employees outside of the faculty and Administration. Helpful librarians, meticulous Business Office workers, patient switchboard operators—these and other members of the University staff perform jobs vital to the successful operation of the school. But the significance of their contributions is easy to forget.

These are people students know by name and accept. But they are also people necessary to efficient functioning of a Christian institution. They are secretaries who keep accurate records. They are dormitory hostesses who see that life in women's dormitories is wholesome. They are dietitians who attempt to plan healthful meals in the Cafeteria. They are essential to TCU.

Right
Cafeteria workers during the 60s, before Black students were integrated. *Courtesy of the* Horned Frog, *1960.*

exist, but to be faced with limitations and exclusions while still being expected to promote the university's aspiration of excellence.

It is clear that there has always been a foundational Black presence on TCU's campus—even when at times it was deemed nonexistent or invisible, they were there. However, the places and positions that the Black population did engage with at TCU prior to integration only took place in one of two forms. The first would be that of service roles and positions. Early Black TCU staff members were found either as janitorial or food hall staff hires where their responsibilities were simply to clean, cook, and care for the campus. Ironically, the very same Black staff members who were "valued" enough where their labors were needed for the university to function, were simply unable to reap the benefits of their employer's main purpose, which was to provide an education to the open and able mind.

The second point of Black engagement on TCU's campus during the early years would be that of entertainment. Though TCU would not permit Black students to enroll on campus as undergraduate students until the 1960s, during the 1940s and 1950s, Black performers would be routinely hired for student homecoming and dances. Names such as jazz legend Duke Ellington and famous rock 'n' roll Fort Worth Native Ray Sharpe were among those welcomed to perform on campus for the all-white audiences at TCU. The photos of the all-white audiences enjoying the rhythmic melodies of Black artists revealed the dissonance behind observed segregationist practices that were not attuned to true principles of racial harmony.

Some of the same students who paraded in blackface or performed taunting pranks towards Black staff enjoyed the meals and other living situations being made convenient at the expense of Black people at TCU. The practice of having Black performers and service workers is not unique to TCU and was quite common amongst other all-white universities. Yet regardless of where it happened, the paradox behind desiring Black talent and service, but not wanting Blacks to enjoy the same benefits as white people at TCU was certainly confounding for any Black body anywhere.

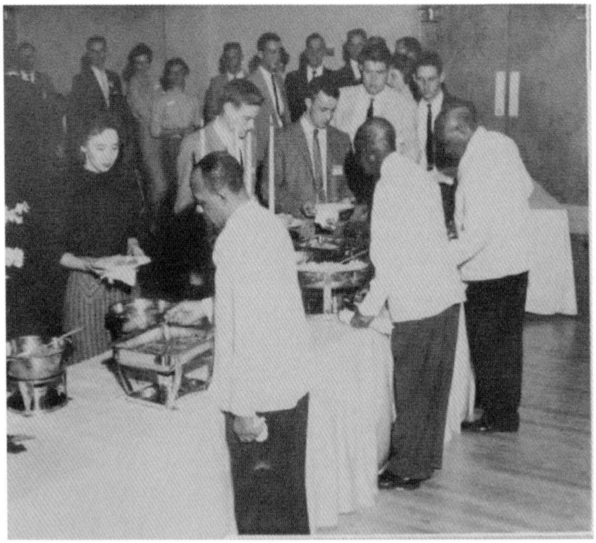

Above (Top)
Black service staff members providing meals for student delegates in the ballroom. *Courtesy of the* Horned Frog, *1952.*

Above
Black women who served as cafeteria employees. *Courtesy of the* Horned Frog, *1954.*

Above (Top)
Duke Ellington and the "Dukes" perform for TCU students. *Courtesy of Brite Divinity, 1948.*

Above
Local Fort Worth native rock 'n' roll artist Ray Sharpe. *Courtesy of the* Horned Frog, *1960.*

Early Attempts

We have come across and acknowledged the evening college classes taken up by Black military personnel in the 1950s at Carswell Air Force Base.[8] Though the university was reluctant to participate, they still entered a partnership with the United States Air Force. This program was not an active push for integration for TCU, but integrated education was being offered by the university. Recipients of this integrated education, such as Sergeant First Class (SFC) Charles J. Branson, made a direct impact on TCU's race relations. However, his story, like the stories of other participants, would not be fully integrated into campus or celebrated within the history of TCU in detail as it deserved. Even when white professors from the TCU School of Education began teaching courses at Gay Street Elementary school for Black public schoolteachers who sought to pursue an advanced degree in the 1950s, the story is brief and vaguely told in parts that do not detail the full experience or outcomes of this exchange.[9]

Even TCU's complicated relationship with Jarvis Christian College tells a story of racial friction that may now be recounted with transparency a story detailed more fully in Chapter 7. The trouble with not telling a full and complete story is that it creates the illusion that growth and expansion are a linear process. It is also the effect of exclusion, for when half a story is told, the full history is erased.

Brite College of the Bible (renamed Brite Divinity School in 1963) would become one of the more progressive presences on TCU's campus through the admittance of James Lee Claiborne, Daniel Goodspeed, and Vada Phillips Felder in 1952—the first Black students permitted to take classes on University Drive.[10] Because of its early integration, Brite would serve as a safe haven for Black students in the late 1960s to eat and commune when the broader campus community neglected to provide such accommodations for Black students. Brite Divinity lived the mission when it acted as an ethical leader. Though it would take the broader TCU campus and community a little bit longer to follow suit, its friendly neighbor Brite Divinity proved that real integration was in sight.

We would not receive TCU's first Black students until Allene Jones and Doris Ann McBride Goree in 1962 broke through the color barrier for TCU's Harris College of Nursing as graduate students.[11] One would think with the success

Above
Gay Street School. Courtesy of L.E. Swanson, "Image of Gay Street School," 1946, *TCU Special Collections.*

of Jones and Goree through the graduate avenues that TCU might have been ready for the Black undergraduate presences on campus. However, when the first few Black undergraduate students came in 1964, they would have a short stay on University Drive that would prove that TCU was not quite ready to embrace Black students within the main campus experience.[12] Though their names were not listed and have been difficult to uncover, they too are just as important to the story we tell ourselves about being at TCU.

These students are just as important to the growing legacy of Black people here at TCU—for those who came and tried, made an effort to better themselves, and ultimately influenced the institution to think critically of how it might not be living up to the idea that it has of itself. In all, Black people, whether students, faculty, or staff, became part of a legacy that allowed them to stand as giants on the shoulders of more giants reaching a little farther up the increasingly browning ivory towers of TCU.

Above
Brite College of the Bible brings Dr. Martin Luther King Jr. to Fort Worth, but he is not allowed to speak on campus. *Source unknown, 1959.*

Left
SPC Charles J. Branson receives service course certificate. *Courtesy of the* Horned Frog, *1955.*

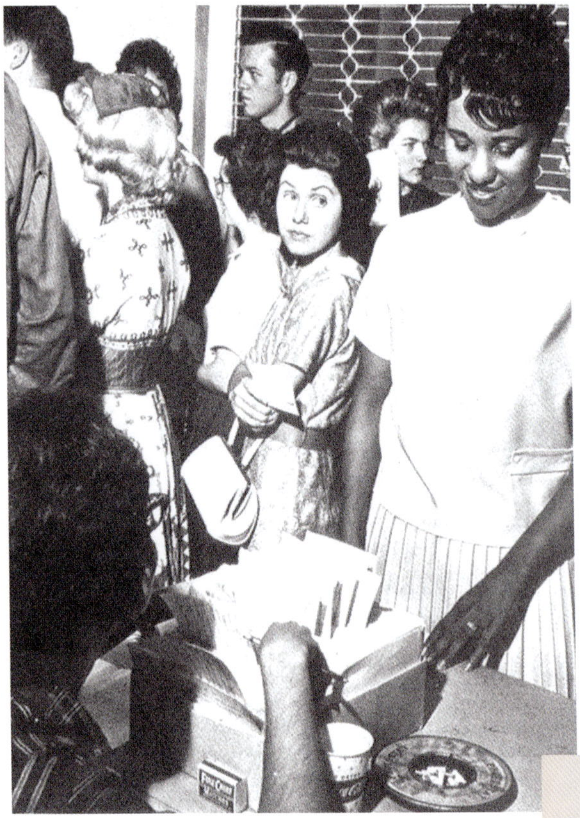

Above
Allene Jones registers for classes at the Harris College of Nursing. *Courtesy of the* Skiff, *1962.*

Below
Vada Felder and James Lee Claiborne. *Courtesy of TCU Special Collections.*

Above
TCU's first Black student athlete, James Cash. *Courtesy of the* Fort Worth Star-Telegram/*Vince Heptig.*

From Out of the Shadows

We would grow more familiar with names and the likeness of such as Dr. James Cash, who in 1966 became the first Black student-athlete at TCU and the first Black basketball student-athlete within the Southwest conference. Followed by Linzy Cole in 1967, TCU's first Black football player; Ronnie Hurdle, TCU's first Black cheerleader in 1969; and Dr. Jennifer Giddings Brooks in 1970, TCU's first Black homecoming queen. But these names are by no means exhaustive of the emergence of Black presences on campus. Quite frankly, they were in the more notable spaces in which Black accomplishments are typically most appreciated at institutions that are predominately white—which is athletics or athletic related. This isn't to downplay or to state these trailblazers were cast into ideal situations in which they did not experience the pressures or *shadows* of being Black in a white institution during the Jim Crow south. If anything, the pressures to perform in highly visible and majority white spaces only illuminated their significance even more with their mere presence, what they faced, and the mark that they created. Which, as a result, makes their accomplishments even richer and more significant and will be discussed in more detail in Chapter 5.

Those four names listed, whose entryway into their positions within TCU came by way of their ability and their likeability, would only prove that Black students had to model a behavior of extreme grace and borderline perfectionism in the face of a TCU that had not fully been ready to integrate. Whether they faced harassing phone calls, letters, taunts, or blatant exclusion, Black students found it within themselves to persevere as they reached higher heights. Additionally, these four students showcased that even within the most visible and pressurized places on campus, they too could find ways to accomplish goals that inspire other Black students to enter pockets of campus with the confidence and willpower to *break through*.

The need to expand to claim pieces of campus where Black students could create the college experience such as their white peers did came with an additional set of challenges. It was one matter to be admitted into a Predominantly White Institution such as TCU; it was a dramatically different matter to find places on campus where Black students would be fully socially accepted. If anything, the five Black students who left the unwelcoming university during the 1964-65 school year proved that integration does not automatically generate a sense of belonging or equal a culture of acceptance.

After athletics, one of the first entryways into TCU's mainstream would come by way of fraternity and sorority life. Even today, the Greek presence on campus has been felt and recognized for decades, as Greeks are the leaders of social events and influence a great deal of the ways in which TCU markets itself. One of the most notable contributors to the student experience of TCU's campus culture, Greek life has been in many ways the social center.

However, for Black students joining this sector of the college experience at TCU during the 1960s and 70s was not a viable option. Given the blatant and or subtle notions of exclusion, Black students were not finding that the TCU Greek life experience was one they could enter, which ultimately limited their ability to create the college experience that their white peers had the access to do.

In the *Skiff*, a 1969 article mentioned how Black students began to enter the sorority rush process but were not met with the desired outcome. The hopeful students that were looking to explore their student experience had this moment cut short by not being selected as a member by any of the campus Greek organizations. One student who was unnamed in the article "was eliminated from any chance of being pledged because of her affiliation with the National Association for the Advancement of Colored People (NAACP)."[13] This student wanted an opportunity to gain membership into Alpha Gamma Delta sorority. However, the members and alumnae had other thoughts on how a student who was associated with a Black organization would be accepted into their sorority. The article continued by stating, "A member of Alpha Gamma Delta, under a pledge of non-attribution, told *The Skiff* that 'rec' sheets from alumnae had recommended one of the women be 'definitely cut' because of her affiliation with the NAACP."[14] This *Skiff* clipping offers the insight into how the idea of integration for Black students did not fully reflect the idea of full acceptance or belonging. For an organization that prided itself on community development and service, it would appear valid to assert that those things are acceptable, as long as a student was not associated or a part of a Black organization that focused on service to Black communities.

Right (Top)
TCU's first Black football player to break the color barrier, Linzy Cole, makes a run for it. *Courtesy of the* Horned Frog, *1970.*

Right
Newly crowned Homecoming Queen Jennifer Giddings. *Courtesy of the* Horned Frog, *1972.*

TEXAS CHRISTIAN

VOL. 68, NO. 2

NAACP Ties Hurt Rushee

For the first time at TCU, black students are going through sororities rush. Of the four black women participating in rush, one probably was eliminated from any chance of being pledged because of her affiliation with the National Association for the Advancement of Colored People (NAACP).

A member of Alpha Gamma Delta, under a pledge of non-attribution, told The Skiff that "rec" sheets from alumnae had recommended one of the women be "definitely cut" because of her affiliation with the NAACP.

"Rec" sheets review the rushees and either recommend them for pledgeship or veto them, according to the sorority source. Because of their status of private property, these sheets are not accessible to people other than the sorority members.

The girl, on a form which asked for organizations and activities, had listed she was a member of the NAACP.

The Skiff was unable to reach either the rushee or the Dallas chapter of the NAACP, the branch she belongs to.

Above
Unnamed student denied sorority bid due to NAACP membership. *Courtesy of the* Skiff, *1969.*

Building Up Community

The struggle for Black students to be accepted into Panhellenic or Interfraternity Councils (IFC) organizations would still be an ongoing struggling in the late 1970s. A 1976 *Skiff* article written by Keith Clark titled "Black Student Denied a Fraternity" details the growing frustrations of Black students being continually denied the opportunity to join an organization.[15] Clark detailed the experience of student Lloyd Higgins, who like other Black students felt he was being denied the opportunity to participate based solely on his race. It was not just the utter disappointment that some Black students felt that brought attention to their exclusion; it was their courage to demand that the university look into the intentionality of racism that Greek life had perpetuated that caused TCU to take this issue more seriously.

It was not that Higgins was looking to prove a point, but just like white college students who were his peers, he wanted to enjoy all of the benefits of being a TCU student. Had his admittance to the university not earned him that? What use would it be to admit Black students without fully providing them access to all resources? Though "separate, but equal" had been deemed illegal, it was as if the new culture was labeled "here, but still separate."

This outcry of student demands led to a civil investigation undertaken by Fraternity and Sorority Life to audit the practices of each of their fraternities to determine if they had in fact partaken in discriminatory practices. Triggered by the growing frustrations of students and supported by associate professor Don Jackson, the conversation became more urgent once students presented administration with a petition to look into the acts of exclusion. As quoted in a March 6, 1980, publication of the *Fort Worth Star-Telegram*, Jackson stated, "There is a continuity of racism among TCU fraternities and sororities." The petition that would be generated emphasized that students would "neither participate in nor condone racism at TCU."[16] Signers of the petition affirmed that they were aware of the problem of discrimination on campus and would not participate in, aid, assist, or condone any organization that continued to be racially discriminatory.

Referred to as the "secret shame" of TCU in a *Skiff* article released a month later, the patterned exclusion of Black students from joining any of the Panhellenic Greek organization brought about a bunch of mixed emotions and perspectives that made it difficult for a practical solution to be devised.[17] At the time of this article's release, there were zero Black students admitted into any of TCU's eight fraternities and ten sororities. This article had reached the light of day in the broader community through the local newspaper, so TCU had now been put into a position of public accountability and scrutiny. This is not to say the surrounding Fort Worth community had become a beacon of racial harmony, but that this internal secret was now open not just to the Dallas-Fort Worth area, but beyond. There was no hiding the fact that Greek organizations had been perpetuating a culture of exclusion that had been established long before. Their efforts to break

Right
Lloyd Higgins interviewed on being denied fraternity bid. (The photo caption misspells Higgins as Wiggins.) *Courtesy of* Image, *1976*

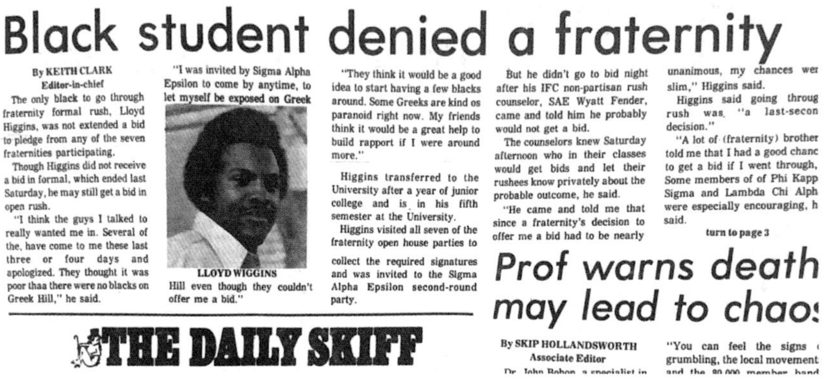

Black student denied a fraternity

By KEITH CLARK
Editor-in-chief

The only black to go through fraternity formal rush, Lloyd Higgins, was not extended a bid to pledge from any of the seven fraternities participating.

Though Higgins did not receive a bid in formal, which ended last Saturday, he may still get a bid in open rush.

"I think the guys I talked to really wanted me in. Several of the, have come to me these last three or four days and apologized. They thought it was poor thaa there were no blacks on Greek Hill," he said.

"I was invited by Sigma Alpha Epsilon to come by anytime, to let myself be exposed on Greek Hill even though they couldn't offer me a bid."

LLOYD WIGGINS

"They think it would be a good idea to start having a few blacks around. Some Greeks are kind os paranoid right now. My friends think it would be a great help to build rapport if I were around more."

Higgins transferred to the University after a year of junior college and is in his fifth semester at the University.

Higgins visited all seven of the fraternity open house parties to collect the required signatures and was invited to the Sigma Alpha Epsilon second-round party.

But he didn't go to bid night after his IFC non-partisan rush counselor, SAE Wyatt Fender, came and told him he probably would not get a bid.

The counselors knew Saturday afternoon who in their classes would get bids and let their rushees know privately about the probable outcome, he said.

"He came and told me that since a fraternity's decision to offer me a bid had to be nearly unanimous, my chances wer slim," Higgins said.

Higgins said going throug rush was "a last-secon decision."

"A lot of (fraternity) brother told me that I had a good chanc to get a bid if I went through, Some members of of Phi Kapp Sigma and Lambda Chi Alph were especially encouraging, h said.

turn to page 3

THE DAILY SKIFF

Prof warns death may lead to chao:

By SKIP HOLLANDSWORTH
Associate Editor

"You can feel the signs grumbling, the local movement

the mold were evidently slow, but not surprising. For the normalcy of their behavior was the very reason the problem existed in the first place.

The pressures that the university now faced within the public that caused an external investigation put TCU in a position to be viewed for its imperfections. It would not be until almost two years into the investigation that sophomore Tyrone Wilson would become the first Black student to accept a bid into Greek fraternity Lambda Chi Alpha. On February 12, 1981, the *Fort Worth Star-Telegram* published a photo of a smiling Wilson faced center around his new white fraternity brothers of Lambda Chi.[18]

Similar to other trailblazers, Wilson's intention was not to be trophied as the first Black student to take a place within a historically segregated organization on campus. Neither was it to be glorified as a celebrated token who was uniquely different from the majority of Black students who had been previously denied. He simply wanted to have a college experience that was memorable and enjoyable.

The public pressures brought about an external investigation, but the investigators determined that because admission into Greek organizations was based upon the vote of all members, they could find no explicit evidence that race was a deciding factor. As a result, we can argue that this verdict discredited a great deal of the experiences of Lloyd Higgins and many other students who felt that they were excluded from opportunities at TCU because of their race, instead of being considered because of what they could contribute as campus members. Their conclusion was by no means far-fetched.

But it is hard to overlook the coincidence that Wilson was admitted during the investigation. It might make one question the sincerity and genuineness of the admittance of a Black man to the historically segregated fraternity, or even the acceptance of Black students into the university to begin with. The experience of Wilson was not documented in detail, but based upon the still-siloed realities of TCU's Greek life, we can infer that race was indeed an influential factor.

Though experiencing different outcomes, the four Black women of 1969, Higgins, and Wilson would energize Black students to continue to advocate for themselves and expose the hypocrisy of the institution in not being as inclusive as preached to be. On the other hand, what these students probably did not realize was that their efforts and voices would echo for generations for Black students at TCU who wanted to also have a full TCU experience. A marker of real inclusivity is when those who are newly included have the privilege of exploring the same or similar options as those who have always been included.

Black students' desire to join the traditional white Greek organizations does not negate the long legacy of Black fraternities and sororities on college campuses and communities. This desire stems from just wanting the privilege to explore all options and to ultimately choose the best fit for them. Though there are not nearly as many traditional Black Greek organizations as Panhellenic or Interfraternity Council organizations, a strong sense of unity and community is re-

Above (Top)
The men of Alpha Phi Alpha Inc.
Courtesy of the Horned Frog, *1972.*

Above
The women of Delta Sigma Theta Inc.
Courtesy of the Horned Frog, *1979.*

Star-Telegram/VINCE HEPTIG
TYRONE WILSON . . . with new Lambda Chi "brothers"

Black TCU student joins white fraternity

Above
Tyrone Wilson is invited and accepts bid into Lambda Chi. *Courtesy of* TCU Magazine/ *Vishal Malhotra, 1981.*

flected amongst their members and gives Black students an opportunity to find a sense of belonging. These Black organizations began taking root on TCU's campus in the 1970s; the popularity began to emerge more amongst the 4 percent of Black students at TCU. Black students found solace and space in fully creating the experience that reflected their needs through the platform of the "Divine Nine."

The Divine Nine is a term that encompasses the nine historically Black Greek fraternities and sororities that are also members of the National Pan-Hellenic Council (NPHC). In the spring of 1971, Lonnie Woods, Charles Daniels, Hal Carter, Billy Davis, Richard Frichman, Billy Taylor, and Hugh Turner would petition to have a chapter of Alpha Phi Alpha Fraternity, Incorporated brought to campus. Originally the fraternity was an extension of the University of Texas-Arlington chapter, because establishment of a chapter required seven members, which forced TCU students to commute off campus to engage in their brotherhood. If anything, that commute proved the members' sheer determination to establish

4 THE SKIFF Friday, December 12, 1969

Passing the Torch, with Feeling...

Above
News Editor Ken Bunting in "Black is Good" T-shirt. *Courtesy of the* Skiff, *1969.*

a sense of belonging through the means available to them. That fall the first recognized Black fraternity to be established at TCU was the Eta Psi chapter of Alpha Phi Alpha Fraternity, Incorporated, the organization's 375th chapter.

In the same effort to create spaces for Black students, specifically for Black women, on April 22, 1972, Glenda Foreman, Debra Beaty, Sandra Johnson, Julia Wilson, Delores Sheppard, Sharon Hobbs, and Evette Kirkpatrick Brazzile established the Iota Eta chapter of Delta Sigma Theta, Incorporated. It would become the first Black sorority to be chartered at TCU.

Additional Divine Nine organizations would soon follow the original two that were chartered at TCU. If anything, this made the cause of Wilson and Lloyd's matter even more urgent. In effect, most Black students did not benefit from these opportunities to explore their student experience, and those who did were not being afforded the same luxury of options as their white peers.

There were three more avenues Black students began to explore that furthered their student experience. One was through the *Skiff* and the other through the Student Government Association (SGA). Both of these would become prime placements for Black students wanting not only to further immerse themselves in campus life, but ultimately to *influence it.*

The Pen and the Sword

The *Skiff* gave students the freedom to write the narrative of the TCU experience through the lens in which they saw it. Before social media, the *Skiff* would become one of the more (if not the only) prominent media in which TCU student voices could be expressed. These moments that TCU students timestamped still stand as testimony to the importance of allowing student journalism to document student experiences.

The writers in the stories printed throughout the 1960s during the integration of TCU attempted to be as impartial as possible, with reporters interviewing Black students or providing just the facts. Such stories lacked the personal insight that could only come from the vantage point of Black contributors.

Even then, having a space at the table and the freedom to express themselves does not mean that the written efforts of Black students would be as valued as stories by their white counterparts. It requires stakeholding positions within the newspaper office for writers to present their views in ways that would fully express Blackness and the expansiveness of the Black voice at TCU. That would come in the late 1960s, when Ken Bunting became the first Black student in the journalism department and the first Black news editor of the *Skiff.*

He influenced not only the paper through the voice and tone of the stories being told, but also the institution. Bunting would go on to be the first inductee to the Bob Schieffer School of Journalism Hall of Excellence and went on to become a reporter for the *Los Angeles Times.*

In a December 12, 1969, article, Bunting is pictured with a cartoon white "Black Is Good" t-shirt.[19] Though the original picture is blurry and hard to reproduce, readers could see that his personal pride in his Blackness also reflected the counterculture that Black students were creating through their individual and collective participation in TCU's campus culture. Could Bunting have been pictured in such clothing had he not held the title of news editor? Certainly, his status as news editor put him in an advantageous position to sport such clothes and advocate for Black pride.

Above
Loretta Gamble, the first Black student elected as a student body officer. *Courtesy of* Image, *1976.*

New Titles

What we may be able to assert is that Bunting's ability to publish such a social message would have been considered extremely radical for a campus such as TCU during the 1960s, given the protest and other outcries of concern that had been documented and will be revisited in Chapter 6. The student government would become another avenue in which Black students would begin to influence the TCU's campus culture for the better. In the social and athletics realm, in 1969, Ronnie Hurdle would become the first Black student to successfully win a campus-wide elected position. He also would become TCU's first Black cheerleader. In 1975, Loretta Gamble would become the first Black student elected as a student body officer. Elected as the vice president of Programming, Gamble would take on the role of programming events both educational and entertainment-wise for the entire TCU campus. Like her peers who also took on roles that marked them as the first Black student to enter that space, Gamble would be required to be and perform at a level of excellence that her white peers may not have had to reckon with.[20] That the first Black undergraduates of TCU had just graduated in 1969, and five years later, in 1974, a Black woman student became responsible for all campus programs displays how impactful the Black presences on campus had became. Surely Gamble was aware of TCU's history and legacy regarding race relations that took place before and while she was a student. Despite this, the East Texas native still made it a mission to not only be on campus, but to make her mark. Another groundbreaking trailblazer is Anthony Cregler, as he was the first Black student to join ROTC in 1967.

In the 2021–2022 academic year, for the first time TCU had a Black Student Government Association (SGA) president for undergraduates and a Black Graduate Student Senate (GSS) president for graduate students in the same year. The historic achievements of both Lau'Rent Honeycutt and Leslie Ekpe were significant individual accomplishments for them.[21] These events also follow the pattern of widening opportunities for the Black presence to shine brightly on the TCU campus, at the same time that they showcase how long it has taken TCU to be a welcoming space for its Black population to climb the ladder of accomplishments.

Through athletics, Greek Life, SGA, and the *Skiff,* Black students during the 1960s would forge their way into main-

Above
The first Black student to join TCU ROTC, Anthony Cregler, in 1971. *Courtesy of the* Horned Frog, *1971.*

Right
Students for the Advancement of Afro-American Culture (SAAC) host their student-led fashion show. *Courtesy of the* Horned Frog, *1970.*

SAAC

TCU's history as an integrated institution is not a long one. It was somewhat of a novelty, then, for an organization for blacks to be established on campus.

SAAC, the Students for the Advancement of Afro-American Culture, held its most successful activity when it presented the SAAC style and fashion show in the fall. The show not only raised money for the organization, but it also acquainted many members of the TCU community with Afro-American styles such as the dashiki.

ORGANIZATIONS

Above
The first Black graduate and undergraduate student body presidents, 2021. *Courtesy of* TCU Magazine, *Spring 2022.*

Right
Voices United gospel choir gathered around a piano. *Courtesy of the* Horned Frog, *1976.*

stream TCU life. Even though these spaces were not being occupied in large numbers by Black students, they continued to build upon their momentum, eventually creating their own organizations and spaces. Black students began to carve out a piece of campus for and as their own, at the same time influencing the younger generation of Black students and pushing TCU to think critically about how it might be failing to create a sense of belonging.

The counterculture that Black students brought with them onto TCU's campus would further push the envelope for Black students beyond the four main avenues of athletics, Greek life, SGA, and the *Skiff*, into creating their own organizations and clubs such as the Students for the Advancement of Afro-American Culture (SAAC) and Voices United.

Lift Every Voice

Though the official start date and founders' names have not be found, we did find that in the spring of 1969 Black students created an official organization centered on Black culture to serve as a collective voice supporting the interests of Black students. The formation of the Students for the Advancement of Afro-American Culture (SAAC) was foundational, providing students the option of their own space as opposed to having to integrate white organizations on campus. Though Black students had pushed hard to enter spaces where they could more fully explore their student experience, creating their own spaces allowed them to explore and express themselves in a place they felt secure to be themselves.

SAAC was able to create study systems for Black students, establish Black cultural events through such venues as the Black Fashion Show, and serve as a collective advocate on behalf of the sociopolitical needs and interest of Black students. Student President Eddie Miles stated that the purpose of the organization "to advance Afro-American culture at TCU and its immediate community through academic, service, and social activities."[22]

One significant item that helped ensure Black students were privy to the resources noted was the "Black Student Information Guide" produced in the 1970s by the office of Intercultural Affairs under Pat Kane, who had returned from a conference in Atlanta, Georgia, with ideas about how to better support the retention of Black students. With the "Black Student Information Guide" Kane was able to provide a guiding resource for Black students that identified the kinds of support available on campus.[23]

Connecting Black students back to the city Fort Worth was another way to tap important resources that TCU itself did not provide. Black businesses and locations found on the historic Southside, Como, and other predominantly Black neighborhoods of Fort Worth were able to provide Black students with a sense of belonging and community not always readily available on campus.

In this same spirit of creating space for their own, Black students found that creating and crafting of their own Black gospel choir was another outlet for their energy and talent. Established by Carolyn Bailey in 1974 alongside another group of students, Voices United became a traveling choir that expanded beyond the TCU campus and into the Dallas-Fort Worth metroplex area.[24] Bailey's vision was part of the continuum of Black presence growing and making their mark on campus. As Voices United began to gain new membership, it also carried out their work within the community by conducting workshops on campus and at local churches. They notably maintained a partnership with Shiloh Missionary Baptist Church of Fort Worth.[25]

The Climb Up

The breakthroughs that reflect the achievements and accomplishments of Black TCU were not solely the result of student efforts. Alongside them stood the brave Black faculty and staff who, like the students, faced the ever-present realities of being Black at an institution rooted in exclusion and not yet culturally ready for inclusion.

A trailblazer as one of the first Black graduates of TCU, Ms. Allene Jones would return to become the first Black professor at TCU. It is one thing to take instruction as one of the very few Black students on campus, but to return to take up the rank of professor only five years after graduating in 1963 speaks volumes about Jones's foresight and her commitment to help TCU become what it aspired to be. Despite whatever exclusions she faced as a student, Jones understood that there would be students coming behind her, and that the work she was doing should ensure that their door of opportunity remained open. Jones returned to the College of Nursing, where she would teach clinical and psychiatric nursing.[26]

In efforts to continue to diversify TCU, Dr. Cornell Thomas would become the first special assistant to the chancellor. Under his role and during Chancellor Michael Ferrari's tenure, Dr. Thomas would be responsible for overseeing diversity and community for the institution.[27] Dr. Thomas was hired as an assistant professor in 1990. One of the major projects that would come from Dr. Thomas is the TCU Community Scholars Program in the late 1990s. To date, over five hundred students have gone through the Community Scholars Program and have been able to receive full ride scholarships to TCU. [28]

Following the pathways of faculty, Vice Chancellor Tracy Syler-Jones would become TCU's first Black vice chancellor in 2006. Syler-Jones's ascension to the cabinet level of TCU would represent and reflect the ascension of the Black presence into some of the most influential positions on campus.[29]

The Black population on campus ascended into the structures at TCU's core, creating a counterculture that helped create wider opportunities for the Black students and faculty that followed. From the early contributions of Charley and Kate Thorp to the custodial staff, the early students of Brite Divinity, the graduate students of the class of 1963, the undergraduate students of 1964, and all other Black faculty, staff, and students that have come behind them—all would contribute to the counterculture that would challenge TCU's historic pattern of exclusion and racism. When we return to the question of "what is the story we tell ourselves about being at TCU?" we must ensure that our answers require us to think critically about how these breakthroughs, which are typically overlooked or written out of the narrative, are consistent with who we say we want to become.

Chapter 3

University Life

Vive la Différence

Cuando Vuelva a Tu Lado was a 1934 Spanish-language hit song written by Mexican songwriter María Grever and later covered by Black songstress Dinah Washington in 1959, in what is likely one of the track's more popular versions. In fact, Washington's version was so popular it earned her the 1959 Best Rhythm and Blues Performance Grammy Award—one of the international music industry's highest honors. Known in English as "What a Diff'rence a Day Makes," the song rose as high as number eight on the *Billboard* "Hot 100" listing and reached the top slot on the *Billboard* Hot R&B Sides. This track was also successfully recorded again in Spanish by Los Panchos with Eydie Gormé in 1964.

What a difference a day makes indeed. Up until January 22, 1964, Texas Christian University was a private, coed institution of higher learning that was growing in reputation, size, and popularity, but it was racially segregated. That is, until January 23, 1964, when TCU officially renounced racial segregation as a policy.[1] This book's content would be markedly different without such a diff'rence of a day.

But as our inclusion of TCU's *Land Acknowledgment* at this book's beginning indicates, TCU indeed has had relationships with the world and therefore other people of color since its very inception. How well-established and recognized these relationships are remains to be debated. We hope TCU's Native American Nations and Communities Liaison office will only continue to strengthen the university's recognition of Indigenous influence, particularly with the Wichita and affiliated tribes upon whose homeland the university currently stands. Further, TCU's *Civil Rights in Black and Brown Oral History Project* features a repository of film clips that connects TCU to local Mexican American history with numerous oral history interviews—but as Project Director Max Krochmal would likely opine, there are still numerous gaps to be filled with respect to the vast history of Mexican Americans and TCU in Fort Worth, Texas.

Yearbook photos, such as that of transfer student Mateo Alvarez De Molina of Valencia, Spain, not only show Molina graduating in 1916 with a BD degree, but also demonstrate that Spanish-language speakers received formal TCU educations well before 1964.[2] Other yearbook photos, such as this 1915 portrait of Vida Cantrell,[3] raise questions about how observing the "rules" behind segregation was based upon a definition of "whiteness" that may have been more fluid than fixed. In other words, Ms. Cantrell's picture introduces the possibility that she and others may have been "passing,"[4] or navigating life as a Black person who never interrupts society from bestowing upon them the legal benefits and social graces of appearing to be "white." A profound and poignant question, the answer to which is we likely shall never know! Otherwise, the historical record has scant and varied references to

Above
Ms. Vida Cantrell, 1915. *Courtesy of TCU Photo Collection.*

the "valuable, yet invisible" Black service staff in addition to various disparaging references to Black life generally within the student newspaper, the *Skiff.*

We call this chapter "University Life," but it will focus mostly on TCU's transition to integration for students and faculty. This focus is not to ignore the fact that there was a Black presence on campus before the 1964 pronouncement, but it was simply different. If anything, Black presence was felt from "Day One," meaning that Black labor contributed materially and substantively to the institution's early developmental stages. But when there are no Black students enrolled, no Black faculty on the payroll, and the only Black staff on campus play "valuable, but invisible" (that is, mostly manual and labor-intensive) roles, there is simply only so much Black presence to discuss. Additionally, with respect to documenting early Black staff, such a study is limited by the fact that more detailed personnel records were not routinely kept by TCU officials until roughly the 1960s, making the early years more difficult to factually document demographic data organized by race. But we are more fortunate to have a much larger historical record to generally draw from whilst peering into the window of time called *Transition to Integration.*

Transition to Integration

Of all the components that comprise university life, arguably one that receives more than its fair share of attention is that of the "paying customer." Conceivably, there is no university that exists without a group of individuals who decide to enroll and take classes for tuition in exchange for recognized credit—this curious group of individuals we shall call "students."

TCU first opened its doors to tuition-paying students in 1873. While TCU most definitely distinguished itself as one of the few "forward thinking" universities west of the Mississippi that held coed classes,[5] TCU did not integrate with Black students consistently until the 1960s, nearly a century after it was in operation. For the university not to be fully integrated racially for nearly two-thirds of its existence is significant and cannot be overlooked, as it has a continuing effect upon campus relations.

Because TCU was *seen* as not being fully welcoming in this manner for so long, this perception may unduly linger *even if it is not presently the case,* thereby obfuscating attempts to create new narrative impressions that can only be trusted after they've proved consistent over time. It is not as if no Black student ever set foot onto TCU's campus—after all, in 1935 the Wiley College Forensic Society—the same legendary team that was featured in the Denzel Washington-directed 2007 Hollywood movie *The Great Debaters*—was invited to go up against TCU in Fort Worth.[6] TCU "became the first all-white debate team from a university in the South to host historically Black Wiley College on its campus," even though there was no adjudged "winner" since the debate was not sanctioned. The "nonjudgmental approach" was likely for the best, as "Wiley's debaters had become such a phenomenal force that few colleges (Black or white) dared to challenge them."[7] But alas, while Black students were invited to debate, the topic of actually enrolling Black students at TCU was not yet up for debate. So now is as good a time as any to engage the question "Then when exactly did TCU fully integrate?"

The TCU Five-Step

The Texas "Two-Step" dance is yet another example of Texas's outsized cultural influence, likely connected to the overt pride associated with the sheer gargantuan size of the state. In other words, the partner, shuffle-based, circular pattern dance known generally as the country western "two-step" becomes colloquially known as the "Texas Two-Step." Here, in answering the query "Then when exactly did TCU fully integrate?" rather than provide a perfunctory and dissatisfying response such as "it depends," we offer a more nuanced and historically contextualized response that says, "there are potentially five different ways to answer this question." Quite succinctly, TCU engaged Black integration in at least five different steps in time, a choreography of separate yet connected movements that led to the current state of integrated affairs. We affectionately label this dance, the *TCU Five-Step*.

The five different steps in which TCU engaged Black integration are as follows:

- 1942, via the military
- 1952, via Brite College of the Bible
- 1954, via the College of Education
- 1962, via the Harris College of Nursing
- 1964, via TCU's main campus

Allow us to explain.

<u>***Step 1*** - 1942, via the military</u>

In a November 2, 1951 article entitled "Negroes Attending TCU, Sadler Says," the *Skiff* reported that TCU President M. E. Sadler issued a statement earlier that week "acknowledging the fact that Negro students have been admitted to TCU."[8] This was a public admission of what had been privately observed without much fanfare, apparently dating back to World War II. The article goes on to report that Sadler's press release downplayed the revelation that two or three soldiers attending the Evening College was "nothing new because colored soldiers were taught at the school during World War II."

This revelation only extends a poignant but painful narrative that likely is understudied and therefore not fully understood; the "citizen-soldier" model routinely employed by Black Americans with checkered results. The citizen-soldier model essentially holds that Black Americans could prove or even "earn" their citizenship by sacrificing the very thing that establishes citizenship and presence in the first place: the very lives inside their bodies.[9] Many Black Americans joined the cause (but were unable to pick up "arms") during the Civil War upon the faith and belief that their participation would be rewarded not just with "freedom," but with the liberty to actually exercise the theoretical freedom bestowed upon each and every American citizen.

While serving in the armed forces is noble and to be admired, it is also not a requirement for any individual to enjoy the fruits of citizenship. Yet in World War I and again in World War II, this model was employed by many Black Americans—so much so that disenchanted and disillusioned World War II veterans returned to the United States of America waging a new campaign upon the war's conclusion. The campaign was entitled "Double V," which advocated for a "V," or victory against fascism abroad (e.g., Adolf Hitler in Germany, Benito Mussolini in Italy, or Francisco Franco in Spain), and a second "V" against racism domestically.[10] In other words, one can only imagine how soul-crushing and intellectually painful it would be to suit up, engage "the enemy" abroad, and return successfully after risking one's life as a Black American only to be told—in uniform—that you would have to go to the back of the restaurant to get served while German Nazi Prisoners of War (as in Holocaust) were able to get served in the front of the very restaurant that you risked your life to defend overseas.[11]

With respect to how the citizen-soldier model is relevant to the TCU story, Black participation within TCU's educational space was "explained" as a strict matter of color-blindness with an exclusive, myopic focus upon the color green: 1) TCU simply abided by a contract with the Army and did not question who the Army selected to obtain the training necessary for their objectives, so long as the United States government honored its agreement to pay tuition, and 2) in the armed forces, differences are typically minimized in favor of unifying principles of soldiers bonded together for one singular cause. Yet President Sadler was careful to clarify that this limited, temporary arrangement with the military establishment did not affect the way TCU did business—which was to preserve a racially segregated space at the time: "There has been no fundamental change in the policy of Texas Christian University concerning the admission of Negro students to our school." Ultimately, these few students were not considered part of the "regular" undergraduate population and their credits did not advance them toward a TCU degree.[12] In other words, if anyone had a problem with this arrangement, they had to take it up with the United States government. This was not a development borne out of President Sadler having an epiphany about race relations while at Sunday service. TCU, in many ways, was merely "following orders."

Step 2 - 1952, via Brite College of the Bible

While the idea of Black students taking classes under any TCU veneer was perhaps explained away as a temporary, wartime necessity with limited impact on the status quo, TCU as an institution took another step closer when the Brite College of the Bible altered its admissions policy to admit Black students[13]—two years before the Supreme Court decision in *Brown v. Board of Education* effectively started the end of formal Jim Crow segregation with the pronouncement to integrate our nation's schools with "all deliberate speed."

Brite College of the Bible was the former name of the seminary school founded in 1914 that we currently call Brite Divinity School. The relationship between Brite Divinity School (BDS) and TCU is quite layered and is the subject for another study, with *A History of Brite Divinity School* being a good place to start.[14] BDS is located on TCU's campus on land that TCU owns, although permission agreements have been sorted to allow BDS routine and regular access to the chapel. Not only did BDS have and make admissions criteria and decisions independent of TCU, but it also has its own school president, as questions of independence and autonomy continue to be negotiated between it and its landlord, TCU. Nonetheless, BDS's bold step toward integration was absolutely a step for the larger machinery of TCU, even if technically a student at Brite College of the Bible was not an undergraduate student at TCU at the time.

In 1952, a major barrier was broken when Brite College of the Bible Trustees voted unanimously on September 6 that the seminary would admit Black students for graduate work.[15] James Claiborne was the first to enroll, but Vada Phillips Felder became the first Brite graduate.[16] Felder, perhaps proving that good gospel travels fast, read of Brite's new admission policy while riding a train on her way home to Fort Worth, which also was the last day of registration. Fortunately, she made it to Brite in time and enrolled, and "as she put it, she walked in with her transcript that afternoon and walked out with a full scholarship."[17] Felder graduated in the spring of 1954 with a masters of religious education, becoming the first Black American graduate of Brite, or TCU. Two other Black Americans enrolled at Brite at this time—James Claiborne and Daniel Goodspeed—but it is important to note that these were trailblazing *graduate*, and not undergraduate students.[18] Thus, while they were less likely to mix and mingle with the traditional undergraduate student population, this development nonetheless shows that the Brite Trustees actively, intentionally changed their admissions policy, although their decision did not directly bear impact upon TCU students until over a decade later.

Step 3 - 1954, via the College of Education

On February 19, 1954, the *Skiff* published an article entitled "Lack of Enrollment Ends Negro Classes."[19] While the article focuses upon low enrollment, it also points out two key details. First, this development did not represent a full-fledged opening of the proverbial "floodgates" in that the article observes: "The main obstacle in maintaining a larger enrollment is the inability of the students to use the credits earned towards a TCU degree." Similar to the "arrangement" made with the United States government during wartime, a limited number of Black students took classes through TCU, but these classes did not count toward a TCU degree.

Second, these night classes "were held at the Gay Street (elementary) School,"[20] which shows that TCU, like many other institutions and individuals of the time, observed rigid rules of physical racial segregation. As in the Brite College of the Bible, these Black students were only taking graduate classes. Although "students could use the TCU library," there was no true amalgamation of Black bodies and their ideas into the TCU educational universe. According to Mrs. Juanita Cash, mother of TCU alumnus and trailblazer Dr. James Cash, she obtained her master's degree from TCU after integration in the 1960s, but almost a decade after starting classes off campus.[21]

Lack of Enrollment Ends Negro Classes

Negro classes of the Graduate School have been discontinued because of lack of enrollment, Dean A. T. DeGroot, announced.

Enrollment has averaged 25 per semester. The main obstacle in maintaining a larger enrollment is the inability of the students to use the credits earned towards a TCU degree.

Mrs. Lottie Hamilton, principal of the Gay Street Elementary School, contributed much to encouraging students to enroll. She has earned 30 hours under the program.

Classes were held at the Gay Street School, and students could use the TCU Library.

Mrs. Acklin, 83, Dies

Mrs. Kate Acklin, 83, mother of Miss Pauline Acklin, circulation librarian, died Feb. 8 at Harris Hospital.

Above
TCU's College of Education helped TCU take another (quiet and not well-known) step towards racial integration on campus. *Courtesy of the* Skiff, *February 19, 1954.*

Nursing College To Admit Two Negro Students in Fall

While students were vacationing over the Easter holidays, the administration made changes in University policy.

According to a ruling by the executive committee of the Board of Trustees, qualified Negroes will be admitted to Harris College of Nursing in the fall. Two have been accepted.

Negroes enrolled in Harris or in Brite College of the Bible will be allowed to attend regular undergraduate classes to compensate for deficiencies in their programs.

Faces Problem

"Harris College is facing a grave problem of helping to produce enough trained personnel for our community, but with the new regulations, Negroes will be given the opportunity to receive nursing degrees," said Chancellor M. E. Sadler.

Negroes at area hospitals have in many cases completed preliminary work but need to finish their degrees.

For this reason, Negro coeds may take regular undergraduate courses toward their bachelor of science degrees in nursing.

Students in Brite who need to make up deficiencies in undergraduate school also may enroll in regular courses here. Negroes have been admitted to Brite for more than a decade. However, lack of undergraduate training has prevented some from meeting entrance requirements.

Brite students petitioned the Board of Trustes in March to "establish the means whereby all areas of University life be made available to all qualified students regardless of race or color."

Officials made it plain that the move to integrate Harris was in no way connected with the opinion poll taken during spring elections.

Favors Integrations

However, Brite and Harris Colleges showed a greater tendency toward favoring integration than did the five other schools in the University.

In Brite, 66 per cent answered yes to the question: "Do you favor admission of qualified Negro students to all colleges of TCU?" In Harris College, 51 per cent favored the proposal.

There will be no change in University policy regarding housing or other schools in the University.

Above
The Harris College continued the step towards full integration. *Courtesy of the* Skiff, *May 4, 1962.*

Step 4 – 1962, via the Harris College of Nursing

This fourth step is likely the best known of the five and is rehearsed with more frequency. During the fall semester of 1962, junior Patsy Brown and seniors Mrs. Doris Ann McBride and Mrs. Allene Jones all registered for classes at the Harris College of Nursing.[22] This is a significant step insofar as formal registration was observed for these three. It should be noted, however, that it is not without consequence that the first four steps in the TCU Five-Step involve opportunities that still speak to Romantic Racialist ideas of the nurturing skillsets traditionally associated with working Blacks: providing labor through service in the armed forces, or education to fulfill service-oriented roles (i.e., divinity school, elementary teacher education, and nursing). The idea of a liberal arts education, where Blacks would be free to pursue topics such as sixteenth century Russian art, for example, were still far and foreign.

Moreover, the three new TCU nursing students were not exactly new to education: "Two are seniors and graduates of St. Joseph Hospital School of Nursing and the Wichita General Hospital School of Nursing. The other is a junior and attended Dillard University in New Orleans."[23] Further, Allene Jones is likely the best known of the three within TCU circles, since she not only graduated but she returned to become TCU's first Black professor in 1968.[24] Allene Jones was lauded for taking a page of her integration experience out of the Jackie Robinson playbook—the Black male who is credited as being the first to integrate Major League Baseball in 1947, with the entire league wearing his #42 on Jackie Robinson day.[25] Tellingly, Jackie Robinson was heavily praised for his ability to "turn the other cheek," as counseled by Branch Rickey, for the concern was that if Robinson reacted—albeit justifiably—to any instance of racist vitriol, it would only fan the flames of public opinion ready to condemn Robinson and the whole integration enterprise as a waste of time and resources.

A specialist in psychiatric nursing,[26] Jones was constantly complimented for her calm demeanor and even temperament, with one example coming when her classmates were apparently more upset than she was when the owner of a private property refused to rent the location to the entire class on account of Jones's expected attendance.[27] Yet it is important to note that Jones at the time was not a traditional first-year student—she was nearly thirty years old and had prior schooling experience in an integrated institution. Says Jones: "I think the sheer fact that I was an adult and married made it easier for me than if I was a younger student."[28] Jones's respected temperament, in combination with her extended relationship with the university upon her return, likely contributed to her becoming the namesake of the Allene Jones Trailblazer Award by the TCU Harris College of Nursing and Health Sciences Alumni Association. Although Harris first started classes in September of 1962, she graduated with her degree in May 1963, and did not matriculate on a traditional four-year undergraduate plan.

Step 5 - 1964, via TCU's main campus

For the fifth and final step, on January 23, 1964, the university declared "From this day henceforth..."[29] effectively terminating racial segregation. This move came swiftly on the heels of mounting public pressure, as the previous December 1963 a student resolution was passed by vocal TCU student body president, Mark Wassenich.[30] In fact, white male Wassenich was a devoted Dr. Martin Luther King Jr. admirer who made desegregation part of his campaign. True to his word, after his successful election, he leveraged his position as president to guide TCU's Student Government Association toward passing the resolution denouncing continued discriminatory practices. His position was not occupied by a Black student until the election of Lau'Rent Honeycutt as the first Black TCU student body president in 2021.[31]

The board of trustees were originally scheduled to vote on the issue of desegregation in late November 1963, but those meetings were canceled due to President John F. Kennedy's assassination in nearby Dallas, after President Kennedy spent his last evening in Fort Worth. Says Wassenich: "The public schools got ahead of the private schools in integrating . . . Increasingly, progressive people related to the private schools." Wassenich and a growing chorus of others objected. "'Wait a minute. We shouldn't be dragging our heels on this. We should be leading.'"[32]

James M. Moudy, who succeeded Sadler as chancellor in 1965 and was instructed to write the integration statement, said: "I thought it was natural. I thought it was Christian. I thought it was time. It helped address a historic wrong."[33]

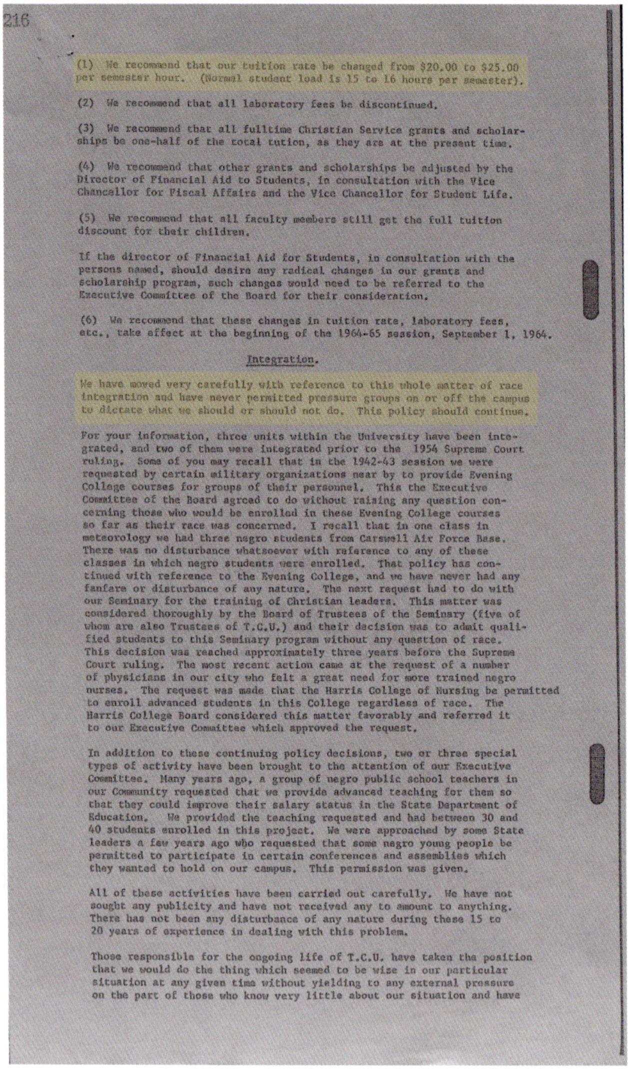
216

(1) We recommend that our tuition rate be changed from $20.00 to $25.00 per semester hour. (Normal student load is 15 to 16 hours per semester).

(2) We recommend that all laboratory fees be discontinued.

(3) We recommend that all fulltime Christian Service grants and scholarships be one-half of the total tution, as they are at the present time.

(4) We recommend that other grants and scholarships be adjusted by the Director of Financial Aid to Students, in consultation with the Vice Chancellor for Fiscal Affairs and the Vice Chancellor for Student Life.

(5) We recommend that all faculty members still get the full tuition discount for their children.

If the director of Financial Aid for Students, in consultation with the persons named, should desire any radical changes in our grants and scholarship program, such changes would need to be referred to the Executive Committee of the Board for their consideration.

(6) We recommend that these changes in tuition rate, laboratory fees, etc., take effect at the beginning of the 1964-65 session, September 1, 1964.

Integration.

We have moved very carefully with reference to this whole matter of race integration and have never permitted pressure groups on or off the campus to dictate what we should or should not do. This policy should continue.

For your information, three units within the University have been integrated, and two of them were integrated prior to the 1954 Supreme Court ruling. Some of you may recall that in the 1942-43 session we were requested by certain military organizations near by to provide Evening College courses for groups of their personnel. This the Executive Committee of the Board agreed to do without raising any question concerning those who would be enrolled in these Evening College courses so far as their race was concerned. I recall that in one class in meteorology we had three negro students from Carswell Air Force Base. There was no disturbance whatsoever with reference to any of these classes in which negro students were enrolled. That policy has continued with reference to the Evening College, and we have never had any fanfare or disturbance of any nature. The next request had to do with our Seminary for the training of Christian leaders. This matter was considered thoroughly by the Board of Trustees of the Seminary (five of whom are also Trustees of T.C.U.) and their decision was to admit qualified students to this Seminary program without any question of race. This decision was reached approximately three years before the Supreme Court ruling. The most recent action came at the request of a number of physicians in our city who felt a great need for more trained negro nurses. The request was made that the Harris College of Nursing be permitted to enroll advanced students in this College regardless of race. The Harris College Board considered this matter favorably and referred it to our Executive Committee which approved the request.

In addition to these continuing policy decisions, two or three special types of activity have been brought to the attention of our Executive Committee. Many years ago, a group of negro public school teachers in our Community requested that we provide advanced teaching for them so that they could improve their salary status in the State Department of Education. We provided the teaching requested and had between 30 and 40 students enrolled in this project. We were approached by some State leaders a few years ago who requested that some negro young people be permitted to participate in certain conferences and assemblies which they wanted to hold on our campus. This permission was given.

All of these activities have been carried out carefully. We have not sought any publicity and have not received any to amount to anything. There has not been any disturbance of any nature during these 15 to 20 years of experience in dealing with this problem.

Those responsible for the ongoing life of T.C.U. have taken the position that we would do the thing which seemed to be wise in our particular situation at any given time without yielding to any external pressure on the part of those who know very little about our situation and have

Above and Opposite
Photocopy of TCU Board of Trustee Minutes from the Special Meeting on January 23, 1964, addressing the university's altered position on segregation. *Courtesy of TCU Photo Collection.*

217

no responsibility for the maintenance of satisfactory life in our Institution.

I believe we have gone far enough now to draw some rather definite conclusions with reference to this matter.

No matter what units within the University it might seem wise to integrate at any given time we will never have very many negro students enrolled. This is due to two or three basic factors. Our admissions requirements and course requirements are being raised increasingly, and very few negro students could qualify for admission. Our tuition and fees will be raised from time to time, and relatively few negro people would have the funds necessary to finance the kind of education we offer here. The third factor grows in part out of my experience as a Trustee of a negro college and a negro university. No matter how much integration previously white colleges and universities might allow, almost all negro college students will want to attend their own institutions of higher learning. For the next half century it will be the relatively few negro students who cannot find in their own colleges exactly the kind of higher education they desire and who have unusual intellectual abilities and financial resources who would want to enroll in previously white colleges and universities.

For the past six months we have had some students meeting with some Trustees to discuss racial issues. One purpose which we had in mind in starting these discussions was to let our student leaders understand something of the problems and difficulties which are in the thinking of some of us who are more mature in our connection with life and with T.C.U. At the same time I wanted some of our Trustees to become acquainted with the reasonable attitudes which most of our student leaders have concerning this and other matters pertaining to our situation. It is our hope that these informal conversations can be continued and increasingly enlarged.

Wills and Bequests

Those of you who listen to radio and television very much hear frequent reference concerning the importance and needs of higher education in the United States. Dr. Frank Sparks was a very successful businessman before he decided to go into education. After he completed his education he went as President of Wabash College in Indiana. Because of his successful business background and educational experience, he was selected to lead the privately controlled Council for Financial Aid to Education. This Council is responsible for the numerous statements concerning education which we hear over radio and television frequently. It has been extremely helpful.

I have know Dr. Sparks for perhaps 15 years. In one of the conferences which he conducted he made this suggestion which impressed me most favorably. In effect, he said we should get all persons who are at all friendly to our institution to mention the Institution in their wills even though they were not in position to leave a bequest. As he put it, it would be extremely impressive if it could be stated in numerous wills that the person writing it had T.C.U. in mind even though he might not be in position to include any bequest. In his talk Dr. Sparks said that some such paragraph as this might be in the will of a person who had very little resources and could not do anything in a material way to help:

> "I believe in the work of ______________________
> and would like to leave something to help undergird
> the future development of this significant institu-
> rion if I were able to do so."

If we could get a campaign of this nature started and if it could spread throughout the Southwest so that when numerous wills were read the name of T.C.U. would be favorably mentioned, whether or not the person felt able to contribute anything it would have a most wholesome effect. It is likely that many people would decide they could leave something to T.C.U.

Income Tax Credit For Tuition And Fees

Most of you will remember that about three years ago the possibility of income tax credit for college tuition and fees was discussed in our Board meeting. The idea was unanimously approved, and some suggestions were made that I might talk with groups of college representatives in different areas with reference

223

SPECIAL MEETING OF THE BOARD OF TRUSTEES
January 23, 1964

A special meeting of the Board of Trustees was held in the Board of Trustees Room at 3:00 p.m. on Thursday, January 23, 1964, with the following persons present:

Mr. Clyde Tomlinson, Vice Chairman	Mr, Granville Walker
Mr. A. D. Weatherly	Mr. Bonner Frizzell
Mr. Sol Brachman	Mr. Theodore Beasley
Mr. B. B. Fuqua	Mr. W. Oliver Harrison
Mr. Y. Q. McCammon	Mr. Drew Ellis
Mr. Sidney Latham	Mr. L. C. Wright
Mr. Sam P. Woodson	Mr. Murray Kyger
Mr. Marion Hicks	Mr. Newton J. Robison
Mr. Beeman Fisher	Mr. Carlos Ashley
Mr. W. M. Sherley	Mr. Fred Erisman
Mr. Andrew A. Bradford	Mr. M. M. Neeley
Mr. Ralph B. Shank	Mr. Harold Herndon
Mr. Larry Blackmon	Mr. Lester Clark
Mr. Bryant M. Collins	Mr. Gean B. Turner
Mr. J. A. D. Green	Mr. Earle B. Barnes
Mr. Glen Turbeville	Judge Jack M. Langdon
Mr. W.C.C. Conner	

Chancellor M. E. Sadler, Assistant Chancellor Amos W. Melton, Vice Chancellor for Fiscal Affairs L. C. White, Secretary Dean Jerome A. Moore.

Mr. Clyde Tomlinson, Vice Chairman, presided in the absence of Mr. Lorin Boswell, who was in a hospital.

The invocation was pronounced by Dr. Granville Walker.

After a preliminary clarification of the purpose of the special meeting; Mr. Tomlinson called on Chancellor M. E. Sadler.

Chancellor Sadler read a statement characterized by historical accuracy, completeness of details, and statesmanlike approach to the question under consideration, concerning which he recommended.

"That from this day henceforth students be enrolled at T.C.U. without reference to race, creed or nationality, and that the Board of Trustees trust the administration to carry out this responsibility."

Mr. Harrison moved adoption of the recommendation as read by Chancellor Sadler. Mr. Brachman seconded the motion.

Mr. Sherley made a substitute motion that T.C.U. not be further integrated than it now is. Mr. Latham seconded the substitute motion.

Mr. Sherley and Mr. Latham withdrew their substitute motion and Mr. Beasley moved that no action be taken at this time. Seconded by Mr. Sherley.

Mr. Blackmon moved that the substitute motion by Mr. Beasley be tabled. Seconded by Mr. Ashley. Mr. Balckmon's motion passed (18 for, 9 against).

A vote was then called for on the original motion by Mr. Harrison, as seconded by Mr. Brachman, that approval be given for enrollment of students in T.C.U. without reference to race, creed, or nationality, and that the administration be entrusted to carry out this responsibility from this day forward. The motion passed (21 for, 4 against).

The text of Chancellor Sadler's statement is attached to these minutes as Appendix "A". Perhaps it should be recorded in these minutes that the consensus of those present was that Chancellor Sadler's statement and replies to questions were a model of educational and spiritual statesmanship, that Mr. Tomlinson's ability and fairness as chairman were unsurpassed, and that the exemplary conduct of all who spoke, whether for or against the motion adopted, was a demonstration of the character of the Board which continues to make our University great.

Secretary

(Mr. Tomlinson passed away before he had an opportunity to sign these minutes.

Growing Pains

Unlike solving a simple problem like changing out a burned-out light bulb, however, solving the problem of desegregation on TCU's campus was considerably complex. As the famous Dinah Washington song waxes on about "What a Diff'rence a Day Makes," it may have only taken a day to announce a new TCU policy, but it may take considerably more time to truly implement and integrate said policy. Unfortunately, it did not take long after the first full-time, "traditional" undergraduate Black students were admitted to TCU for attendant tensions—or growing pains—surrounding this "new" Black presence to appear. And reappear.

For example, less than half a decade after official integration, before a TCU home football game against visiting in-state rival Southern Methodist University, the first Black scholarship athlete in the Southwest Conference, Jerry LeVias, received death threats. Apparently, in addition to the young man juggling being a student athlete with his academic obligations, he had the additional consideration of watching out for bullets that could possibly end his life while playing a game out under the sun—the same one that shone on the majority white crowd in the stands. The threat was taken seriously, for "during every down, Fort Worth police and the FBI watched for an assassin from locations throughout the stadium. Even the Boy Scouts working as ushers were looking out for the sniper."[34] It is as amazing as it is alarming to read LeVias's account of how he ran to the sidelines for cover between plays and how his coaches called numerous plays for him to be "in motion," to make him a more difficult target. Obviously, some readers may wonder why even play the game, but to LeVias and his teammates, playing despite the risk was perhaps an act of resistance to the fear the death threat was supposed to produce. We tip our hat to such bravery in the face of such cowardice.

If anything, this dramatic response to the same Black bodies who traditionally share intimate spaces with whites while cooking, cleaning, and caring for TCU's campus, sitting inside classrooms as purported peers fits a larger pattern of resistance. Immediately after the Civil War, during the failed Reconstruction period, race relations, which arguably were already problematic if you count enslavement as an affront to basic civil liberties, actually worsened following the end of enslavement, as many citizens were reluctant and recalcitrant to let go of a civilization "gone with the wind."[35] Many forget that extrajudicial lynchings, the rise of the Ku Klux Klan, convict leasing, sharecropping, and unchecked racial vigilantism all were new developments that occurred *after enslavement*, not during.

Ronald Hurdle in 1969 dared to become the university's first Black cheerleader, but at a personal cost. Although he simply wanted to become more involved in mainstream college life, Hurdle's experience demonstrated that not everyone would necessarily cheer him on as he embarked upon his solitary, trailblazing path. For hours, his white roommate would field harassing phone calls, some replete with the n-word, from enterprising individuals who had discovered his phone number. Aside from his own safety, Hurdle was made to worry about other people—namely the white female cheerleaders with whom he worked. Says Hurdle, "It became obvious to me that they didn't want these contact cheers done because now they had a Black male in the midst of a bunch of white students."[36] After much discussion and spilled ink, an entire year later in 1970, TCU finally decided to "allow" Hurdle to touch his fellow white female cheerleaders.[37]

While TCU itself, as an institution, did not explicitly deploy the Confederate flag or other Confederate paraphernalia on campus, its rhetoric about race was nonetheless problematic. After integration, TCU faced the thorny issue of convincing a potential new market that they were open for such integrated business, while at the same time not "upsetting" older white and affluent donors.

In fall of 1970, Jennifer Giddings made history when she was elected TCU's first Black Homecoming Queen. While Giddings was pleasantly surprised at her successful election by her peers, she likely was also surprised to learn that the 1970 TCU Homecoming Queen would not be invited to the Cotton Bowl. The then TCU student body president Mike Usnick explained that "for the last two years, invitations to the Cotton Bowl game have been sent for the student body president, the cheerleaders, and the TCU Sweetheart. Since Angela Ambrose was this year's sweetheart, she, and not Jennifer Giddings, got the invitation to participate."[38] While the record is unclear as to what was communicated or miscommunicated to Giddings, the bottom line is that although TCU elected its first Black Homecoming Queen, it was the TCU Sweetheart and not the TCU Homecoming Queen who received an invitation to represent the school nationally at the Cotton Bowl in 1970. While undoubtedly Ms. Giddings's successful election was a tangible sign of "linear progress," in actuality her qualified and limited moment of glory was a tangible sign of the more cyclical nature of differing treatment, or discrimination, believed, perceived, and received by Black people.

In October of 1974, TCU's Forums Committee invited David Duke, Grand Dragon of the Ku Klux Klan, to speak at the university.[39] After much campus debate and activism by mostly Brite Divinity students in the form of a petition with hundreds of signatures, Duke's appearance was canceled, and he did not come to campus.[40] At least Duke had an invitation that needed canceling; Dr. Martin Luther King had no such luck. Granted, free speech is a necessary component for a university that should remain open to the robust and vigorous exchange of ideas—however, it is interesting to note that just over a decade earlier, TCU student body president Mark Wassenich said he and "the Student Congress tried to invite Martin Luther King Jr. to speak on campus. Wassenich said the administration and Fort Worth community leaders felt if King spoke on campus, it could easily lead to riots in the TCU community."[41] Apparently, with Duke's event, the same concern for riots had dissipated, even though the country did indeed witness a national breakout of riots and protests in the aftermath of Dr. King's assassination in 1968. Interestingly, many moons later, the same institution would host renowned Black scholar and equal education advocate Beverly Tatum, and civil rights activist and surviving cousin of Emmett Till, Reverend Wheeler Parker Jr., within a few weeks of one another.[42]

A decade after Jennifer Giddings integrated TCU public life in 1970, in the early 1980s, TCU took its first step toward racially integrated fraternity and sorority life on campus. In 1981, Tyrone Wilson became the university's first Black student admitted to a white fraternity when he accepted a bid from Lambda Chi. Wilson received the bid as soon as a two-year investigation by TCU's Student Organizations Committee was completed. Yet the fraternity declared the bid was not in response to the investigation of "alleged racial discrimination among the traditionally segregated social fraternities and sororities."[43]

Perhaps racial tensions could be expected to be high initially, as the transition to integration created novel scenarios that were new for all involved. Yet, in the late eighties, evidence of racial tension still reared its head. In 1988, TCU's University Minister, Reverend Jesse Truvillion, found a Black cat with its throat slit dying on top of his vehicle.[44] Apparently, Truvillion held a "South African Simulation Game" after hosting African visitors to campus, during a time when promoting dialogue and awareness over apartheid was growing, with freedom fighter Nelson Mandela still in jail (released in 1991). In addition to obscenities hurled in Truvillion's direction, he was told directly before approaching his car, "You're a dead cat, buddy." It is unknown whether the dog-loving individuals were TCU students or not, but they were clearly individuals who had knowledge and information about an activity held on campus for TCU students on a Tuesday evening in early April. It would not be until a decade later, in 1998, when TCU reintroduced the Black Studies minor as a means to foster, for lack of a better word, education around the topic of race relations.[45]

Perhaps earlier integration of such Black Studies curriculum would have assisted local Fort Worth Police in restraint before they cast such a wide net of suspicion over every Black male breathing when the campus scrambled to respond to a series of sexual assaults. On February 11, 1999, the *Daily Skiff* reported that thirty mostly Black males attended a session on campus led by attorneys from the American Civil Liberties Union to understand their rights.[46] Many were concerned that in efforts to "solve a crime," authorities had questioned too many Black males fitting the vague description of "a black male, 20 to 30 years old, approximately 5 feet 10 inches tall and weighing between 160 and 180 pounds." Many of the Black males in attendance at the information session shared that they were "unnecessarily stopped and harassed by officers on separate occasions since the sexual assaults began in January 1998."[47]

One of the attending students, Joe Briggs, asserted that the already negative narratives surrounding virtually any Black male were only worsened in the wake of the campus assaults. "Being a Black male on campus is becoming very burdensome . . . people whisper when you walk by." Briggs was a TCU senior at the time he shared his thoughts, exclaiming "I can't wait until I don't have to walk around with a yoke on my neck. . . . I think it will go on as long as Black males are around TCU." Only time will tell whether Mr. Briggs's prophecy will be proven false. On the other hand, Briggs in 1999 may have unwittingly planted seeds of a growing Afro-pessimism movement that has numerous Black intellectuals wondering aloud whether true fundamental, systemic change will ever occur and release Black Americans from the continued frictions and restrictions they face.[48] While Briggs offered insightful social commentary as a young man on TCU's campus, TCU is fortunate to now count upon Joe D. Briggs's insights as one of the few non-white board of trustees members since 2015.

To conclude this section and to return to its opening analogy about switching out a burned-out light bulb, it is no indictment to state that improving race relations on TCU's campus or any other campus is not as simple as "flipping a light switch." We often overlook how two-and-a-half centuries of enslavement preceded the failed Reconstruction and Jim Crow periods that spanned the first two-thirds of TCU's existence. These old—albeit racially problematic—habits do not fade away as quickly as some would like to think upon the public pronouncement of a practical policy. This contextualization perhaps helps explain why or how from 1959 to 1984, there were at least seventeen "slave auctions" on campus—although they were innocently designed as a fraternity and sorority effort to raise funds for a "good cause."[49] It goes without saying that despite the philanthropic intent, the resulting impact is that such a framing is tone-deaf, to say the very least.

The Ambivalence Equivalence

While it is clear that the decision to integrate TCU changed its future trajectory, what is less clear is why TCU ultimately arrived at this decision after ninety-one years of largely uninterrupted and unchallenged racial segregation. The delicate matter here is when discussing TCU's decision to integrate, proper recognition of instituting an egalitarian and morally just policy is justified; but should an institution receive adulation and commemoration for finally instituting what arguably it could have and should have done from the onset? While this is the type of question that is neither asked nor answered fully in the prevailing historiography, we aim to do so here.

At a special meeting of the TCU Board of Trustees, on January 23, 1964, Chancellor Sadler read a statement: "That from this day henceforth students be enrolled at T.C.U. without reference to race, creed or nationality, and that the Board of Trustees trust the administration to carry out this responsibility."[50] Before TCU arrived at this decision, however, the archives reveal an ambivalence toward desegregation by upper-level administrators who never explicitly or expressly prohibited racial integration—it was just tactfully and consistently avoided.[51] Thus, to see change over time in policy and position is proof positive that institutions can undergo profound change, insofar as the entire body and leadership invests in principles of reconciliation.

However, there are additional details to point out in the *same document* that allow for us to "celebrate" this integration edict with the proper perspective. Not only did the same memorandum include a recommendation to increase tuition "from $20.00 to $25.00 per semester hour," but Sadler offers three key rationales to assuage the public that even in the face of an edict endorsing integration, the proverbial "floodgates" allowing for massive Black infusion would simply not occur. Sadler first states, "our admissions requirements and course requirements are being raised increasingly, and very few negro students could qualify for admission." While seemingly opening the door, Sadler appears content with the calculation that not many Black students will even be able to walk through the door.

Secondly, Sadler continues, "our tuition and fees will be raised from time to time, and relatively few negro people would have the funds necessary to finance the kind of education we offer here." Again, while the doors of the university are technically open, Sadler reasons that the cost is too expensive for many Blacks to afford the investment, notwithstanding the possibilities of individual savings, scholarship, or federal loan aid. Further, such an economic assumption speaks volumes about Sadler's possible working acknowledgement of systemic, structural barriers that make economic prosperity difficult for Black people, thereby making the price of TCU just a bit out of reach—even if legally affordable to anyone who wishes to enter.

Finally, Sadler opines that "no matter how much integration previously white colleges and universities might allow, almost all negro college students will want to attend their own institutions of higher learning."[52] This last reason defies logic, for if TCU is a high-quality institution that should attract the best and the brightest, then why would Black students not be attracted or intrigued by the prospects of obtaining a TCU degree like any other? The idea that Black students will want to self-segregate justifies an unfair system of disparate resource allocation which they bore no responsibility in creating. It is important not to myopically focus on the few lines declaring integration when there is considerably more accompanying text in the full memorandum that paints a larger picture of a policy that sounds great in theory, but in practice was designed to keep the university feeling, looking, and operating much like it did before the desegregation decree.

Furthermore, over a decade before the 1964 edict, it appears Chancellor Sadler was noncommittal on the issue. When he was quoted in a November 2, 1951, *Skiff* article stating, "For the past ten years, we have wanted to avoid any action which would cause any people to point to us and say 'Texas Christian University is pioneering and pushing out in the matter of non-segregation,'"[53] Sadler seemed to downplay the fact that Black students were actually receiving intellectual instruction from TCU faculty, but only due to an economic and possibly patriotic arrangement with the federal government, with two or three Black soldiers attending the Evening College.

Sadler's economic interest is clear with the statement: "If the University attempts to render this service for the military establishments it does not feel it should bar any students sent in by the military to take the courses which they contract with us to give." But even Sadler's logic to justify this small deviation from the societal status quo (which was Jim Crow segregation) suggests a gravitational pull to the ultimate truth of equality, ergo desegregation. The idea that honoring the contract with the government to teach pupils—no matter who they are—speaks to the basic, universal concept of equanimity. Sadler understands this logic when he expands, "when they select these people for various educational courses, they do not check to see whether or not they are Whites or Negroes." Unfortunately, that logic did not yet extend to Black students willing to sign a contract to pay tuition to TCU for a high-quality education at that point in time.[54]

This ambivalence is also apparent in a letter dated January 4, 1952, addressed to Mrs. Betty Wilkes Pederson. In the letter Sadler reassures the TCU alum that "I regret exceedingly the disturbed attitude which you have concerning Texas Christian University, because of what you think we are doing in the field of Negro education. I believe if we could explain the facts, you would not be disturbed at all." Pederson composed a letter the day after Christmas, or on December 26, 1951, expressing disbelief over the prospects of racial integration. She made sure that the economic consequences of her opinion were clear when she stated, "I will never contribute to anything our ex-school needs and will never let my children attend a school with negroes!" But in strict observance of formal graces, Pederson does not fail to include a dash of Southern etiquette when the last line of her letter reads: "I might add that we are all terribly sorry this had to happen."[55]

Sadler responded, "In the sense in which you evidently think of it, we do not have Negroes enrolled in Texas Christian University. We are providing certain special work for them which they have no possibility of getting elsewhere and which I do not believe has at all raised the problem of non-segregation in the minds of any of our students or friends on the campus." Sadler then concluded with the phrase, "When we are so careful in our approach to it, it disturbs us very much when those who are supposed to be our friends take an adverse attitude." The year was 1952, and rigid rules of segregation were not just observed at TCU, but within Fort Worth and across the South. For instance, in August of 1953, Lawrence and Ava Peters purchased a home at 109 Judkins Street, and in so doing became the first Black family to cross the segregated boundary of Fort Worth's Riverside neighborhood. On November 2 of that same year, the Peterses' car was bombed and destroyed in an attempt to intimidate them for daring to live the American Dream by becoming homeowners.[56]

When Students Educate the University

In looking at how TCU can change over time, perhaps a key clue can be found with the "paying customer," or students. As more students wrestled with the 3Es (i.e., lack of education, exposure, and experience), more became vocal about how being informed and inclusive contributes to an improved university environment. For example, on November 4, 1960, the *Skiff* published an editorial entitled "Immature Segregationists" that called out and criticized members of the TCU community who apparently were not polite hosts to a recent campus speaker.[57] The campus speaker was professor Kenneth Henry of Jarvis Christian College, a Historically Black College or University (i.e., HBCU) who spoke on campus on October 24, 1960, with a speech entitled, "The Negro's Quest for Fair Play." Thus the student newspaper gave air and voice to a TCU student reporter who condemned the behavior of students who defaced posters advertising Henry's talk by crossing out the word negro and writing in the n-word instead.

But let us not overlook how Brite Divinity School's first Black graduate, Vada Phillips Felder, actually hosted Dr. Martin Luther King Jr. a year earlier at her own home in 1959.[58] King spoke on October 22, 1959, about "A Great Time to Be Alive" at the Majestic Theater to an audience of roughly four hundred people.[59] The semester following Professor Henry's visit, a March 1961 article in the *Skiff* discusses how the TCU Student Congress "has accepted a proposal to sponsor a seminar that would discuss objectively race relations in the United States." The date was set for May 5–6, 1961, and showed perhaps growing interest in the topic generally when the proposal "passed by almost a 2-1 margin."[60] So in May 1962 TCU students had the opportunity to hear in person United Nations undersecretary and Nobel Prize winner Ralph Bunche as "the first highly visible Black leader on campus."[61]

This growing interest apparently started spreading to upper administration when Vice Chancellor James M. Moudy delivered a six-page statement to the board of trustees on June 7, 1963. Moudy opened by stating, "I believe that our longstanding policy of excluding Negro students from Texas Christian University has served its purpose and that in the future we should rely on an admissions policy which excludes only persons who are judged to be unable to profit from curricula at TCU." The sense of equality is subtly tied to the growing "economic equality" theme, whereby if the individual is unable to "profit," then TCU will not be worth their expenditure of time, money, or energy—but according to Moudy's logic, TCU would not be to blame when it is up to the individual's free economic decision.[62]

Then in December 1963 TCU student body president Mark Wassenich helped lead the charge for students to vociferously offer their view, with the student congress passing a resolution, "26-0, for the administration to remove admission requirement barriers by the end of the academic year."[63] All of these events provide a glimpse into the bevy of steps TCU took up until January 23, 1964, with many more steps yet to be discovered and added to our existing foundation of understanding.

The Dance of Interest Convergence

In returning to the history-altering date of January 23, 1964, Vice Chancellor Moudy, who became chancellor in 1965, was tasked by Chancellor Sadler to write the desegregation statement that he expressed was overdue. Sadler was quoted as saying, "For Christian reasons, it should have been sooner. For practical reasons, it was not done sooner. The reason we were late in doing it was because we were a little fearful in what the parents would think, what trustees would think and what donors would think."[64] In fact, Student Body President Wassenich said that he spoke to Chancellor Sadler by phone after the historic board meeting. TCU "'only lost $5 million in pledged endowment (because of the vote),' Wassenich said. 'He was afraid he could lose three to four times that amount.'" To his credit, Sadler was not too concerned about the bottom line when he stated "'Once people settle down, I'll get that money back . . . we were late in doing it. It was past time.'"[65]

As time would tell, shifting an entire ontology of thought overnight was not as simple as issuing a memo. While the 1964 edict does state that no barriers will be erected for Black admission, the initial statement does not detail or mention a recruiting or admissions plan to implement the policy, nor is there evidence of collaboration or consultation with local Black constituents. But even an institution must learn to crawl before it can walk.

Before we paint this part of the integration picture with a stroke of altruism, however, we must also consider broader forces that may have contributed to TCU's decision to open its doors. This brings us to the principle of interest convergence, a simple concept that shows how individuals or institutions often operating in their own best interest will align themselves with others to the extent that a benefit can be extracted. By way of brief example, consider how an eager teenager may "offer" to get groceries, otherwise a chore, if able to use the car to sneak in a quick visit with their new paramour who happens to live near the very same grocery store where the teenager offered to complete the shopping. In other words, while the eager teenager is indeed offering assistance to their parent, the teenager's conduct is highly incentivized by the prospect of personal gain. This analogy prompts us not to discount wholesale with skepticism the actions of an institution like TCU to engage racial equity issues, but rather that in addition to altruism, there may be other motivating reasons to consider as well.

Rice University is similar to TCU in that it is a private university located in Texas. Rice University is *dissimilar* to TCU in that it is a Research 1 University (TCU is classified as "R2")[66] that has significantly more resources. Rice was also dissimilar in that it was expressly provided by the founder's will to educate only "the white inhabitants of the City of Houston, and State of Texas." Further, the Rice University Woodson Research Center states Rice "was one of the last private schools in the South to desegregate because of the trustee's false sense of financial security."[67] So what changed,

Right
On November 11, 2022, Dr. James Cash was honored with a statue in the Schollmaier Arena, the first statue of a Black individual on campus. Additionally, Dr. Cash was awarded an Honorary Doctorate and honored with official statements from leaders of Tarrant County and the City of Fort Worth, declaring November 11 Dr. James Cash Day. *Courtesy of TCU Athletics/Sharon Ellman.*

prompting Rice University to finally desegregate? Was it an urgent and burning sense of righteous justice that could not be abated any further? Or would it surprise the reader that monetary resources may have also played a factor?

With research organized under a heading entitled "Between Decisions," the Research Center explains that as the school grew over the years since its founding, so did its need for additional resources and revenue. Fortunately, Rice University's Board of Trustees Chair George R. Brown's "ties to Lyndon B. Johnson provided a chance for Rice to work with the newly formed NASA (1958) and its Manned Spacecraft Center."[68]

Interest convergence here would suggest that as Rice University was quite desirous of lucrative federal contracts, the NASA contract and others "were also in jeopardy because of the federal government's strict enforcement of racial non-discrimination clauses. The charter prohibiting the trustees to admit black students and charge tuition forced Rice between a rock and a hard place."[69] Suddenly, if not magically, Rice University's interest in working with NASA right outside of Houston now meant that "we have a problem" with racial discrimination. Once an effective enforcement mechanism was in place (i.e., withholding of federal dollars), Rice University decided to change "the way it does business" by formally amending its charter on September 26, 1962, and hiring lawyers to alter the course and complexion of its campus forever. In other words, "justice" may have been part of the decision-making process, but such justice also conveniently intersects with Rice University's desire to avail itself of a significant funding source that would have been denied based upon its prior "whites only" policy.

With respect to TCU, Jerome A. Moore in *Texas Christian University: A Hundred Years of History* reminds us that in 1963 TCU, "following the lead of the University of Texas, joined with the other members of the Southwest Conference in dropping all racial bars to University admission and participation in athletic sports."[70] TCU's desegregation edict closely follows in early 1964. It is unclear to what degree it was a factor, but it is a possibility that the prospect of lost revenue if they were unable to participate in racially integrated intercollegiate sports may have been a factor. All we know is that these two events happened closely in time, with not enough evidence currently to conclusively draw a solid connection.

Ultimately, the sincerity of TCU's future efforts toward diversity are simply a story that will continue to be told in time, with the presumption that time always tells the truth.

Chapter 4

Athletics

Pregame

The Horned Frogs have a history as a relatively small institution with a highly competitive sports program. The entry area of the Ed and Rae Schollmaier Arena details the school's trophied glory from the twentieth century, which saw the institution rise to national prominence first through its football program and then by the success of its other sport programs. Now the Horned Frogs hold national recognition in sports such as basketball, track and field, rifle, soccer, golf, tennis, and more. Football, however, was the foundation around which TCU would build its athletic identity. From Hall of Fame football coaches Dutch Meyer to Gary Patterson, the leadership of storied coaches would guide the program into national prominence. Both legends have statues erected in their honor as leaders to be celebrated and appreciated for what they were able to accomplish during their tenure.

It is common within the sports world that head coaches are the play callers, responsible for building a culture and recruiting and molding players that will fit into their systems to win games and championships. When teams are successful, we remember the star players as well as the coaches who led the team to victory. However, when programs struggle, it is just the coach who is blamed and possibly even fired or demoted. Thus, heavy is the head that wears the headset, for the responsibility of being a head coach comes with the weighty task of building and maintaining a winning team year in and year out.

The Scouting Report

The head coach position is one of the most important and remembered positions within sports. Coaches are the individuals who are seen as responsible for the direction and success of a team. Especially in major college athletics, where winning teams help generate revenue and attract students and donors to an institution.

Though it is typically the coaches whose tenure and name become associated with a school's success, it is the student athletes who risk their bodies for the name on their helmets or jerseys. Dedicating themselves fully to practice, play, and performance to compete at a high level, student athletes are the engines behind college athletics and an institution's athletic successes. Furthermore, succeeding at a rigorous TCU is only half of the game; performing and winning on the athletics field is one-half of the assignment. Being full-time students, dedicating time to study, and excelling within the classroom is no easy feat. While balancing school, college life, and performing on their respective playing fields, student athletes become the true champions and models of the TCU brand and legacy. This is not to say that they are the sole and only group of students who push forward the institution, but simply to acknowledge that being both students and athletes is a large task. By offering up their time, energy, effort, and bodies, student athletes give a lot of themselves to contribute to the success of their team, and thus, the university. But how is success measured in sports? Obviously, the score-

Left
Evans Royal being lifted up by fans after a win. *Courtesy of Linda Kaye, 1971.*

Above
TCU Women's Basketball Team celebrates a big win over Vanderbilt University. *Courtesy of Linda Kaye, 2002.*

board and trophy case recount a program's success. But if college athletics are also viewed as a tool to help shape practical skills of discipline, partnership, strategic thinking, and leadership, how is the success of that tool measured? Success in athletics does build morale for the campus (and community) overall. Non-athlete college students are highly impacted by how their school performs.

Black student athletes who helped integrate TCU were trailblazers and champions who pushed the university to look internally on how it might be losing this "game" of inclusion. At times this game demanded more of its Black student athletes than it did of the institution, in that it forced student athletes to shoulder the work of being the first while making room for their difference. This is not to say that there were not plenty of supporting coaches, teammates, fans, and supporters of Black student athletes or coaches who were breaking color barriers or helping the school to integrate. But more so to acknowledge that these students are the ones that had to take center stage and not just offer up their physical bodies, but demonstrate their mental and emotional equity as scholars.

To the extent that TCU had a reputation for being a bit lethargic with its integration efforts, such a skeptical narrative may have been well-earned for the numerous decades prior to integration where essentially the only spaces and places that "allowed" for Black bodies within the power structure were those of subservience. If an institution had not allowed Black students to matriculate because it did not see them as equal, how could we expect them to welcome competition? Nonetheless, in 1935 TCU would become the first white institution of the South to invite and host an all-Black school down to compete in debate. That institution they invited was Wiley College of Marshall, Texas. Reports from this competition indicate that "the Wiley team experienced no traces of racism at TCU, before, during, or after the debate. Jarrett recalled that the Horned Frog team rushed across the stage at the end of the debate to congratulate Wiley team members."[1] This suggests that TCU held to the idea that Blacks and whites could compete and be seen as equal. A later *Skiff* article, however, indicated that "a section of the auditorium will be set off for negroes."[2] The totality of this historic meeting between two vastly different institutions and the responses from those who attended is lost to time, but the fact remains that audience members were not permitted to sit together, indicating that racial tension and distance still existed within the space.

Even though the TCU and Wiley College debate was not an athletic competition, it was indeed a competition of mind and thought. One would assume that, given the racial context of the 1930s and the climate found in Texas regarding race, to display Black intellectuals competing and outperforming white intellectuals on a white campus would be dangerous.

Above
Jerry LeVias makes a dashing cut with his eyes on the endzone. *Courtesy Collegiate Images/Getty Images.*

Jump Ball

But we could find no reports of repercussions of that debate. Nearly thirty years later, however, when competition took new form and a sole Black student athlete arrived on TCU's campus, the outcome was different. One would also think that as time progressed, people's attitudes toward race would also progress. SMU's Jerry LeVias, the first Black scholarship student athlete of the Southwest conference, would learn of the TCU attitude toward race when the rival programs met in Amon G. Carter field in 1965. LeVias was greeted with harassment and death threats stating that if he set foot on TCU's campus he would be seriously harmed, or worse, killed.[3]

The National Football League would pursue integration nearly twenty years earlier, in 1946, with the integration of Marion Motley, Kenny Washington, Bill Willis, and Woody Strode.[4] LeVias was the first Black student athlete to integrate the historic Southwest Conference that TCU had been members of since the 1920s.[5] How could a young college student be expected to perform under such circumstances? As LeVias navigated the season as the only Black player on the field, his opponent, TCU, remained on the wrong side of the field regarding this "game" of inclusion.

LeVias's experiences were similar to those of many Black student athletes across the US who were attempting to find opportunities at newly integrated institutions and conferences in the sixties. Black student athletes had to navigate a "game within a game."

We would be remiss if we did not include LeVias's experience in relation to TCU's integration efforts and breakthroughs with athletics. Intentionally or not, SMU's LeVias may have served as a sacrifice that instigated TCU's first recruitment of Black student athletes. For TCU would bring in their first Black student athlete shortly after their competition with LeVias. We did not uncover stories from TCU Black student athletes whose experience was as extreme as LeVias's when he competed against TCU; however the protest of 1971 would indicate that Black student athletes did have an adverse experience of some sort.[6] One can only wonder whether the purple uniform served as a certain level of protection, acceptance, or obliviousness for TCU regarding

Above
Members from the football team Terry Diennan, Mike Luttrell, Steve Patterson, Jeff Heinicken, Scott Walker, Guy Morriss, Charlie Davis, Lyle Blackwood accept their end-of-the-year awards in 1973. *Courtesy of TCU Special Collections.*

Right
Thomas Bledsoe shoots a hookshot. *Courtesy of Linda Kaye.*

Right
Members of the TCU track team. *Courtesy of TCU Special Collections, Linda Kaye, 2002.*

its race relations. Had the university decided that recruiting Black student athletes would cure its racial problems?

To be successful at an institution that has expressed, overtly or subtly, its disdain for those who are Black demands a level of fortitude that cannot necessarily be coached or game-planned. Black student athletes who played for TCU would find it challenging to try to win on and off the field, while competing against an institutional culture that may not have been fully ready for them. What they were able to accomplish was far greater than championship banners or wins; they helped open up opportunities for additional Black student athletes and coaches to compete at TCU. Further, these Black student athletes widened the path for Black people who came to TCU to expand their scholarly work, and in fact strengthened the institution as a whole by expanding its cohorts' ability to *think and act as ethical leaders and responsible citizens in the global community.*[7]

To fully understand the importance of athletics in the game of inclusion, certain individuals must be highlighted. While we are unable to give time and attention to every name that has made meaningful and significant contributions to TCU's athletic history, we elected to profile a few names that will sketch out our portrait of TCU in purple, white, and Black.

The Starting Five

Dr. James Cash

Dr. James Cash is integral to TCU's early integration and success on the hardwood. The six-foot, six-inch forward was a basketball standout for the Horned Frogs, leading the Southwest conference in rebounding and averaging a double-double with thirteen points and eleven rebounds that established a one-thousand-point career and a place in the Southwestern Conference Hall of Fame.[8] His numerous accomplishments include being an Academic All-American, a published author, a member of the TCU Board of Trustees, a tenured professor in Harvard's business school, and board memberships on Fortune 500 companies. Cash was a trailblazer for Horned Frogs athletics and for TCU as a whole.[9] But the extent of Cash's career goes far beyond what he has done for the game of basketball and for the companies he has worked for. The Fort Worth native and I. M. Terrell graduate may have been recruited to play hoops, but his mere presence on campus in 1966 proved to be groundbreaking in ways that he may not have considered during his time at TCU. Cash may not have endured LeVias's scalding experience, but he certainly felt the pressure of succeeding on the court and off the court within a highly visible, newly integrated space. And Black Fort Worth now had an individual who came from their side of town who had established himself in a part of the city that rarely welcomed Black people.

The retired and framed #54 jersey in the Ed and Rae Schollmaier Arena stands as a testament to the giant that came and succeeded as the first Black student athlete at TCU. In his wake more Black student athletes, new coaches, and other staff members were able to enter into Horned Frog Athletics. His statue is the first Black statue on campus, and one of very few in North Texas. It celebrates the champion James Cash, who came and changed the game.

Linzy Cole

Linzy Cole would become instrumental in breaking the color barrier for TCU's football program. Unlike Cash, Cole had already begun his college football career at Trinity Valley Community College, where he was a certified star on the field and became a two-time All American.[10] The five-foot, nine-inch dazzlingly fast and agile receiver would contribute right away as a junior entering TCU by leading the Horned Frogs in receiving. Knowing of LeVias's experience on the same football field, Cole would line up on the side of the field that at one point did not seem to be ready to have a Black player compete.

Despite attending two different schools, Cole and LeVias would forge a friendship and connection that allowed the two to share an experience on and off the football field that only the two of them could understand.[11] Though they competed against each other on the field, they were still playing for the same team off the field. That is why during the summer of 1967, the two decided to become roommates in Fort Worth, which provided a sense of brotherhood, or perhaps support, that their teammates could not fully share or understand.[12] In an interview conducted in 2012, Jerry LeVias recounted that "I'm nowhere without him" referring to Cole. LeVias would go on to mention the lack of interviews that covered Cole as well

Right
From left to right, cheerleaders Ron Hurdle, Mark Hill, Josh Huffman, and Steve Benton share a laugh during the 1970-71 season. *Courtesy of Linda Kaye.*

as the sheer perseverance that Cole would exhibit. "Could you smile after getting kicked in the ribs? Would you try to win someone over after they told you to burn in Hell?" LeVias asked. "Linzy could. And he did."[13] Cole became a starter in the game of integration for TCU.

When we look at how men's basketball and football generates millions of dollars, you have to credit the perseverance of Cole and Cash. Currently, there is no shortage of Black males on either team. The Black student athletes who play on these teams make up a large percentage of TCU's Black male population. What do we make of this? How does a university find eligible Black males to join their sport programs, yet struggle to find Black male students who are not athletes? This is not to blame athletics or the administration for whom it does or does not recruit, but more so to ask a simple question, "What changed and what has stayed the same?"

The game that Cash and Cole played would not stay between the two of them. For as their success grew, other Black student athletes would find their way into the fold. They passed the ball or rather the baton in order to continue the race.

Attorney Ronnie Hurdle

Ronnie Hurdle became another star player within TCU's athletic program. The Dallas native took the opportunity to pursue his academic career by moving to Fort Worth to be a Horned Frog. Hurdle was the first Black cheerleader at TCU and in the Southwestern Conference. Cheerleading was arguably a more interesting and nuanced sport in which to compete in 1969.[14] Cash and Cole were recruited to play in their programs; Hurdle ran for the cheerleading position and was voted in by the student body. That he was voted onto a team by his peers shows there had been a slow change in the culture of TCU. Black students were slowly gaining access to other parts of campus life.

Although Cash and Cole faced tough opposition on the field, their focus was on the game, and they did not have to face *all* of their opposition all of the time.

Hurdle's physical proximity to white women drove some TCU fans and alumni to express their objection to his role as a TCU cheerleader. His closeness and having to touch white female student athletes while cheerleading did not sit well with some. Hurdle recalled that once when the spirit team was scheduled to compete, they were notified by the administration that a TCU alum had written letters stating Hurdle should refrain from touching or picking up the white women student athletes.[15] His squad mates stood up to show their support for Hurdle in protest of the request.

Hurdle's perseverance shows that even in the face of adversity, Black student athletes were willing to perform. Unlike other athletes, his position as a cheerleader required him to constantly face many of those who did not want him there—but Hurdle still cheered loud for TCU.

Dr. Jennifer Giddings Brooks

Dr. Jennifer Giddings Brooks would become the fourth member of this starting lineup for diversity in TCU's athletics program. Like Hurdle, Dr. Brooks's accomplishment came by way of a vote by her class peers, who chose her to be TCU's 1970 Homecoming Queen. For a storied football program like TCU, the homecoming event is a major celebration of legacy, culture, and history, one that invites the entire TCU community to come together and celebrate their common experience as Horned Frogs.

To be named to the homecoming court is an honor that reflects the respect and admiration of one's peers. A homecoming queen can serve as an ambassador for the university within the community and at outside events. Brooks became not only the first Black homecoming queen at TCU but also the first in the Southwest Conference. As it was with the three Black athletes, Dr. Brooks's highly visible achievement came as a surprise to many within TCU—and it also came as a big surprise for her.

But the win came with its own set of challenges. In 1971, the January following her election as Homecoming Queen, she was not invited to attend the historic Cotton Bowl parade. Dr. Brooks said, "I am disappointed to know that the students selected me to represent them, but I was denied this opportunity on January first. I know that some people would say 'Well, that would happen anyway,' but sometimes you think a little differently when you are black."[16] Like Hurdle, she faced restrictions. Although she had gained access to a highly visible and previously always-white position on campus, she was still barred from participating in the same capacity as her white peers. As a result, Brooks and Black members of the 1970-71 football team staged a press conference to demand apologies and accountability for the treatment that they had been receiving.[17] Brooks's use of her platform proved that she was in fact a true "Horned Frog" by standing up for what she believed was right and just.

'Our Fred' (See Pages 11, 12) / The Skiff / Volume 69, Number 21 Friday, November 13, 1970

Texas Christian University • • • • Fort Worth, Texas 76129

Miss Jennifer Giddings
1970 Homecoming Queen

Above
Homecoming Queen Jennifer Giddings on the front cover of the *Skiff.*

Like her trailblazing peers, Brooks opened pathways for Black students to be voted into highly influential places on campus—and demonstrated that Black students did not have to physically compete in order to be celebrated at TCU. Yendor Reese, the first Black homecoming king, would not be voted into court for another thirty years.[18]

Vernell "Minnie" Armstrong

Before Title IX[19] there had been little space in school athletics for any women—much less Black women. Once legislation was passed in 1972, institutions slowly began incorporating more opportunities for women to participate in college athletics. It would be another five years—1977—before TCU started a women's basketball team, and the game at TCU would be changed in a major way when North Carolina native Vernell "Minnie" Armstrong put on the Horned Frog uniform. She became a dominating force on the team from 1977 to 1980 by notching a career total of 1,102 points and 718 rebounds in the total of three seasons.[20] Totaling a thousand-point career would be impressive in a typical four-year career, but Armstrong did it in three. She led the way for more Black women to find a place in male-dominated spaces. TCU announced its first Black female Hall of Famer in 2003 with track and field star Donna Wilson-Thomas, '85.[21]

Minnie Armstrong graduated TCU *cum laude*—a stellar athlete whose classroom performance matched her skill on the court.

It is the legacy of these starting five Black student athletes that paved the way for TCU greats like NFL Hall of Famer LaDainian "LT" Tomlinson, Kurt Thomas, Donna Wilson-Thomas, and many more. Because of those first five Black athletes, these giants serve as legends in TCU's purple, white, and Black.

Above
Vernell "Minnie" Armstrong jumps high for the ball. *Courtesy of Linda Kaye, 1977-78.*

Left
NFL Hall of Famer LaDainian Tomlinson during the 1997 football season. *Courtesy of Linda Kaye.*

The Other Four

Speaking out was not the only way to protest exclusions Black students experienced at TCU. Walking out could be just as loud a protest—if not louder. Students who chose this route should be recognized as true champions of the cause. Larry Dibbles, Hodges Mitchell, Raymond Rhodes, and Ervin Garnett decided that it was not their responsibility to fix TCU's racial problems, so they turned away from TCU's football team and from the university as a whole.[22] One might argue that their leaving was the easy way out, but it could also be argued that they were just as influential and important to the TCU athletics story as the "starting five" listed previously who stayed and became the first to integrate their respective sports. We celebrate wins and championships, but it is mostly from the losses that we learn how to improve for the next game.

Halftime

Black student athletes were the first to integrate the athletics realm, but it was a long time before Black head coaches followed suit. Though we have come across the names of Black assistant coaches during this period, head coaches are the ones given the authority to recruit, influence, and make their way into the history books when their careers are successful. The first Black head coach at TCU would appear nearly two decades after James Cash broke the color barrier as a student athlete. There was a glass ceiling for Black athletic coaches throughout the sports world when it came to accessing decision-making positions.

Ultimately, TCU would break the color barrier with head coaching and administrative hires during the 1990s and early 2000s. Though some coaches' tenures were longer, more successful, or more memorable than others, being the first is a celebratory and worthy accomplishment within the game of inclusion. Again, while we are unable to profile every single Black coach or athletics administrator within these pages, a few key profiles follow.

Shell Robinson

It was more than a decade after Minnie Armstrong graced the team that another significant color barrier in TCU women's basketball would be broken. In the 1992–1993 season, Coach Shell Robinson would start her coaching career as an assistant coach for the TCU Horned Frogs.[23] The McKinney, Texas, native joined TCU's coaching staff under Coach Fran Garmon as an alumnus of the University of Texas at Austin Longhorns, the 1982 AIAW National Championship runners-up.[24]

Robinson would not only become the first African American coach for the TCU women's basketball program, but the first Black American head coach at TCU at the start of the 1993–1994 season.[25] Being a woman head coach in general can be seen as a very difficult experience, since the sports world was not fully ready for woman head coaches. Moreover, Robinson filled the role at an institution that had very little experience with diversity in decision-making roles. Robinson's tenure was not long, but it was indeed impactful, and her promotion to the status of head coach was surely a banner worth displaying.

Ron Parker

After a brief stint in the National Football League (NFL) with the Chicago Bears, Ron Parker returned to TCU in an influential role. Parker was hired as the assistant athletic director under Athletic Director Frank Windegger. Parker would serve two years with the responsibility of TCU's recruiting strategies and efforts between 1978–1980.[26] Years later Parker would become the longest-standing TCU trustee as an African American.

Kim Johnson

Kim Johnson was the first Black American woman to join the ranks of senior administration in athletics in 2008.[27] As stated in TCU's staff directory, she has "managed and supervised men's and women's golf, equestrian, men's and women's swimming, and currently has oversight of women's basketball, women's soccer, men's and women's track and field, men's and women's tennis programs, and the Bayard H. Friedman Tennis Center. . . [she] leads the department's gender equity goals and initiatives. In 2022 Johnson serves as a campus Deputy Title IX Officer, working with the Title IX Office to help provide a safe learning and work environment for student athletes and staff."

Cornelius Aaron "Neil" Dougherty

After leaving the powerhouse of the Kansas University Jay Hawks as an assistant coach, Coach Cornelius Aaron "Neil" Dougherty became TCU's first Black head coach for the men's basketball program in 2002, a decade after the women's program had broken that color barrier. He took the reins from the fast-paced motor offense of Billy Tubbs.[28] At his peak, during the 2004–2005 season, Dougherty led the Horned Frogs to a 21-14 record and a quarter final appearance in the NCAA National Invitation Tournament (NIT).[29]

Trent Johnson

Joining from Louisiana State University, the 2008–2009 SEC Coach of the Year recipient Coach Trent Johnson would make his way to Fort Worth to lead the Horned Frogs into a new era of Big Twelve sports, becoming the second Black head coach for men's basketball and the first to usher in the new era of a power five conference.[30] Though his tenure was not long (2012-2016), at his peak Johnson led the Horned Frogs to a 13–0 record and a ranking of twenty-fifth in national polls[31]—an achievement which had not been accomplished by TCU basketball in over a decade.

Darryl Anderson

Coach Darryl Anderson was the longest-serving Black head coach at TCU, with eighteen years at his position in Track and Field after starting his tenure in the fall of 2004.[32] Under his tenure, Anderson has coached and produced nine National Champions, over twenty individual Big Twelve Champions, and 104 All Americans.[33] Additionally, Anderson has coached three conference championships and eight Olympians during his career. What Coach Anderson has accomplished during his almost two decades as head coach has been testament to the culture he has been able to build within the program and the coaching culture he has contributed to taking the track and field program to national prominence.

Eric Bell

In 2011 Coach Eric Bell became the first Black head coach of the soccer program at TCU and only the third head coach in the program's existence.[34] Though it was an extremely young program compared to other TCU sports teams, Bell would lead the Horned Frogs to national heights in his ten seasons, making it to six national championship tournament appearances, two regular season Big Twelve Championship finishes, and attaining national rankings.[35] His record has made Bell one of the most decorated and successful TCU coaches of the past decade.

Overtime

The success of Coach Bell, like others, has been a part of a larger story of Black student athletes and coaches slowly building on the successes not only of James Cash, but all other Black faculty, staff, and students whose mere presence continued to widen the path of opportunity at TCU.

It is not just the jersey that will hang, or the trophies that will shine in cases that will help us remember the valiant efforts of these star players. It is the impact that they had not only on the game they played or coached, but on the institution that they played for. Without them and their ability to stand at the plate, TCU would have missed out on the opportunity to reflect on its wider mission—to acknowledge and view how it might be sitting on the wrong side of the "game" and how it could better support future Horned Frogs who would wear purple, white, and Black.

Above (Top)
TCU's first Black female coach, Shell Robinson, gives instruction to forward Stacy Price. *Courtesy of Blake Sims/MBR, 1996.*

Above
TCU's first Black coach for its men's basketball program, Coach Neil Dougherty. *Courtesy of Linda Kaye.*

Right
Karen Davis (1987-88 season) makes a dribble move to get past her defender. *Courtesy of Linda Kaye.*

Left
New recruit poses with a TCU basketball,
Courtesy of Linda Kaye, 1971.

Above
Vanessa Clementino posts up for the ball.
Courtesy of Linda Kaye, 2006.

Chapter 5

Alumni

When documenting the Black student presence at TCU, it is important to consider the impact of the church as a primary factor in attracting African American applicants, especially in the first two decades that followed integration. During an interview with representatives of the Race and Reconciliation Initiative, Mr. Larry Dickson, class of 1969, explained: "my dad being a minister [...], we knew about the school and we knew about the denomination and how it interacted with the school [...] I thought I would run into some people who were decent people," despite his knowledge of racism and segregationist practices that took place on campus.[1] The demographics of their previous institutions are an important variable that seems to affect how Black alums remember their years at TCU. Indeed, alums who came from integrated schools prior to attending TCU (i.e., Allene Jones, Lillian Warner-Green, Ron Parker) tend to view their racial experience in more positive terms, and perceive their acceptance as relatively effortless.

On the other hand, graduates of predominantly Black high schools often reported that they were expected to perform at an exceptionally high academic level in order to qualify. Many did just that. Dr. Ronnie Hurdle (Class of 1971), for instance, explains: "I was in the National Honor Society, [and looked to participate in] all the things that lend some credence to your academic capabilities."[2] I. M. Terrell, a historically Black secondary school, is the high school alma mater of numerous TCU African American alums. These students benefited from I. M. Terrell's rigorous education, which was the product of its highly knowledgeable teaching body, with alumnus Dr. James Cash (Class of 1969) counted among their proud number.[3] Cash recalls that a large number of his teachers held doctorate degrees, but because of segregation, did not have access to careers in their fields or in academia. They were overqualified and set uncommonly high expectations for all their students, resulting in a college-ready, academically proficient student population. Likewise, Marian Brooks Bryant, an I. M. Terrell graduate who enrolled at TCU in 1964, states: "Black people were not accepted to work in many fields. They didn't really have their choice of what they wanted to do. They had to settle for whatever they could get, and quite often it was less than what they were trained for."[4]

Far from being exhaustive, this chapter considers the legacy of a handful of African American TCU alums, highlighting their achievements upon leaving the university and their post-graduation contributions to the institution. It centers on the individuals who have remained connected to the university, mainly through philanthropy, mentoring, and academic and administrative service.

Philanthropy and Mentoring Programs

Dr. James Cash

Dr. Cash is a bona fide TCU success story. His academic, athletic, and professional excellence are only paralleled by his commitment to service. In 1965, he saw in TCU a school where he could grow, and where he could contribute his

Above
Dr. James Cash, Class of 1969, received the RRI Plume Award in 2021. *Courtesy of TCU Race and Reconciliation Initiative.*

talents, despite the paucity of racial or ethnic diversity at the time. He broke the color barrier in 1966 as the first Black basketball player in the entire Southwest Conference and the first Black athlete at TCU, leading the university to two consecutive SWC championships. After graduating from TCU, Cash worked in the computer industry, then enrolled at Purdue University, where he completed a master of science and a PhD program. He immediately started teaching at Harvard Business School, where he remained until retirement. In addition to becoming co-owner of the Boston Celtics in 2003, Cash also chaired and sat on the boards of countless companies, including The Chubb Corporation, General Electric Company, HBS Publishing, Alcon Laboratories, the American Academy of Arts and Sciences, General Electric, the Harlem Children's Zone Project, Massachusetts General Hospital, Microsoft Corporation, the National Association of Basketball Coaches Foundation, the Smithsonian Institution National Museum of African American History and Culture, Walmart, and WinStar.[5]

Dr. Cash's other "firsts" include being the first Black TCU Trustee and the first Black tenured faculty member at Harvard Business School, where he introduced computer-based systems and technology into the curriculum, and where he is the first Black American to have a building named after him: in 2020, the school's faculty housing building was renamed The Cash House.[6] Among countless philanthropic initiatives, he cofounded the Juanita Cash Fellowship at TCU, which funds graduate school tuition for local teachers.[7] This fund was created in memory of his late mother, Mrs. Juanita Cash, also among the "firsts": she was one of the first Black students to receive a master's degree in education from TCU in 1965.[8] With the collaborative input of TCU's Race and Reconciliation Initiative, a statue of Dr. Cash (the first monument depicting a Black individual in TCU history) was erected in 2022 in the Athletic Complex, and he was awarded an honorary doctorate.[9] The same year, Fort Worth mayor Mattie Parker declared November 11 Dr. James Cash Day.

Attorney Leon Reed Jr.

Leon Reed Jr. (Class of 2000) is an attorney from the Como neighborhood in Fort Worth. A non-traditional student, Reed applied to TCU while serving in the military overseas. He grew up in one of Fort Worth's lowest-income neighborhoods, where the mindset was that "TCU wasn't necessarily a school for us. [...] We're a shadow of the university."[10] Nevertheless, Reed joined the institution determined to live his campus experience to the fullest extent. He was instrumental in organizing the inaugural Frog Camp, and he was named Chair of the Student Concerns Committee within the House of Student Representatives in 1994. As such, he tackled a wide and diverse range of subjects (racism, pollution, parking, athletics, communication systems in residence halls), directing them to the highest levels of the administration. He notably coordinated a forum with local lawyers to educate his fellow male Black students on their civil rights in the face of the racial profiling that occurred after a serial rapist struck victims in the vicinity of TCU. After graduating in 2000 with a bachelor's degree in political science, Reed attended law school at Texas Tech, then started in own criminal law practice.

Despite clear instances of racial discrimination, Reed thinks rather fondly of his years at TCU. His attachment is attributed to the fact that he was actively involved in campus life. As Reed explained to TCU's Race and Reconciliation Initiative's Oral History team,[11] he has remained committed to "paying his blessings forward."[12] He regularly holds legal clinics in

Above
Attorney Leon Reed, Class of 2000. *Courtesy of TCU Race and Reconciliation Initiative.*

Above
The Honorable Zuberi Williams, Class of 1998. *Courtesy of TCU Race and Reconciliation Initiative.*

Fort Worth to enable people who cannot always afford legal counsel to know and understand their basic rights, especially when stopped by the police. Along those lines, Reed made headlines in 2020 when he led a two-hundred-mile walk from Fort Worth to Austin to meet Texas Governor Abbott and share his data-driven ideas on police reform. Although the meeting did not occur, Reed has remained vocal in his activism against police brutality in Fort Worth.

Judge Zuberi Williams

The Honorable Zuberi Williams (Class of 2000) is originally from Southern Maryland. The son of a Guyanese immigrant mother and a South Chicagoan father, Williams grew up as a Black Baptist, as his parents were champions of Black empowerment. His spiritual upbringing led him to select TCU as his school of choice, unaware of the institution's racial demographics: "If I did, I might not have come. It was probably a blessing that I didn't know," he shared during an oral history interview with TCU's Race and Reconciliation Initiative.[13] Williams recounts that when he joined TCU in 1996, the Black population was so sparse and academically scattered that he struggled to find fellow African American students to collaborate with within his initial Department of Computer Science. In addition, the recurrent racist microaggressions he experienced contributed to a decline in his disposition to academic success. To counter this feeling of isolation, he opted for a marketing major and increased his participation in student life. Williams joined the House of Student Representatives during his sophomore year.

Williams enrolled at the American University to pursue a law degree as well as a master of business administration. After a relatively brief career as an attorney, Williams became, at age thirty-six, one of the youngest judges in the state of Maryland. He is also the very first graduate of the American Bar Association's Judicial Intern Opportunity Program (a boot camp internship for law students who are from marginalized racial and ethnic groups) and then became a judge. Now a camp instructor himself, Williams is part of an initiative that has trained over thirty interns and eighty mentees. He is purposeful in seeking program recruits among TCU graduates.

As he had announced even before finishing his degree,[14] Williams is an active member of the Black Alumni Alliance, a group formed in 1998 to reunite Black TCU alums and mentor current Black students to help them navigate the university microcosm. As an avid supporter of the Horned Frog soccer team, he still visits the campus often.

Above
In 2019, the Harris College of Nursing unveiled a portrait of Allene Jones, Class of 1964, painted by 2018 TCU alum Melissa Perkins. *Courtesy of Melissa Perkins and the TCU Bob Schieffer College of Communication.*

Faculty and Staff Alums

Allene Jones

When Jones enrolled in TCU in 1962, she did not fit the profile of the typical college student. A high achiever, Jones had graduated from high school two years earlier than her peers. She had college experience, having attended St. Joseph School of Nursing, an integrated Catholic institution. She had professional experience, having worked as a licensed vocational nurse in Fort Worth. Given her prior college credits, Jones only remained a TCU undergraduate for two years. After obtaining her master's degree in psychiatric nursing from UCLA, she returned to TCU, this time as a clinical and psychiatric nursing professor. She remained at the Harris College of Nursing and Health Sciences until her retirement in 1998, but by way of her emeritus status stayed involved in the institution. Thirteen years later, the college's Alumni Association acknowledged her contributions with the creation of the Allene Jones Trailblazer Award, a prize that recognizes Harris-associated individuals who break social and professional barriers.[15] Jones passed away in 2015, but is ever remembered as one of the greatest "firsts" in TCU history.[16] In 2019, she was posthumously honored with a portrait as part of TCU's ongoing Diversity, Equity, and Inclusion's initiative.[17]

Dr. Jennifer Giddings Brooks

Dr. Brooks graduated from TCU in 1971 with a bachelor's degree in speech pathology. Known for being the first Black Homecoming Queen at TCU and in the entire Southwest Conference, she was also a student activist advocating for the rights and recognition of Black American students on campus.[18] She now remembers her college experience with fondness, despite and perhaps because of the challenges she faced: "TCU with the various experience which certainly helped me in terms of my growth [. . .] into becoming an adult in terms of my goals and objectives, it helped all of us."[19]

Brooks went into education after graduation, working as a speech pathologist at first. She worked for the Crippled Children's Society in Los Angeles County, providing therapy from a mobile Winnebago in lieu of a center location, as low-income families often struggled to find transportation to the CCS center. She then transitioned to the university level at University of North Texas, where she earned a master of science and obtained her EdD degree at Texas Woman's University.[20] Teacher training and community support have been the core of her work, and Brooks has remained connected to her alma mater professionally and socially. She would later become the inaugural director for the Center for Urban Education, connecting future teachers to the larger Fort Worth community.[21] She now serves on a long list of nonprofit organizations with the purpose of elevating the Fort Worth community and histori-

Above
Dr. Jennifer Giddings Brooks, Class of 1971. *Courtesy of TCU Race and Reconciliation Initiative.*

cally Black institutions and organizations like Jarvis Christian College, I. M. Terrell High School, and the Black Fort Worth Genealogical Society, and she is still extensively involved in countless TCU programs and events. Thanks to the efforts of the Race and Reconciliation Initiative, TCU recently honored her contributions and achievements by way of a portrait in the rotunda of the Dee J. Kelly Alumni Center, as well as with an honorary doctorate degree.

Alums as Administrators

Ron Parker

Mr. Ron Parker joined TCU as a transfer student from Blinn Junior College. As a student athlete, he played tight end until he graduated in 1976 with a bachelor's degree in political science and government. That same year he was drafted

Above
Ron and Paula Parker, Class of 1976, 1977. *Courtesy of TCU University Advancement.*

by the Chicago Bears, but later went on to work for a petroleum company. In 1978, Parker came back to his alma mater, where he worked as assistant director of TCU Athletics, leading athlete recruitment nationwide. He then transitioned to a series of managerial positions, including a long career with PepsiCo. He is presently the president and CEO of the National Association of Securities Professionals and serves on numerous boards, including the Association of Governing Boards of Universities and Colleges, Procter & Gamble, and Baylor Scott & White Health.

Now a TCU Trustee, Ron Parker has continued his involvement in TCU in numerous arenas. He is a champion of the Community Scholars Program, as he explained to the Race and Reconciliation Initiative: "systems of power can be changed only if you have the courage to ask."[22] He has served on the Chancellor's Advisory Council, the Neeley School of Business's International Board of Visitors, and the Commission on the Future of TCU. He is also a member of several TCU organizations: the Addison & Randolph Clark Society, Frog Club, the Lettermen's Association, and the Black Alumni Alliance. In 2004, Parker was inducted into the TCU Lettermen's Hall of Fame. The same year, he demonstrated his commitment to philanthropy and to the future of TCU athletics as he and his wife Mrs. Paula Parker (Class of 1977) endowed a full football scholarship for players at the tight end position.

Dr. Darron Turner

Dr. Darron Turner (Class of 1987) joined TCU through sports, playing under the leadership of Coach Jim Wacker. As a student athlete, Turner experienced the constant contradictions of his environment, moving between his ethnically diverse football team and a classroom environment where he was in the minority.[23] He returned to TCU as a doctoral student, obtaining an EdD in 2011.

Darron Turner initially worked with Dr. Cornell Thomas behind the scenes as they both mentored minority students. For example, the both of them annually would take ten students to the National Conference on Race and Ethnicity (NCORE), and at the end of each day would debrief and discuss goals for the upcoming year.

As a staff member within Student Affairs, Dr. Turner was considered the hands-on, go-to person for numerous students. He assumed a variety of roles: director of Minority Affairs and Commuter Student Services, director of Intercultural Education and Services, and vice chancellor of Student Affairs, among other positions. After Dr. Thomas left his position as chair of Chancellor Ferrari's Council on Diversity, Turner in a sense succeeded him. He became the inaugural Chief Inclusion Officer in 2017, under the chancellorship of Dr. Victor Boschini. Throughout his career at TCU, Turner advocated for the general student body to have greater interaction with students of color and to grow more comfortable discussing race. He retired from the university in 2021.

Above
Dr. Darron Turner, Class of 1987, 2011.
Courtesy of TCU Magazine.

Black Alumni Alliance

The Black Alumni Alliance (BAA) was founded in the summer of 1999 by Correlia Allen Henslee (Class of 1989). This group aims at providing support to current Black TCU students and cultivating school spirit among Black TCU alums. While the organization currently has formal social media outlets, the BAA grew out of the oral tradition, in alignment with the Black American subculture: "Here has always been a need for a group created to support and encourage Black American students. By word of mouth, the alliance has attracted over six hundred members, and the numbers continue to grow."[24]

As of this writing, the BAA is led by Dr. Zoranna Jones, who is also the newly appointed assistant dean for the TCU College of Science and Engineering. Unlike the previous generations, Dr. Zoranna Jones joined TCU in 1993 as a first-generation college student. Dr. Jones describes the Black student

Above
Dr. Zoranna Jones, Class of 1998, 2002. *Courtesy of TCU Race and Reconciliation Initiative.*

community of the 1990s a tight-knit group.[25] Under the mentorship of Minority Affairs Director Darron Turner and Program Director of Campus Life Phyllis Bodie, she was involved in all aspects of campus life: student ambassadors, athletics, band, and Greek life—one of the most challenging race-related experiences, as she recounts. After graduating from TCU in 1998 with a nursing degree, then a brief four-year stint at a local hospital, Dr. Jones returned to TCU in 2002 as coordinator of Recruitment, Retention, and Alumni Relations. Dr. Jones completed her master's degree in communication and human relations at TCU, then obtained a PhD in public and urban administration from UTA. Jones is the current associate dean of the School of Interdisciplinary Studies and the president of the Black Alumni Alliance at TCU. Moreover, as a former student of the trailblazing Professor Allene Jones, the first Black nursing student and first Black TCU professor, Dr. Zoranna Jones (no relation) has further carried on the spirit of communal advancement by initiating a STEM Scholars program cohort.[26]

Chapter 6

Student Activity & Activism

Introduction: the Elevator Is Broken

Major shifts in campus culture and breakthrough events in TCU history were to a large extent student-initiated. A salient feature that appears in the history of student advocacy is the constant change in the nature of Black American students' attitudes and activism over time. Most of the first Black enrollees reported facing racist microaggressions in the 1960s, but resolved to adopt the philosophy, "If the elevator is broken, take the stairs." As the number of students of color grew by the next decade, Blacks on campus started to understand and claim the power of their presence in improving the university's image as a non-racist, accepting space. In the 1970s, students strategically utilized the media and publicly denounced the university's discriminatory policies. Four African American athletes walked off of the football team and transferred to other institutions in 1971, leading to a series of losses in that season. This chapter chronicles the evolution of these acts of resistance and activism, leading to a more recent series of demands for change.

Students Lead On

The origins of TCU's modern racial history lie within student activism. Mark Wassenich, whose father was actively involved in the integration effort of Fort Worth counters and lunch accommodations in 1963, was the student body president in 1964, at a time when only two major institutions in the state of Texas were still segregated. Under his leadership, the student body drafted a formal request, addressed to the board of trustees, demanding that the university officially and unequivocally cease segregationist and discriminatory practices regarding enrollment.[1]

1964–1965 class: "If the elevator is broken, there is no way up."

Based on testimonials from the Race and Reconciliation Initiative's Oral History Project, the majority of African American students elected to pursue their college programs at TCU both because of its academic reputation and its Christian tradition.[2] Once the main campus officially dropped racial barriers to student enrollment, five African American students were admitted in the fall of 1964. They came from highly educated households and were academically talented.[3] Nevertheless, as is often the case with transformative policies, there was a significant cultural lag on campus, and the new policy ran counter to the campus's racial climate.

Mrs. Marian Brooks Bryant, oldest sister of Tarrant County Commissioner Roy Brooks (2007–), was among the group of five. Her testimony illustrates discriminatory practices in the academic arena: "I was very good at math and took advanced math classes in high school. And I took the placement test for

Above
Mark and Linda Wassenich, Class of 1964, 1965.
Courtesy of TCU Gives Day.

math and they told me that I needed to take remedial math. So, I was very disappointed with that. And I talked with my parents about it and we decided I was not going to take remedial math. I took calculus. And I don't remember what grade I got in it, but I can guarantee you it was no less than a B."[4] Jimmy Isum, another African American student among the five, came to TCU from an integrated high school in Arkansas in 1964. He reported similar frustrations in the social arena as well. Black American students made up a small percentage of the overall student body population, which only added to the feeling of isolation for these students. "They just decided they were gonna do this and brought five Black kids on campus. The atmosphere was not welcoming. [. . .] It's like they didn't really want us there. They just did it because somebody decided that it's time to do it."[5]

Rejecting the alienating climate, the five students elected not to re-enroll. Withdrawing from the university (and therefore withholding financial support) can be considered the ultimate form of protest. Nevertheless, because their departure remained largely undiscussed for decades, very few people were made aware of the hardships these students endured.

1965–1969: "If the elevator is broken, take the stairs."

The next year, fourteen African American freshmen were admitted.[6] They would all be part of the first integrated graduating class on TCU's main campus, the class of 1969. Testimonies on the racial experience differ among these alumni, but all agreed that they would remain at TCU until they graduated, and that they would graduate in May 1969.[7] Strong bonds of solidarity and friendship were a key strength to ensure their resilience, as several of them admitted being subject to race-related hostilities. They were aware of the school's discriminatory attitude, but made efforts to work within the system despite its unfairness.

1971: "If the elevator is broken, let's ride elsewhere."

By the late 1960s, it had become clear that the integration of athletics allowed universities to increase their diversity ratios and to become more competitive on the field and on the court. In 1971, TCU Football Coach Jim Pittman's policy that all players be clean-shaven and well-groomed was formulated as a race-neutral requirement. However, out of the sixty-two players who made up the Horned Frogs football team, only six had facial hair and voluminous hairdos: Danny Colbert, Larry Dibbles, Ervin Garnett, Larry Harris, Hodges Mitchell, and Raymond Rhodes. These six men also happened to be the only Black American players on the team. As they shared their frustrations with their fellow Black students at TCU, they compiled a series of written complaints and demands to address the discriminatory treatment of African American students on campus, discussed in further detail in Chapter 8, *Ongoing Challenges*.

The Black student leadership expressed outrage at the fact that the 1970 Homecoming Queen Jennifer Giddings (now Giddings Brooks), who was also the first Black homecoming queen at TCU and in the Southwest Conference, was not invited to participate in the Cotton Bowl parade. In 2021, during an interview with TCU's Race and Reconciliation Initiative, Dr. Brooks explained that although the homecoming queen was not traditionally part of the parade, there were serious instances of miscommunication and misunderstandings, which

Above
Lillian Warner-Green, Class of 1969, looks at a 1968 *Skiff* article before an interview with the Race and Reconciliation Initiative. *Courtesy of TCU Race and Reconciliation Initiative.*

Right
"Walkout Spurs Black Outcry," 1971. *Courtesy of TCU Digital Repository.*

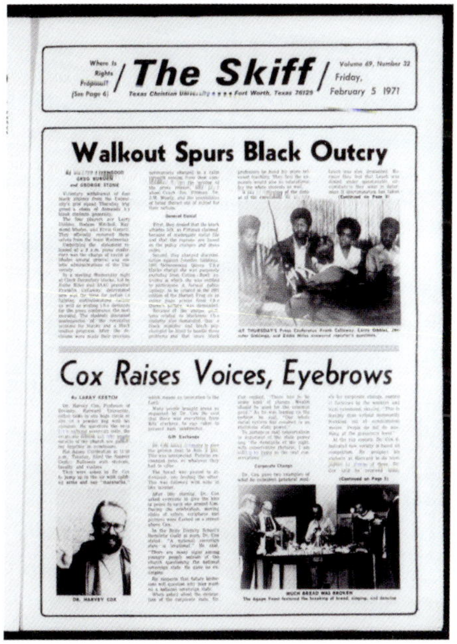

Where Is Rights Proposal? (See Page 4)

The Skiff

Texas Christian University • • • • Fort Worth, Texas 76129

Volume 69, Number 32
Friday, February 5 1971

Walkout Spurs Black Outcry

By [illegible] GREG BURDEN and GEORGE STONE

(Continued on Page 3)

AT THURSDAY'S Press Conference Frank Calloway, Larry Gibbles, Jennifer Giddings, and Eddie Miles answered reporter's questions.

Cox Raises Voices, Eyebrows

By LARRY KEETCH

Gift Exchange

Corporate Change

(Continued on Page 3)

DR. HARVEY COX

MUCH BREAD WAS BROKEN
The Agape Feast featured the breaking of bread, singing, and dancing

could have been mitigated with better dialogue between the white student body and the African American student population at TCU.

The list of demands addressed in February 1971 included the integration of "black-oriented courses" in the curriculum, leading to a Black studies minor. The document also asked for an increase in Black faculty. At the time, there were three African American faculty members at TCU, the first one being Dr. Allene Jones, who had been hired to teach at the Harris College of Nursing in 1968. In his response to the demands, former Vice Chancellor for Academic Affairs James Newcomer detailed that with the university's recent hiring of two additional Black instructors TCU was "doing pretty well," and that he had no intention of giving preference to Black faculty applicants over white ones based on their race.[8] In addition, in 1972 TCU attempted a "Black Studies" minor, but the program was not rigorously organized, and instruction was administered by only white professors.[9]

Finally, the Black student leadership requested the hiring of a Black campus minister, counselor, or psychologist. Vice Chancellor for Student Life Howard Wible initially indicated that the university did not compensate any ministers besides the Minister to the University. Nevertheless, in 1972, Roy Maiden was hired as the first African American counselor. In 1979, the Office of Intercultural Affairs developed a Black Student Guide to help with minority student retention and provide emotional and mental support for Black students. Perhaps in belated response to the 1971 demands, TCU finally added a Chief Inclusion Officer in 2018 with the appointment of Dr. Darron Turner. Unfortunately, Larry Dibbles, Ervin Garnett, Hodges Mitchell, and Raymond Rhodes all left TCU in 1971 and played football at other institutions. Dibbles was drafted into the NFL in 1973. Rhodes was drafted in 1974 and became the head coach of the high-flying Philadelphia Eagles in 1995.

Spokesman Ray Turner Explains NAACP Complaints

By Rich Doty

Last spring the campus chapter of NAACP filed complaints against the University with the Health Education and Welfare Department (HEW) and the Equal Employment Opportunity Commission (EEOC). **Image** interviewed NAACP spokesman and executive committee chairman, Ray Turner, about the events that led to the complaints. The EEOC complaint dealt primarily with hiring and advancement of employes; the HEW complaint covered a wider range of charges.

Turner stated the complaints were filed as a last resort by the NAACP. "These complaints were filed in an honest effort to improve this University. We feel that education should be diversified. Everybody should have the opportunity to have this diversified education but there are so few minorities in teaching or professional positions here that the opportunity is being denied, not just to blacks, not just to Chicanos but to whites also.

"The recognition of these problems come out of an honest consideration of the facts and statistics and years of observation. This was not done to be sensational or done on the spur of the moment. It was given a lot of thought.

"If we had tried to make it sensational we would have had a big press conference, mentioned names and accusations. We did make the statistics known to the government and we honestly hope that something can be done," Turner said.

Turner said the University should be under an Affirmative Action report. Affirmative Action is an HEW program in which corporations, businesses or institutions which hire

13

Above
1974 Yearbook coverage. *Courtesy of TCU Digital Repository.*

1974: "If the elevator is broken, sound the alarm."

In 1974, a series of formal complaints echoed the frustrations of 1971. Students had now united, however, under the umbrella of TCU's chapter of the National Association for the Advancement of Colored People. Led by NAACP chapter president Bronaugh Bridges and then by his successor Ray Turner, the student organization collected statistical data regarding the lack of faculty of color, the poor recruitment strategies to attract students of color or to inform potential students about financial aid, the all too common derogatory rhetoric from professors in the classroom, the uneven athletic performance expectations from Black student athletes compared to their white counterparts, and the racist activities conducted by Greek organizations on campus grounds.[10]

The group also met with fraternity and sorority members, the dean of admissions, the dean and associate dean of the university, and the director of financial aid in order to get TCU to establish a government-approved Affirmative Action plan. When dialogue yielded no results, the NAACP filed a charge against the university at the Health, Education and Welfare Department (HEW) and the Equal Employment Opportunity Commission (EEOC) in April, under Title VI, which outlaws racial discrimination in education institutions that receive federal funds. Unlike the 1971 walkout that strategically used the media and brought public blame on the institution, the NAACP sought to follow the proper chain of command and show good faith, as Turner later explained: "This was not

Above
Founding members of Tau Chi Upsilon gathered for an interview with the Race and Reconciliation Initiative, 2021. *Courtesy of TCU Race and Reconciliation Initiative.*

done to be sensational; [if so] we would have had a big press conference."[11]

This suit at the federal level accused TCU of discrimination "against Negroes and Spanish-surnamed Americans in its recruitment, hiring, qualifications, and placement." The investigation was planned to start in December and was aimed at developing a formal process of reconciliation. Should such a process fail, TCU risked being taken to court and losing the 7.5 percent of its budget that came from federal funding. However, the case was not treated as a priority, because both the HEW and the EEOC claimed "backlog" delays in the investigation. Two years later, no report had been officially filed. No conciliation processes were established, and the university retained its federal funding.[12]

1979: "Step into my elevator."

Despite various indicators of social progress on campus, discrimination and racist activities in Greek Life would remain a thorn in the Interfraternity Council (IFC)'s side. Minstrel and slave auction programs were commonly advertised in the *Skiff* until 1984. In 1979, however, John Mark Williams founded the first fraternity to be fully integrated from its beginnings. The IFC initially opposed the organization's nonconformism, but Williams's perseverance led to the eventual recognition of Tau Chi Upsilon as an official Greek organization.[13] Since the brotherhood had but one individual and independent chapter, there were no major membership requirements, and any male student willing to join was accepted: "It was a complete hodgepodge of individuals: rich, poor, color, non-color."[14] Tau Chi Upsilon had relatively low membership, and the organization eventually shut down in 1995.

The first formal organization on campus formed to counter feelings of isolation and disillusionment among Black students was the Students for the Advancement of Afro-American Culture, established in 1969. This group was very involved in campus activism, especially with the 1971 walkout.[15] In 1982, African American students reorganized with the creation of the Black Student Caucus. The new name indicated a broader inclusion of Black issues and a potentially stronger impact on campus culture. The organization would change its name to the Black Student Association in 1997.

1988: "Riding a broken elevator could be deadly."

In the 1980s, Black students at TCU took the fight against South African apartheid to heart because it echoed the systemic, constitutional racism of Jim Crow. American segregation and racism were a reality to which their white counterparts were not necessarily sensitive, but South Africa provided the distance needed for white Americans to consider the severity of the greed, entitlement, and injustice that marked the South African regime. The Black South African Scholarship Committee was a group of faculty and students who raised awareness and funds to provide a TCU education to Black South Africans. John Rodenberg, a senior in religious studies, led the student division and chaired the committee under the guidance of Rev. Jesse Truvillion, TCU minister to minority students and adjunct professor at Brite.

Truvillion, an African American clergyman from East Texas who grew up under Jim Crow, was actively involved in the civil rights movement, worked with Black-majority student organizations such as Students for Democratic South Africa (which in 1987 protested against TCU's investments in companies with ties to the South African apartheid regime), and the Black Student Caucus.[16] In April 1988, the committee organized a simulation game that reenacted apartheid conditions at the Student Center. The event was to be followed by a speech by Rev. Truvillion. Instead, two white men verbally assaulted him in the parking lot, concluding their rant with "You're a dead cat, buddy." As Truvillion turned around, he found a dying cat in the back of his car. Students rallied in protest against this despicable act, but it was not treated as a priority case by police.[17] By the fall semester of 1988, Institutional Analysis statistics reported that Black enrollment was "the lowest it's been in thirteen years."

Above
Rev. Jesse Truvillion. *Courtesy of* Springfield News.

1990: "It takes a whole campus to fix a broken elevator."

The establishment of the Dr. Martin Luther King Jr. holiday as an official TCU holiday provides a tangible example of the potential university-wide influence of Black student activism when paired effectively with faculty support. Students' and student athletes' voices coupled with the mobilization of interdepartmental forces constitute a game-changing power, and the potential impact of this voice is still largely untapped

Three years after MLK was declared a federal holiday, students in Dr. Linda Moore's all-white social work class expressed their desire to have TCU adopt the holiday. At the time, TCU was the only university in the region that had not. The request was addressed to the Faculty Senate, unsuccessfully. The turning point in this fight was when the Black Student Caucus decided to partner with the football team, a group that had been relatively sheltered from the numerous microaggressions that nonathlete Black students reported.[18] L. Michelle Smith (Class of 1993) was a cheerleader, columnist for the *Skiff*, and student activist at the time. She solicited the Horned Frogs' cooperation and support, and helped initiate a campus-wide march in support of the holiday.[19] Smith shared her testimony: "The football team was brave. We decided that we'd give it a trial run and have the guys walk off the field during practice, with the threat that they'd do it again during Saturday's game. We were on pins looking across the quad, waiting to see if they'd actually march from the stadium to the student center. And before long, there they were, arm-in-arm, walking alongside Coach Jim Wacker, who agreed with their stance."[20]

Above (Top)
In 1990, Dr. Linda Moore's social work students developed an initiative to support and advocate for a Martin Luther King Jr. holiday on campus. *Courtesy of TCU Race and Reconciliation Initiative.*

Above
L. Michelle Smith, Class of 1993. *Courtesy of TCU Race and Reconciliation Initiative.*

1999: "Broken elevators are code violations."

In January and February of 1999, a series of rapes on campus spawned a climate of fear and mistrust. The perpetrator's description, "black, looking in his 20s or 30s, having an athletic build and standing between 5 foot 6 inches and 5 foot 10 inches tall," and between 160 to 200 pounds, depending on the accounts, was so broad that any male walking the TCU grounds was considered a potential suspect.[21] Black male students reported being systematically stopped and questioned by the police when they would walk or run errands outside after dark.

In order to "narrow down" the list of suspects, TCU Police Chief Steve McGee and Lt. M. C. Slayton and his office decided to contact all African American male students, individually, to request that they come to the station and donate DNA samples to clear their names. Some students, not knowledgeable concerning their rights, gave samples which have remained in the system's database to this day, because they did not understand that samples were to be given willingly: "the police, when they interview you, don't make it seem like they're asking," stated Attorney Leon Reed Jr., who was a TCU senior student and chair of the Student Concerns Committee at the time of the investigation.[22]

This act of racial profiling triggered general outrage in the black student population. It promoted a climate of racial fear and hatred. Joe Briggs, who at the time was TCU quarterback (as of this writing a lecturer at Georgetown and a TCU Trustee), stated that the police stops and rhetoric soured campus attitudes toward Black males: "Being a Black male on campus is becoming very burdensome. People whisper when you walk by."[23]

In February 1999, the Student Concerns Committee, with the help of Professor Don Jackson, who was also a member of the ACLU, called an assembly to discuss students' rights and obligations, and the unethical practice of racial profiling.

This forum featured several local lawyers, who explained safe and strategic responses for Black men when stopped by the police. While this gathering was an act of activism, the larger narrative at TCU was not particularly empathetic. The TCU Police Department was quick to distance itself from any claim of harassment, stating that the Fort Worth Police Department were the ones making the stops. The rhetoric in the media coverage was not favorable either.

For instance, a *Skiff* headline story was split into two sections.[24] The first section, on the right side of the front page, was titled "Vigil lights way to help victims, unite campus." Its illustration at the center of the front page was a close-up photograph of eight students at the vigil, seven white women and one white man. The gathering meant to provide a sense of unity and community. The other portion on the left side of the front page, titled "Black males discuss rights during forum," detailed events and testimonies in response to the police stops that alienated them from the very community lauded in the previous section. The illustration of their meeting is a smaller photograph, placed below the first section's picture, that zooms out on the auditorium, giving the impression that the meeting was sparsely attended, even though there were more than thirty men there. TCU alumnus Judge Zuberi Williams (Class of 2000, marketing), who witnessed the uproar, would later comment that despite the insulting nature of racial profiling, the Black Student Caucus was to be applauded, and there was a silver lining: "It brought us together."

2015–2016: "Fix the elevator already!"

The spring and fall semesters of 2016 were a turning point. In response to all-too-numerous incidents of police brutality against African American men, a number of Black student activists mobilized on campus. In 2016 there was silent protest during national anthem at the football games.[25] Shanel Alexander (Class of 2017, political science) was the main organizer of this event. The same year, inspired by coursework on racism and civil rights, Alexander and two other senior students, SGA Director of Diversity and Inclusion Diona Willis (Class of 2017, political science) and Emily Laff (Class of 2017, journalism, managing editor for *TCU 360*) drafted a letter addressed directly to Chancellor Victor Boschini.[26] The letter included a series of complaints along with demands for structural and academic reforms on campus. The document

TCU DAILY
Skiff
THURSDAY
FEBRUARY 11, 1999
Students denounce area violence
Vigil lights way to help victims, unite campus
Black males discuss rights during forum

Above
Coverage of the same story from different angles, 1999.
Courtesy of TCU Digital Repository.

sparked much controversy, as the TCU community was still polarized when it came to racial matters.[27]

Despite the activist student efforts of 1971 and 1974 to include Black studies in the curriculum, it would take the university forty-five years and another round of student demands to achieve it. Thanks to the efforts of students such as Samantha Koehler, Alma Luna, Richard Thomas, Diona Willis, Adam Powell, Emily Laff, and Shanel Alexander, a minor for African American and Africana Studies was established in 2017, which helped contribute to the founding of the current Comparative Race and Ethnic Studies Department in that same year.[28]

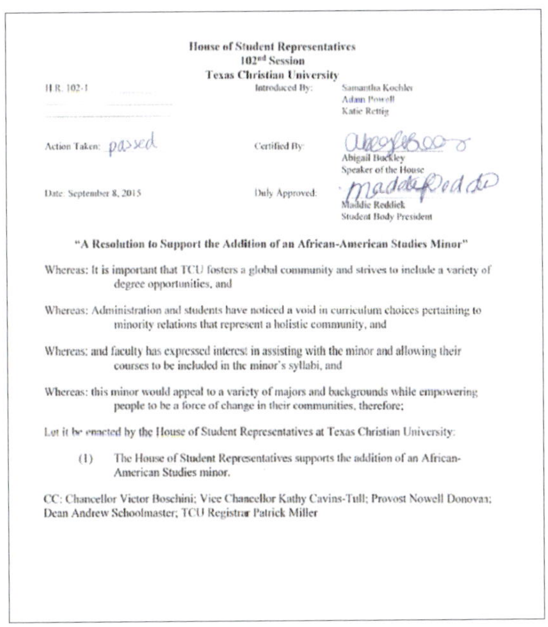

House of Student Representatives
102nd Session
Texas Christian University

H.R. 102-1

Introduced By: Samantha Kochler, Adam Powell, Katie Rettig

Action Taken: passed

Certified By: Abigail Buckley, Speaker of the House

Date: September 8, 2015

Duly Approved: Maddie Reddick, Student Body President

"A Resolution to Support the Addition of an African-American Studies Minor"

Whereas: It is important that TCU fosters a global community and strives to include a variety of degree opportunities, and

Whereas: Administration and students have noticed a void in curriculum choices pertaining to minority relations that represent a holistic community, and

Whereas: and faculty has expressed interest in assisting with the minor and allowing their courses to be included in the minor's syllabi, and

Whereas: this minor would appeal to a variety of majors and backgrounds while empowering people to be a force of change in their communities, therefore;

Let it be enacted by the House of Student Representatives at Texas Christian University:

(1) The House of Student Representatives supports the addition of an African-American Studies minor.

CC: Chancellor Victor Boschini; Vice Chancellor Kathy Cavins-Tull; Provost Nowell Donovan; Dean Andrew Schoolmaster; TCU Registrar Patrick Miller

Above

Sit-ins at football games were a form of silent protest against racism on campus. *Courtesy of* TCU 360*, 2016.*

Left

House of Student Representatives motion to support the creation of AAAS, 2015. *Courtesy of the School of Interdisciplinary Studies.*

Chapter 7

Community

Location Is Everything

Southern cities with ties to racism, confederacy, or slavery display contemporary patterns of "different realties, same place." It may be a cliché, but the past is indeed reflected in the present, and the experience that members of a community have will depend upon their race and which side of the tracks they live on. This is not unique to southern cities: intentional city planning to keep races separate has marked communities throughout the United States.

As defined by the Aspen Institute, structural racism is "a system in which public policies, institutional practices, cultural representations, and other norms work in various, often reinforcing ways to perpetuate racial group inequity."[1] Many aspects of what once was a legally segregated country still have the remnants and residue of "separate, but equal."

The West Begins Here

The city of Fort Worth is no stranger to the separation and segregation of races. Making the fifteen-mile drive from one end of Berry—East Berry—to the other the end—West Berry—will confirm how big a difference location can make. This phenomenon has roots that began as white settlers from the Deep South began to make new homes on land that once belonged to the now destroyed Wichita tribes and establish what is now known as Tarrant County.

How Fort Worth became the thirteenth most populated city in the country in its short history is an amazing feat.[2] The military base that was established to protect families moving west of the Mississippi would soon become a stopping and settling point that would eventually be considered the gateway to the West. Entitled by the scurrilous doctrine of Manifest Destiny, those looking to start a new life found attractive possibilities here and beyond the frontier.

> In an attempt to establish control over North Texas, the Republic of Texas attempted to set up a line of "ranger" (militia) forts on the frontier. When ranger stations proved inadequate, the U.S. Army stepped in and took over the job of watching the frontier. It adopted a "picket line" strategy of establishing forts every 100 miles or so, stretching from the Rio Grande in the south to the Red River in the north. The security provided by the U.S. Army. In the next four years, the number of settlers grew to some 350 hardy souls. . . . On Sept. 17, 1853, the fort was vacated. Troops were redeployed as the line marking the Western frontier made another push toward the Pacific Ocean.[3]

A growing Fort Worth became a central location for those working in cow herding or railroads. Its location allowed those who were looking for new beginnings to find their new start in close proximity to a developing Dallas. Once settlers found the potential of expanding the cotton empire west, they not only relocated their families and lives, but also their enslaved Black laborers, who would build their wealth. So as the indigenous population were moved off of their land, Black bodies were brought in to build the town's financial landscape. The contributions of Black people to the history of Fort Worth, like their contributions to the development of much of the US, is underrepresented and often completely written out of the story that is told about Fort Worth.

Early white Fort Worth settlers such as Colonel Middleton Johnson, Major Ripley Arnold, or Captain J. C. Terrell are prominent names that are celebrated and documented.[4] However, the names of the enslaved people who helped build their fortunes are not. Richard Selcer in his *A History of Fort Worth in Black & White* writes, "There is no historical consensus about the number of slaves living in the county between 1850 and 1865, and even less agreement when it (slavery) comes to Forth Worth."[5] However, historians of Tarrant County and Fort Worth did note that as the area began to develop more, there was an increase of Black enslaved laborers being bought and sold to work the lands of the West.

The "Texas Troubles"

The early relationship between Black and white residents in Tarrant County is not well documented. With enslaved Blacks being restricted from reading and writing, there is very little documented literature that details their experiences, thoughts, and feelings from their perspective. As a result, most of what we do know is from the perspective of white settlers, through their deeds, journals, letters, and court records. This one-sided narrative presents a slanted story in terms of race relations.

However, there is one story documented by news articles that stands out as one of the most significant moments in race relations in the newly established county. Referred to as the "Texas Troubles," this moment in Texas history would slowly fade and become less relevant in modern history, but those who lived through it or heard of it most likely had this history ingrained in their minds for time afterwards.

As the presidential election of 1860 drew close, conversations about abolishing slavery and insurrections increased. White slave owners began to fear losing their Black subjects.[6] This fear (and ultimately hysteria) would devolve into a campaign of terror against white abolitionists and local enslaved Blacks.

On July 8, 1860, a fire destroyed a square of downtown Dallas business districts. Soon after the fire, news articles and letters would be sent throughout the North Texas region encouraging white slave owners to stay on alert for possible slave uprisings. A rumor spread that an abolitionist had set the fire, and the push to apprehend those responsible increased. A letter from Charles C. Pryor, editor of the *Dallas Herald*, claiming that the fire had been started by an abolitionist to inspire an uprising was sent out to other newspaper editors.[7] Apparently those who were pro-slavery were not just fearful of revengeful Blacks; they also feared—or used the excuse—that Black men were becoming attracted to and might rape local white women.[8] It is reported that over one hundred white and Black men were lynched throughout the Tarrant County region.[9]

Historians would note some immediate impacts from the "Texas Troubles." One of these was that the incident helped push Texas toward secession. Second, some white Northerners and abolitionists became doubtful of their efforts and left the North Texas area to avoid violence. Enslaved Blacks had few options but to stay and endure the threat of terror or try to run away and relocate to surrounding territories such as Oklahoma. Without any just legal procedures, enslaved Blacks were either lynched or burned to death for suspicion of involvement. The "Texas Troubles" was one of the most concerning and impactful panics against slaves since Nat Turner's slave revolt in the 1830s.[10]

The fear engendered among whites was that the institution of slavery was in danger, threatening their way and understanding of Southern life. On the other hand, enslaved Black people in North Texas, whose emancipation would come five years later, needed to find ways to protect and establish their own safe communities. On top of legal segregation being the law of the land, white vigilantes also had a toxic and detrimental influence on the lives of Black people without real or consistent consequences.

Therefore, Black families who decided to stay in Fort Worth or surrounding Tarrant County would have to do as many newly freed Blacks, race colonies, freedman towns, and maroon communities throughout the US would have to do: learn how to find resources to build and support their communities by their own means.

Black Neighborhoods and Negro Districts

After emancipation, the newly free Black population would begin to look to establish their new lives Fort Worth. With few resources, the ex-enslaved had to rely on sharecropping, squatting, and/or renting out land to work and live on because they could not afford mortgages. Even as Blacks began spreading out within Fort Worth, they were forced to live on some of the most undesirable lands or "bottoms" that were still owned by whites.[11]

With little to no resources, Black residents were forced to figure out ways not only to support their immediate families, but also to support the growing community of Black Fort Worth. Seeing little support from the city, community leaders took it upon themselves to support the needs of Black residents. For example, pioneer Amanda Davis, born sometime around 1865, was responsible for helping establish what would become one of the first historic Black neighborhoods in Fort Worth.

> Davis would go on to buy property several miles southeast of town at the bargain rate of $45 an acre. She purchased several acres and built a home—a crude cabin without electricity or running water—but it was hers free and clear, which was more than the tenement dwellers could say. In the beginning, her nearest neighbors were miles away, and the city did not know she existed. Fortunately, Village Creek ran through the area and provided a reliable source of water. Other blacks followed Davis, like the Cowans, the Stalcups, and the Brockmans, and together they created a rural family-oriented community that they named Cowanville.[12]

Eventually Cowanwille would become known at the Stop Six neighborhood, its name taken from the train line that ran to Dallas. This model of self-preservation was repeated and represented throughout the south and east sides of Fort Worth. Black residents continued to build their neighborhoods and communities within the confines and capacities of their areas. Black-owned businesses, barbershops, hospitals, dentist office, churches, and boutiques were being supported by their growing Black working and middle-class residents.[13] As segregation was the law of the land and enforced by many white citizens, Black residents found that the resources they were in need of were not accessible to them in the white parts of town. Therefore, establishing their own businesses was vital.

One would be remiss not to include the financial and political gains made by Black communities that also contributed greatly to their dynamic and rapid growth. The political pursuits of Blacks and the collaboration of a growing communal network permitted people such as William Madison "Gooseneck Bill" McDonald to becoming the manager of the first Black-owned bank in the state of Texas.[14] The Fraternal Bank and Trust was opened for business on January 12, 1912. In the local newspaper, The Fraternal Bank and Trust would openly publicize that it was "owned, operated, and controlled by Negroes."[15]

By 1928, The Fraternal Bank and Trust had garnered over one thousand depositors.[16] The bank had become a staple and foundational block to the growing Black Fort Worth community, and Bill was the facilitator. His contributions to the community did not end there; Bill would go on to secure locations for drug stores, physician offices, barbershops, and other entrepreneurial ventures in the vicinity around the bank.

As Bill continued to grow his financial empire, he would become essential to providing loans for Black businesses as well as bailing out failing white businesses. One of the finest contributions Bill provided to the growing community was the Jim Hotel, known as a haven for travelers venturing through the South, and listed in Victor Hugo Green's *The Negro Motorist Green Book.*[17] Additionally, the Jim Hotel would become a mecca for Black jazz artists to perform and build their fame. Ray Charles, Ella Fitzgerald, Count Basie, and Louis Armstrong would make their stops in Fort Worth successful due in part to the Bill's financial investment and development of what would be known as "Fort Worth's Black Business District."[18]

Like many slowly forming Black communities and sections of white cities, Black residents in Fort Worth shared a sense of communal responsibility for development. The collaboration between schools, businesses, and churches became foundational to the development of Black Fort Worth and has a long-standing legacy.

Above
Mount Gilead Baptist Church, known as the mother of Black Baptist Churches in Fort Worth. © *University of Texas at Arlington Library to The Portal to Texas History at UNT Libraries, Fair use image.*

Black Churches

One of the more influential institutions of Black life, particularly in the South, is that of the Black church. For Black Fort Worth, the church was not only a way to build and nourish their spiritual connection, but a way to foster their community networks. It is important to note that the "Black church" is a broad umbrella term that encompasses the factions and various Christian-based denominations that Black churchgoers attended.

For the early inhabitants of Fort Worth, there were three main denominations that were relevant: Baptist, Methodist, and African Methodist Episcopal church. The three denominations would provide similar services for their members: a place to worship, connect with community members through networking, and find resources.

Now known as Allen Chapel, which has historical roots dating back to the late 1780s, the African Methodist Episcopal Church was one the oldest churches in the city, and it had great influence on the growing Black population. With functions that began before emancipation, the Allen Chapel and other smaller, church-like gatherings of Black worshippers were the cradle of the Black community. It would not be until 1870 that the church would officially organize, but within three years, in 1873, the congregation had erected its first building.[19]

It was not only spiritual development that the Black church had to offer: it was also a place where education—reading and writing—could be provided. Under the leadership of Belle Murray Burchill, Allen Chapel would reportedly house one of the first private schools for Blacks in Fort Worth in 1873.[20]

The first Baptist Black church in the Fort Worth area is recorded as opening in 1875. Mount Gilead Baptist Church would become known as the "mother church" of Fort Worth's black Baptists churches. Only ten years after emancipation, the Black churches became a central piece in facilitating

Black community. Community leaders typically were also pastors or church officials, so that the Black church functioned as the social-political voice of the people.

As the Black population continued to grow, the responsibility of the church also continued to expand. As mentioned, one of the church's most important services was that it provided education for Black members before an official school system was established.

> Black churches were important because they filled many needs besides spiritual nourishment, such as the three R's. With public schooling for blacks unavailable before 1882 and extremely limited even after that, the school-church connection was very important. Between Sunday worship services church buildings could be turned into classrooms for neighborhood children. In 1894 the South Side Colored School rented space from Mount Zion Baptist Church (Rosedale and Louisiana). Twenty-five years later when Mount Zion built a magnificent new building (1101 Evans Ave.), they included an Educational Annex, and not just for holding Sunday School classes. Other churches no doubt were also committed to faith-based schooling, only their names did not make it into the history books. Once a grammar school system was in place, some churches turned their attention to higher education.[21]

Black Education in Fort Worth

Even after news of emancipation reached the region of North Texas in June of 1865, the racial dynamics and separation were still intact and in place. While Black churches were growing and becoming the centerpiece for community resources, there was also a unique case in which Black schools were being established outside of the church. In 1873, alongside the efforts of the church, a collective of schools for newly freed Blacks was also being established in Fort Worth by Confederate veteran Charles Cummings.[22] Cummings's ties to the Confederacy coupled with his desire to encourage the education of newly freed Blacks is a story of nuanced character, but not totally uncommon.

Though Cummings's intentions in becoming instrumental in Black education are unclear, his impact still warrants acknowledgment. If anything, Cummings's decision could be one of political gain. Regardless, unlike the Black churches that had already begun to host and build private schools as an attachment to their church, Cummings had to be a little more strategic in his planning. Therefore, as Cummings began to ascend in the Fort Worth political chambers by becoming county judge, he would approach community leader James A. Cavile to help him in the efforts of establishing a "colored school system" for Black children throughout Tarrant County.[23] The schools would be privately funded through the donations from both white donors and from the fees of Black parents to stay afloat. Needless to say, the quality of both the education and physical landscape of the Black schools were not equivalent to that of the white schools; nonetheless, they were there.

Four years after establishing its public school system, in 1886 Fort Worth laid claim to only one school for Black students. As the city of Fort Worth continued to grow, city officials ensured that more schools and resources were built and made available for its white population and students. With support of local Black citizens, the Fort Worth school district and city council would establish another school, undersized and underfunded, for Black students. Ultimately, in 1921, it was renamed after the "Father of Black education in Fort Worth"—Isaiah M. Terrell. This school had a lasting legacy in the community and would be known as one of the centerpieces for Black Fort Worth. Just like its namesake, I. M. Terrell High School would serve the Fort Worth community for decades, until its closure in the 1970s.

I. M. Terrell

A visionary and trailblazer in education, I. M. Terrell was born enslaved in the southeastern region of Texas which is now known as Grimes County.[24] His travels throughout the state of Texas engendered in him an admirable grit and determination. Illegally learning how to read and write while being enslaved is a testament to Terrell's drive for education. Upon emancipation, Terrell continued his journey by traveling east until he reached New Orleans to attend Straight University. He attained not only his undergraduate bachelor's degree, but his master's as well.

Upon graduating in 1880, Terrell served a brief stint as a teacher in Grimes County before relocating to become one of the very first Black teachers in the city of Fort Worth. Terrell's tenure as an educator in Fort Worth spanned more than three decades of experience and dedication in helping develop Black Fort Worth.[25] Even today, the legacy of I. M. Terrell High School remains prominent for many long-standing residents of Fort Worth who remember the legacy of the first high school that served Black students.

Higher Education Opportunities

As Black citizens of Fort Worth and North Texas continued to become more educated, gain access to jobs, and build up resources in their communities, the desire for higher education became an additional focus. As it was with earlier schools for Black students that had begun in the 1870s and 80s, the Black church and other community leaders began to imagine how a higher education institution might benefit the Black community of Fort Worth. Particularly looking into the idea of vocational training, a collective of Black churches began the process of fundraising to accomplish their new goal.

> Fort Worth's large black Baptist congregations, in particular those of Mount Gilead, Mount Pisgah, and St. James took a strong interest in black education. They were determined to get a "negro college" for Fort Worth. In 1907 the Negro Baptist Missionary and Educational Association of Texas, led by their President Lacey K. Williams, launched a drive to accomplish that. At their national convention that year the association began trying to raise $20,000 to build a new school. Stymied on that front, they decided to move Hearne Academy (founded in 1881 in Hearne, Texas) to Fort Worth and rename it Fort Worth Industrial and Mechanical College. . . . [26]

As local Black Fort Worth residents began to work collaboratively to bring this idea into fruition just roughly forty years post emancipation, the formerly enslaved and the children of the enslaved set their thoughts high on the possibility of college education. The sheer determination to build Black

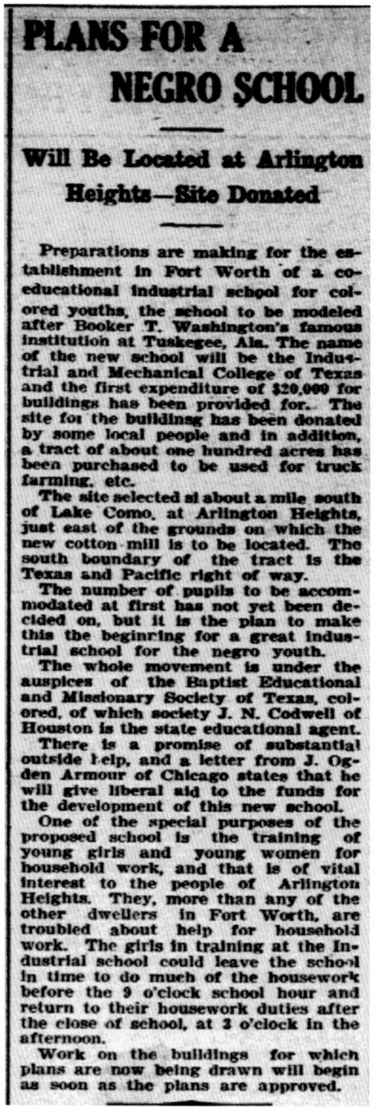

PLANS FOR A NEGRO SCHOOL

Will Be Located at Arlington Heights—Site Donated

Preparations are making for the establishment in Fort Worth of a coeducational industrial school for colored youths, the school to be modeled after Booker T. Washington's famous institution at Tuskegee, Ala. The name of the new school will be the Industrial and Mechanical College of Texas and the first expenditure of $20,000 for buildings has been provided for. The site foı the buildinsg has been donated by some local people and in addition, a tract of about one hundred acres has been purchased to be used for truck farming, etc.

The site selected sl about a mile south of Lake Como, at Arlington Heights, just east of the grounds on which the new cotton mill is to be located. The south boundary of the tract is the Texas and Pacific right of way.

The number of pupils to be accommodated at first has not yet been decided on, but it is the plan to make this the beginring for a great industrial school for the negro youth.

The whole movement is under the auspices of the Baptist Educational and Missionary Society of Texas, colored, of which society J. N. Codwell of Houston is the state educational agent.

There is a promise of substantial outside help, and a letter from J. Ogden Armour of Chicago states that he will give liberal aid to the funds for the development of this new school.

One of the special purposes of the proposed school is the training of young girls and young women for household work, and that is of vital interest to the people of Arlington Heights. They, more than any of the other dwellers in Fort Worth, are troubled about help for household work. The girls in training at the Industrial school could leave the school in time to do much of the housework before the 9 o'clock school hour and return to their housework duties after the close of school, at 3 o'clock in the afternoon.

Work on the buildings for which plans are now being drawn will begin as soon as the plans are approved.

Above
Black churches worked together to bring a bout a vocational school for Black youth in Fort Worth. *Courtesy of the* Fort Worth Star-Telegram, *October 18, 1906.*

JUNE 28, 1908

NEGRO INDUSTRIAL BUILDING COMPLETE

Work has been completed on the first building of the negro industrial college south of Lake Como. Work will begin at once on the second building and patrons of the school hope to open the institution this fall. The first building is a sixteen room boys' dormitory. With the completion of the other building there will be quarters for about 200 students. It is expected this number will enroll the first year.

The college is under the auspices of the Texas Negro Baptist Missionary and Educational Convention. Trades and agriculture will be taught at the institution.

MARCH 9, 1913.

Jarvis Institute Is Memorial to Loved and Faithful Slaves

Mrs. Ida Van Zandt Jarvis Draws Touching Word Picture of Former Feeling Between Master and Man.

BY KITTY BARRY.

Have you ever thought of the immense difference between the well dressed, educated negro of today, who has been to high school, and often to college, who wears stylish clothes, and who holds a salaried position, and the old-fashioned turbaned darkey of slavery times?

And remembering this difference, have you been able to keep in your mind a picture of the charming, loving relation that often existed between slave negroes and their masters?

Mrs. J. J. Jarvis, in a recent address at the opening of Jarvis Institute, a negro industrial school in Hawkins county, graphically depicts this relation, and draws a beautiful picture of the life in the good old days.

The land upon which Jarvis Institute is built, a beautiful piece of timber land 365 acres in extent, was given by Major and Mrs. Jarvis for the erection of this school as a memorial to the tender feeling they had for the slave negro. No more fitting memorial to this sentiment could be conceived than will be developed from this land gift. It is a tribute to all old negro "mammies" and old story-telling uncles of former days.

Above (Top)
What would be known as the Fort Worth Industrial and Mechanical College would open its doors in the Arlington Heights sections of Fort Worth. *Courtesy of the* Fort Worth Star-Telegram, *June 28, 1908.*

Above
Newspaper headline in which Ida Van Zandt Jarvis recalls her appreciation for her faithful slaves that inspired her involvement in Black education. *Courtesy of the* Fort Worth Star-Telegram, *Vol. XXXI, Issue 53, 1913.*

Fort Worth had been a vibrant ethos of the community. The influence of the Black church was working and evident, as members determined what kind of education would be most appropriate and acceptable in the Jim Crow South.

> The idea was to create an "industrial school" modeled on Tuskegee Institute that would provide vocational training for "colored youth" who did not have an affinity for academic subjects but still desired more out of life than farm work. White supporters believed a technical school, as it was also known, would teach practical job skills that would keep young black men from becoming beggars or worse, that old "ethical character" issue.[27]

In 1909, the Fort Worth Industrial and Mechanical College would open its door in the College Heights neighborhood of Fort Worth. This developing neighborhood began to take root near the Como neighborhood in Fort Worth, which is relatively close to present-day TCU. Black leaders of Fort Worth who had been envisioning taking Black education to new heights were now in reach of developing their own Black college. With the expectation that two hundred students would enroll within its first year in Fort Worth, the Negro Baptist Missionary and Educational Convention had achieved an astonishing accomplishment within a few years of its inception.[28]

Unfortunately, as funding slowly diminished, the short-lived institution soon had to close its doors after its graduating class of 1917.[29] What could have been Fort Worth's very own historically Black college and university had become a pipe dream.

Though the dreams of having a Black college in Fort Worth had now long sailed, a new nightmare for some white residents now emerged. With a growing Black population within Fort Worth due to the city's growth and development, some local white residents had growing concerns of the trajectory of the city. Similar to the Texas Troubles, the fear of a growing or perhaps "uncontrollable" Black population plagued the co-consciousness of white Fort Worth residents.

This however, did not stop the continued involvement of white philanthropists in Black education. Like Charles Cummings, Ida Van Zandt Jarvis and her husband James Jarvis, a major in the Confederate army along with two original board members of TCU would become very instrumental in the education of Black Tarrant County.[30]

Despite the interest of the Negro Disciples in Texas that were led by Mary Alphin who wanted to establish their own higher education institution and had begun to do a lot of the ground work, the Jarvis family would become the namesakes of this new school due to their large donation of land in East Texas.

Though this involvement into Black education seems applaudable, some of the discourse towards the institution from the Jarvis family seemed to hold blatant racist and paternalistic tones. In an interview that was conducted right after the opening of Jarvis Institute, Ida Van Zandt would be quoted saying the school was a memorial to her "loved and faithful Slaves."[31] Even if it was not overt, configuring subtle ways to extend segregation, while providing continued educational opportunities for local Black residents, was one of many nuances that come with white philanthropists' involvement in Black education.

> The Christian Woman's Board of Missions was a part of the Disciples of Christ that included Mrs. Ida Van Zandt Jarvis of Fort Worth and her white friends. All three groups believed in "the possibilities and the worthiness of the Negro." All of these groups had one thing in common: they thought African Americans must be educated by whites. They also tried to soothe white fears by putting their schools in areas that already had a sizable black population. They knew the thought of "hordes of Negroes" descending on their communities would alarm white residents. That is why Jarvis Christian College, founded in 1912, was located on rural land in far east Texas even though most of its benefactors were Fort Worth residents. . . . [32]

The Jarvis family's connection to both institutions meant TCU's influence was more prevalent in Jarvis Christian University's development than what it is given credit for. Major Jarvis's close connection to the Clark brothers allowed him the opportunity to serve as TCU's first president of the board of directors.[33] As president, he would be expected to provide direction and insight to the benefit of TCU. Would donating resources to develop a Black institution that would serve Christian Black Tarrant County citizens in a location away from Fort Worth serve that purpose? The arrangement seems to closely mirror the politics of "separate, but equal," in that both TCU and JCU were connected to the Disciples of Christ Church at their establishment yet were as different as the students they serviced. The two institutions would have an interesting connection that would continue to intertwine TCU, Black education, and Fort Worth in the future.

Access to University Drive

Though strides were being made to develop academic opportunities for Black community members in the city, there were still limitations in educational mobility. Although TCU was progressive in regard to admitting women, it was not open to Black students. Originally, the only benefit local Fort Worth Black constituents would enjoy from having TCU in their city would be through employment opportunities as janitorial or culinary staff.

Over time, TCU would slowly become engaged in a role that served as an educational resource for Black Fort Worth. One of these was through a government contract to conduct classes for military officers. Starting in 1942, TCU would provide Carswell Air Force Base with academic support by offering classes and training.[34] Though not directly and intentionally just for Black personnel, Black military men were included in the program.

In the 1950s, Black teachers in Fort Worth would also be the beneficiaries of having a partnership with the university.[35] TCU's College of Education provided classes that were reserved for Black public school educators in the city.[36] However, these programs were held off campus, during the evening at local Gay Street Elementary, and not on the campus of TCU.[37] This brief partnership would last from 1951 to 1953.

A decade after the Gay Street Elementary program ended, TCU would engage in another interesting relationship with the local Black community and education. On behalf of the TCU Student Congress on December 9, 1963, Mike Walsh wrote to TCU faculty and staff asking TCU to help pay a debt acquired by Jarvis Christian College.[38] At the time, Jarvis was on the brink of closing if the debt—resulting from two fires and much-needed repairs—could not be paid. Jarvis's Disciples in Christ Church sibling had begun to devise a strategy to re-intertwine the two institutions.

Although some sympathetic students, faculty, and staff members genuinely wanted to help Jarvis remain open, others had alternative motives. These wanted Jarvis to remain open so that TCU would not become pressured into admitting a

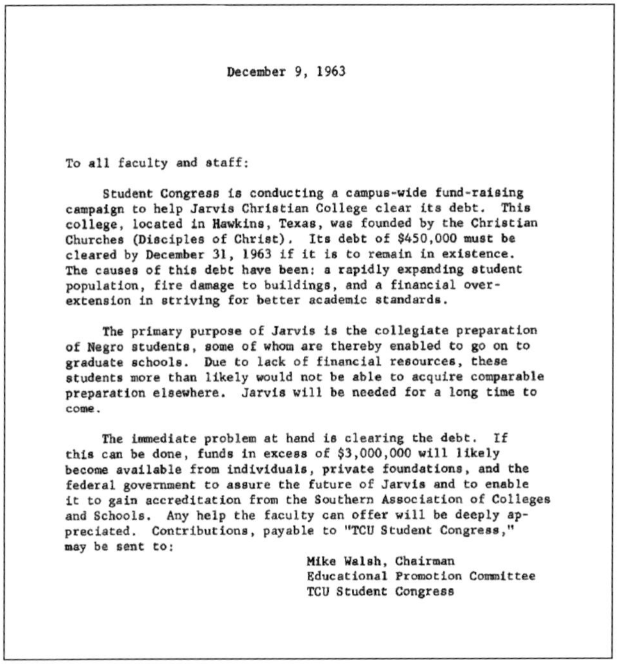

December 9, 1963

To all faculty and staff:

Student Congress is conducting a campus-wide fund-raising campaign to help Jarvis Christian College clear its debt. This college, located in Hawkins, Texas, was founded by the Christian Churches (Disciples of Christ). Its debt of $450,000 must be cleared by December 31, 1963 if it is to remain in existence. The causes of this debt have been: a rapidly expanding student population, fire damage to buildings, and a financial over-extension in striving for better academic standards.

The primary purpose of Jarvis is the collegiate preparation of Negro students, some of whom are thereby enabled to go on to graduate schools. Due to lack of financial resources, these students more than likely would not be able to acquire comparable preparation elsewhere. Jarvis will be needed for a long time to come.

The immediate problem at hand is clearing the debt. If this can be done, funds in excess of $3,000,000 will likely become available from individuals, private foundations, and the federal government to assure the future of Jarvis and to enable it to gain accreditation from the Southern Association of Colleges and Schools. Any help the faculty can offer will be deeply appreciated. Contributions, payable to "TCU Student Congress," may be sent to:

Mike Walsh, Chairman
Educational Promotion Committee
TCU Student Congress

Above
Educational Promotion Committee Chairman Mike Walsh offers a letter of invitation to TCU faculty and staff to help financially support Jarvis Christian College to avoid from closing. *Courtesy of TCU Special Collections, Dec. 9, 1963.*

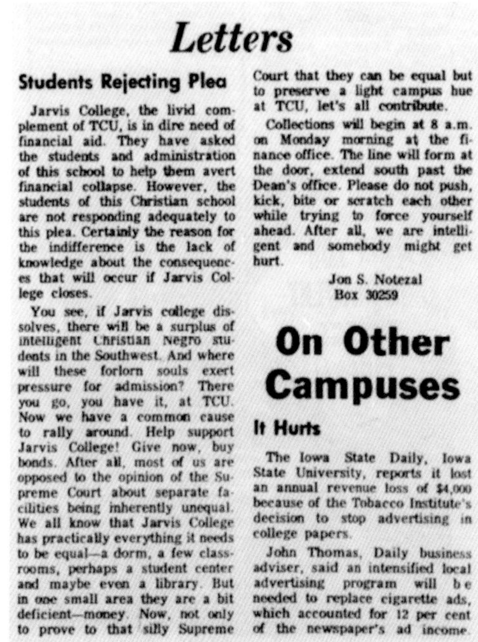

Letters

Students Rejecting Plea

Jarvis College, the livid complement of TCU, is in dire need of financial aid. They have asked the students and administration of this school to help them avert financial collapse. However, the students of this Christian school are not responding adequately to this plea. Certainly the reason for the indifference is the lack of knowledge about the consequences that will occur if Jarvis College closes.

You see, if Jarvis college dissolves, there will be a surplus of intelligent Christian Negro students in the Southwest. And where will these forlorn souls exert pressure for admission? There you go, you have it, at TCU. Now we have a common cause to rally around. Help support Jarvis College! Give now, buy bonds. After all, most of us are opposed to the opinion of the Supreme Court about separate facilities being inherently unequal. We all know that Jarvis College has practically everything it needs to be equal—a dorm, a few classrooms, perhaps a student center and maybe even a library. But in one small area they are a bit deficient—money. Now, not only to prove to that silly Supreme Court that they can be equal but to preserve a light campus hue at TCU, let's all contribute.

Collections will begin at 8 a.m. on Monday morning at the finance office. The line will form at the door, extend south past the Dean's office. Please do not push, kick, bite or scratch each other while trying to force yourself ahead. After all, we are intelligent and somebody might get hurt.

Jon S. Notezal
Box 30259

On Other Campuses

It Hurts

The Iowa State Daily, Iowa State University, reports it lost an annual revenue loss of $4,000 because of the Tobacco Institute's decision to stop advertising in college papers.

John Thomas, Daily business adviser, said an intensified local advertising program will be needed to replace cigarette ads, which accounted for 12 per cent of the newspaper's ad income.

Above
A concerned student offers a letter of encouragement to support the efforts of Jarvis to avoid the "pressure of admitting the surplus of intelligent Christian Negro students in the Southwest." *Courtesy of the* Skiff, *Nov. 22,1963.*

"surplus of intelligent Christian Negro students in the Southwest."[39] The urgency of Jarvis's need was well-documented in the *Skiff.* Not only did the student organization join in with the fundraising efforts, it also included Jarvis in its annual "slave auction" fundraiser. Chancellor Sadler, a Jarvis board member, also began to raise funds through the Southwest region.

A month later, TCU's Board of Trustees agreed to officially integrate on January 23, 1964.[40] This would mark a new direction for an institution that was one of the few in the Southwest Conference that still had not integrated. TCU would purposely increase its tuition and academic requirements, however, while asserting that Black students would want to willingly participate in segregation.[41]

Only shortly afterward, on March 17, 1964, TCU made another important announcement: Jarvis Christian College would become an actual part of Texas Christian University as the ninth academic unit of the institution. The released board of trustee notes stated that "the TCU Board first went on record as expressing belief in a need for the continued existence of Jarvis Christian College and a strong interest in its purposes and operations." As this partnership began, TCU and Jarvis created a mixed board that would oversee the academic and financial affairs of Jarvis. This board included TCU Chancellor McGruder Ellis Sadler (1941–1965), Chancellor James Mattox Moudy (1965–1979), and other TCU dignitaries.

The timing of these events makes the connection interesting. As TCU appears to be opening its doors to Black students, it becomes intentionally involved with a Black college that it could have been working with well before 1964. The same TCU Board of Trustee members who had dragged their feet to integrate now were "expressing belief in a need for the

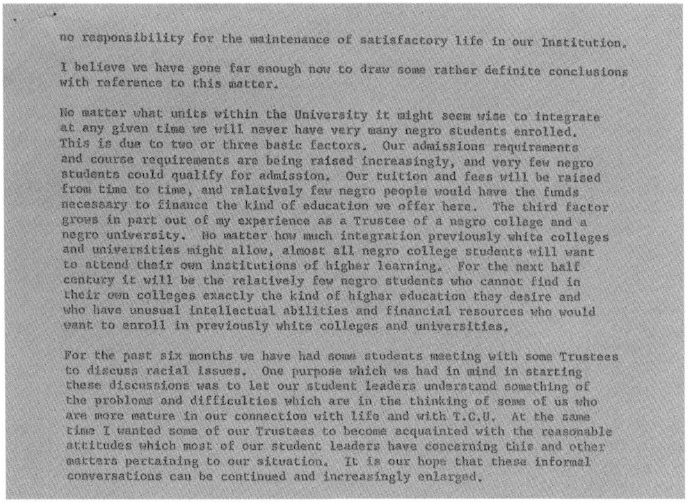

no responsibility for the maintenance of satisfactory life in our Institution.

I believe we have gone far enough now to draw some rather definite conclusions with reference to this matter.

No matter what units within the University it might seem wise to integrate at any given time we will never have very many negro students enrolled. This is due to two or three basic factors. Our admissions requirements and course requirements are being raised increasingly, and very few negro students could qualify for admission. Our tuition and fees will be raised from time to time, and relatively few negro people would have the funds necessary to finance the kind of education we offer here. The third factor grows in part out of my experience as a Trustee of a negro college and a negro university. No matter how much integration previously white colleges and universities might allow, almost all negro college students will want to attend their own institutions of higher learning. For the next half century it will be the relatively few negro students who cannot find in their own colleges exactly the kind of higher education they desire and who have unusual intellectual abilities and financial resources who would want to enroll in previously white colleges and universities.

For the past six months we have had some students meeting with some Trustees to discuss racial issues. One purpose which we had in mind in starting these discussions was to let our student leaders understand something of the problems and difficulties which are in the thinking of some of us who are more mature in our connection with life and with T.C.U. At the same time I wanted some of our Trustees to become acquainted with the reasonable attitudes which most of our student leaders have concerning this and other matters pertaining to our situation. It is our hope that these informal conversations can be continued and increasingly enlarged.

Left
On January 23, 1964, the board of trustees offers that while they will make efforts to desegregate, there will be an immediate increase in tuition and academic requirements. *Courtesy of TCU Special Collections.*

VOL. 65, No. 31 FRIDAY, FEBRUARY 10, 1967

Charity Drive Sets $2500 Goal

Slave Auction Due For Campus Chest

By BARBARA GLASS

Abraham Lincoln's birthday and a slave auction in the same week?

It's true! The annual Campus Chest Slave Auction will be 1-3 p.m. in the Student Center Feb. 15.

Each organization may submit two slaves. Money will be collected only at the time of sale.

The names of the slaves must be submitted to Carolyn Breeding, Campus Chest chairman, by Feb. 14.

Credit for the amount of the sale will be given each organization but the proceeds will go to the four organizations sponsored by the charity drive — Jarvis Christian College, World University Service, Foster Parent Plan and the International Rescue Association.

Professors may be submitted as slaves if they agree prior to the auction.

David Ely will be auctioneer.

$2500 Goal

"The goal for this year is $2500," said Miss Breeding, "but we hope to exceed this figure." The Special Events Committee of the House of Representatives sponsors the

The candidate's name, the organization she represents and an 8 x 10 glossy picture must be turned in with $2 to room 211 in the Student Center by Friday.

Pictures of all Campus Chest Queen nominees will be displayed in the Student Center lobby during Campus Chest week.

"The Ugliest Man on Campus" contest is an annual drive to raise funds for Campus Chest. Any organization may enter a candidate by submitting an 8 x 10 photograph and a nomination blank by noon Saturday.

These may be submitted to any member of Alpha Phi Omega. Deadline for balloting is noon Saturday, Feb. 18. The winner will be announced during half time at the Rice-TCU game and the organization he represents will receive a plaque.

The week's activities will include the Chi Omega caramel apple sale, Vigilette peanut brittle sale and Tri Delta fortune teller's booth. Kappa Delta sorority will hold a garage sale. Alpha Delta Phi has challenged Sigma Chi to a basketball game Thursday, Feb. 16 at 7:30 p.m.

Faculty Representative

CAMPUS CHEST UGLY MAN CANDIDATE LARRY WOOD GETS HELP IN ARRANGING MAKE-UP
Denise Landell, Mary Ann Miller, Patty Horne and Diane Willis, from left, aid him

Left
During February of 1967, TCU students organized the annual Campus Chest Slave Auction in which Jarvis Christian College was one of the four benefactors. *Courtesy of the* Skiff, *February 10, 1967.*

Left
The formal partnership between Jarvis and TCU required a collective board of trustees that consisted of dignitaries fromboth institutions. (1960-64) *Courtesy of TCU Special Collections.*

continued existence of Jarvis Christian College and a strong interest in its purposes and operations."[42] With this new five-year partnership, TCU would take charge of the curriculum, financial operations, and degree programs of Jarvis. Many of those moves reflected some of the early sentiments of Ida Van Zandt Jarvis.

The TCU That Is Learning from Fort Worth

Struggling with low Black admittance and retention numbers, TCU attempted to implement a more aggressive plan to cultivate a Black student body. As mentioned in Chapter 2, Dr. Cornell Thomas noticed the lack of diversity on campus and offered two vital programs that would serve the community. The first would be an ACT workshop program, which started in the 2000s, for local high school students to help improve testing scores so that they would be more competitive in terms of scholarships and placement. Though not every student would go on to attend TCU, this program was useful and aided a historically excluded community.

His other important contribution was the Community Scholars Program. Dr. Thomas created an institutional pipeline program that fully funded matriculation at TCU for eligible Black and Brown students. The program would not only give students financial backing, but also access to services that would help them transition into college life at TCU.

Dr. Thomas would leave the university in the midst of doing groundbreaking work. However, his contributions assured that Black students not just from Fort Worth but from the entire metroplex would be able to gain access to the university. Though TCU would continue to struggle with issues with diversity, the attempt to find ways to welcome Black students on to campus—whether one believes it to be merely politically motivated—would result in many Black students becoming debt-free graduates of the institution.

This program by no means was the end-all to the diversity issues at TCU. TCU still had and will have some distance to go. Even to date, longtime Black Fort Worth residents recall a time when they may not have been welcomed on campus or this side of Berry Street. Despite the matriculation of a few Black students entering TCU, residents were not fully convinced that TCU was ready embrace all sides of Fort Worth.

Above
Ms. Opal Lee receiving an honorary doctorate degree from Chancellor Boschini and Provost Teresa Dahlberg for her commendable leadership in the community. *Courtesy of Glen E. Ellman.*

As local Black Fort Worth community members looked to find ways to build and develop their side of Fort Worth, they stood at a distance while observing the institution that pledged to be inclusive and supportive of all students with valid skepticism.

But while they were still skeptical, there remained a number of bright spots that suggested a more optimistic outlook for the future: individuals and collectives at the institution who truly embodied the spirit of ethical leadership. This called for an invitation to reconcile TCU's past and its relationship with the city of Fort Worth.

Fort Worth natives such as Ms. Opal Lee, the "Grandmother of Juneteenth," who has worked adamantly to push the national awareness of Juneteenth, have also reflected the art of the possible. Although she received an honorary doctorate from TCU, Ms. Lee would have not been admitted to TCU as a traditional undergraduate at the age of eighteen because of her race. However, her leadership has demonstrated that critique can live alongside celebration, and ultimately provide a stronger sense of community. Local Forth Worth members such as Ms. Lee and many others are contributing to our understanding and capacity to think and learn from our past, so that we continue creating bridges of connection.

Chapter 8

Ongoing Challenges

Janus, Be Damned!

As many may recall from their early education in Western Civilization, Janus is the Roman god of doorways and passageways.[1] He was commonly depicted as having two faces: one looking forward and the other looking back. The ability to hover over a space and contemplate the meeting place of the past and present is indeed profound; perhaps it is no surprise that Janus lends his namesake to the first month of our Gregorian calendar year (i.e., *January*), as the first month looks forward, standing on the precipice of a new year while so close to the recent past, with the final month of December still so near, dear, and fresh in memory.

Some of us may have learned that other civilizations have similar ideas. One additional concept that comes to mind is that of *Sankofa*—a west African symbol typically depicting a bird with a long neck craning backward, with an open beak around a seed placed near the bird's rear end. Thus, while the entirety of the body faces forward, the head looks back, illustrating a continual balancing of time and space. Not to mention that it is unclear or open to interpretation whether the bird is about to swallow the seed from the outside, or is offering the seed up from inside—both possibilities can be true.

And so it is with our business here. What is fascinating is how people can share an image or an idea that can carry different meanings based upon personal experience. As TCU looks to move forward in time, how will it keep in memory the past Black experience? Will it look back, or simply keep moving forward?

Considering the Cyclical Nature of Time

This chapter about ongoing challenges revolves around two key concepts: the cycle of time and the sincerity of diversity. With respect to the "cycle of time," the contribution here will be to understand the cyclical nature of time. When traditional historians approach history, they usually employ a chronological approach that has a set beginning and a specific ending, a bracketing of periods in order to make the larger concepts more digestible. Thus, to study change over time, one must typically pick a place in time and continue forward. Our analysis of the Black history at TCU offers another approach—namely that rather than move forward within a strictly linear fashion, we can operate in a cyclical manner. Meaning that even though the dates may be different, the circumstances and concepts of events happening to Black people at TCU are quite similar, thereby leading to the expression, "history repeats itself." History may not repeat itself exactly, but themes can indeed reoccur.

Thus we wish to observe whether TCU's Black history is cyclical, so that we may either better understand and undergird it, or if that is problematic, so that we may figure out how to interrupt the cycle. Although this chapter is entitled "Ongoing Challenges," suggesting contemporary commentary, it mostly reflects upon the past as a potential predictor of what is to come, if the key root issues remain unaddressed.

With respect to the sincerity of diversity, it would be inaccurate to make a blanket assertion that TCU has done nothing to help improve its campus after opportunities were missed in the past. However, what must be discovered are the proper metrics—perhaps even metrics that have yet to be invented—with which to assess the quality and efficacy of good-natured and well-meaning intentions to improve campus culture.

Few matters within the human experience remain static and constant (different from consistent)—for memories can fade, narratives can change, and what we know can always grow. We are only a mere discovery away from uncovering a new way to remember the past. First, we often are afforded a vantage point from which to look back and appreciate just how much has truly changed. Next, as people have done the best they could with what they had to effectuate change over time, we see that the policies may have been noble, but the people executing such noble policies may not have been consistent. This is how we end up with equitable intent, but inequitable results. The fluidity of racism can be understood to be akin to water; it continually seeks to adapt and merely adopt the shape of its latest container.

One pattern apparent is that TCU as an institution will often hire and handsomely compensate high-level administrators and faculty fundamental to providing students innovative, high-quality experiences. Yet it is the students—mostly Black ones—who are supposed to be led who have pushed the university to make structural, institutional changes. Of course, it is a sign of success if faculty help students become leaders via the structured curriculum and related experiences for which students pay tuition. But here, TCU students organically staged strategic interventions that led the university on matters of race relations. As we have at least three such student interventions within half a century of each other, that emboldens us to label it a pattern. Specifically, there were three Black student-led "interventions" in the years 1971, 2016, and 2020 that presently draw our attention.

We will not be so sloppy as to call these actions "student protests," lest they bring to mind rehashed negative narratives of ineloquent and unorganized individuals who are terribly angry with "the system," yet instantly melt and morph into grateful beings when delivered pizzas by the administration they are protesting. The efforts chronicled here will be labeled *student interventions*, in that the university had not taken any previous, definitive action on the cause, but clung to what was otherwise known and agreed to as "normal" protocol. It was not until students *intervened* and interrupted the "normal" narrative that a new narrative was born.

If riots are the "language of the unheard,"[2] then perhaps these interventions are the language of the frustrated. Suffice it to say, racial frustrations have resulted in several interventions over the years at TCU. Predictably, there are few recorded accounts of racialized protests on campus before the 1960s, seeing how there was simply not a critical mass of Black American students physically present on campus. It was not until there was a significant concentration of students whereby the frictions of racial integration became clearer—despite the praised and poised, even-tempered trailblazers (e.g., Allene Jones and James Cash).

Yet, before commencing with an exposition and analysis of the three interventions, it is important to point out that Black students were hardly the first to engage the theater of public discourse. According to the Winter 2016 edition of *TCU Magazine,* students protested the unjust practice of limiting library hours on Sundays in February of 1963.[3] More accurately, likely mostly *white students* protested, since TCU did not officially desegregate until the next year.

If anything, it is possible, if not highly probable, that white students were inspired by the growing wave of social protests sprouting up throughout the country on a variety of key social issues, many of which were fueled by organized Black advocacy, which was obtaining more penetration within the mainstream. We should not take for granted how Black Americans "gradually forged vibrant new social movements to meet the demands of life and labor in the industrial age, movements that insisted upon full citizenship, equality before the bar, and social justice."[4]

In this vein of social justice, in February of 1963, students lobbied library staff for open hours on Sundays—complete with signature protest signs—and cleverly held a "sat out" on the library lawn (as opposed to employing the increasingly popular "sit-in" technique where students would peacefully take over an administrative building, blocking internal passageways by sitting on the floor). One sign in particular read, "If the library were open, we'd be inside." The 1963 *Horned Frog* yearbook described the protest thusly: "Not a shot was fired. Not a battle cry was heard. But it was still a revolt."

Not only did students successfully obtain their objective of additional hours on Sunday (currently it is customary for the Mary Couts Burnett Library to be open for twenty-four-hour periods during the academic year), but they also became included on the university's library committee for the first time.[5] This protest and resolution was an excellent example of students raising their voices over an issue they deemed important; they were able to broker a new outcome after negotiation, and more importantly obtain reconciliation with a systemic, substantive change that would include student voices in future decision-making protocols. Now, we shall turn our attention to the three Black interventions with an eye on how such interventions were received and resolved.

1971: We've Only Just Begun

The first documented Black student intervention was in 1971, a mere seven years after the first full-time cohort of Black students were officially permitted to take classes at TCU. On February 3, 1971, four Black American football players—Larry Dibbles, Ervin Garnett, Hodges Mitchell, and Raymond Rhodes—gave notice that they were quitting the football team and subsequently held a press conference to share their reasons why.[6] At the press conference, only football player Larry Dibbles was present, but he was joined by Eddie Miles and student athlete advisory committee president Franklin Callaway, in addition to another individual who had her own personal reasons for speaking up and speaking out—1970 TCU Homecoming Queen Jennifer Giddings. The students were organized and had a list of four demands prepared to share with the press.

First, the football players asserted that they left the team for reasons of underlying and unstated racial discrimination by both TCU administration and the athletic department. For them, this issue crested for "reasons based on the athletic department policy changes and dress codes." Newly installed football Coach Jim Pittman instituted an appearance code which called "for all football players to be clean-shaven, to wear shoes, socks, and belt, and to have reasonably short hair," but as Black men with Afro hairstyles that stand out on a predominantly white campus, they felt that this "universal" policy was designed with them in mind.[7] We have no evidence to contest or confirm this assertion.

Second, the group felt that Giddings "had been purposely excluded from Cotton Bowl Activities in which she was entitled to participate. A formal public apology was demanded to be printed in the 1971 *Horned Frog*." We were unable to find evidence of an apology; however, on February 9, 1971, the *Skiff* published an op-ed authored by J. L., who offers a point-by-point analysis of each of the demands, and "finds" most of them reasonable (per the article's title, "Most Pleas Were Reasonable"). This editorial response, while it does indeed engage sympathetically with the Black students' concerns, is simultaneously dismissive and condescending when it adjudged the Black students' claim over Giddings's Cotton Bowl exclusion to be "a mistake. This goof marred the overall presentation of the Black students, and reveals a failure on their part in the channeling of communications."[8]

We are unsure where one student divines the authority to "render judgment" about the experience of another, especially against the backdrop of an environment that traditionally and historically has been limited in education, exposure to, and experience of the nuanced plight of a person of color on a predominately white campus with strong statements such as: "The incident concerning Jennifer Giddings and the Cotton Bowl activities is another example of the black assuming the worst in a situation involving one of his own."[9] As this is a direct quote, take note of the pejorative, general group reference employed with the phraseology, "the black" from the prior sentence.

Thirdly, the group demanded "a Black campus minister and psychologist (counselor) be hired by the school to help Black students with their unique problems. They felt that more Black professors should be hired, too." Fourthly, the students requested "a full investigation of an incident involving Black student Jimmy Leach" who they felt "had been denied admission under questionable circumstances." However, when the *Horned Frog* yearbook staff made inquiries about the admission of Jimmy Leach, the Business Office stated that Leach had not cleared his bill for fall, 1970.[10] While no Black minister was hired, in direct response to this 1971 Black student intervention, a Black Studies minor was attempted in 1972 before dissipating in the 1980s due to inadequate enrollment and support. Additionally, a Black counselor was hired in 1971.

Yet a mere three years later, in the 1974 *Horned Frog* yearbook, *IMAGE*[11] ran a story about how the TCU campus chapter of the National Association for the Advancement of Colored People filed complaints against the university with the Department of Health, Education and Welfare and the Equal Employment Opportunity Commission. *IMAGE* interviewed NAACP spokesman and executive committee chairman Ray Turner, who explained that such filings were a "last resort." Since only one individual filed paperwork—albeit federal-level paperwork that prompted a formal and public response—this activity does not rise to the level of "student intervention" for our purposes. Turner's actions did raise awareness, as did the 1971 press conference, but after filing the initial paperwork, there was very little continued student involvement. Nonetheless, it is important to note Turner's rhetoric that "Everybody should have the opportunity to have this diversified education, but there are so few minorities in teaching or professional positions here that the opportunity is being denied, not just to blacks, not just to Chicanos, but to whites also."[12]

History may not repeat itself, but events can occur that seem reminiscent of times past. Much of what Turner advocated for was similar in tone to the 1971 intervention. Some of the main areas of the formal complaint centered around hiring, advancement, admissions, and recruitment.[13] Turner said on the lower level of an employment scale, "all you see in the cafeteria and maintenance are blacks and Chicanos. We're saying why can't we see that many blacks and Chicanos on the higher levels of the employment scale here?"[14] The citizen-soldier model can be questioned because of its potential payoff to the volunteer, but Turner appears to adopt a citizen-consumer tack. Said Turner, "When I'm paying tuition the same as white students I don't want to be insulted in class. I shouldn't have to put up with this sort of thing."[15] Turner chose to make a statement based on his investment at a core economic level, which makes him equal to anyone else paying the same amount of tuition, rather than make an appeal to conscience or an attempt to engage in the moral suasion typical of the Black Freedom Movement before it blossomed into the larger civil rights movement.

Turner's decision comes right on the heels of Mrs. Allene Jones becoming the first Black professor hired at TCU, where the university can rightly state that in 1968, progress was made. But if Turner is to be believed, such progress demonstrates how progress must be a continual process, because a single milestone does not obviate the need for continued pressure for positive change. The distinction of the first Black tenured professor goes to Reva Bell, who was a tenured assistant professor in the elementary education division of the school of education, obtaining tenure in spring 1980—a disparity issue that dogs many universities still.[16] Bell also invoked a similar "citizen-consumer" argument to articulate the logic of equal treatment for all of her students who dared to wear purple, whether white or black, when she said "although Blacks were not allowed to be seen visibly on TCU's campus, Blacks had the same financial requirements as white students."[17]

On April 17, 1974, Turner filed the EEOC complaint seemingly out of exasperation when he stated, "We've talked, we've talked, we've continued to talk, but something has to be done."[18] While clever to file under Title IX of CRA—which "forbids racial discrimination in educational institutions receiving federal funds," unfortunately for Mr. Turner's filing, he graduated shortly thereafter that May, and likely shifted his concentration elsewhere. And the EEOC—although only instituted a decade earlier with the passage of the 1964 Civil Rights Act—was deluged with complaints from many aggrieved individuals seeking assistance outside of their ineffective workplace structures, causing a significant months-long backlog.[19]

In fact, the same reporter for the *Skiff* picked up the story thread again two years later in 1976, with an article entitled, "HEW Report Caught in 'Backlog': No Results Yet from 2-Year Investigation." NAACP member Bronaugh Bridges indicated that investigators informed him that "the charges (against the university) were substantiated." Carrying the torch lit by Turner, Bridges was equally exasperated by the tardiness of the final report. Said Bridges, "TCU hasn't taken any steps (to correct discrimination) from what I can see. That's the biggest wrong of this thing taking two years."[20] The bitter irony in this development is that after TCU opened its doors to desegregate and after the federal government created mechanisms designed to address disparities, from the perspective of Black students living and enduring the educational experience in the early years of integration, the struggle merely continued—albeit in a different form.

2016: Students Expect More

In the fall of 2016, three students started leading silent interventions while the national anthem was played at TCU home football games.[21] What was similar to the 1971 intervention was that students leveraged a topic of importance to the larger TCU community in order to heighten awareness: football (which in Texas, is akin to a religion).[22] Similar to the 1971 event, the organizing students had a list of fourteen demands to articulate their position. One difference of note, however, is that the three organizers, Shanel Alexander, Diona Willis, and Emily Laff, were not only all female, but they presented a multiracial coalition with Alexander and Willis identifying as Black and Laff identifying as white.

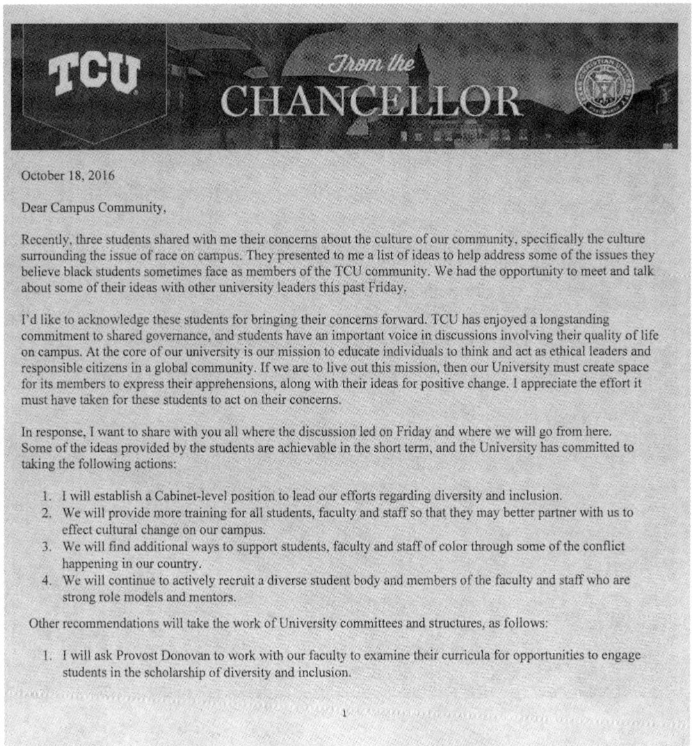

October 18, 2016

Dear Campus Community,

Recently, three students shared with me their concerns about the culture of our community, specifically the culture surrounding the issue of race on campus. They presented to me a list of ideas to help address some of the issues they believe black students sometimes face as members of the TCU community. We had the opportunity to meet and talk about some of their ideas with other university leaders this past Friday.

I'd like to acknowledge these students for bringing their concerns forward. TCU has enjoyed a longstanding commitment to shared governance, and students have an important voice in discussions involving their quality of life on campus. At the core of our university is our mission to educate individuals to think and act as ethical leaders and responsible citizens in a global community. If we are to live out this mission, then our University must create space for its members to express their apprehensions, along with their ideas for positive change. I appreciate the effort it must have taken for these students to act on their concerns.

In response, I want to share with you all where the discussion led on Friday and where we will go from here. Some of the ideas provided by the students are achievable in the short term, and the University has committed to taking the following actions:

1. I will establish a Cabinet-level position to lead our efforts regarding diversity and inclusion.
2. We will provide more training for all students, faculty and staff so that they may better partner with us to effect cultural change on our campus.
3. We will find additional ways to support students, faculty and staff of color through some of the conflict happening in our country.
4. We will continue to actively recruit a diverse student body and members of the faculty and staff who are strong role models and mentors.

Other recommendations will take the work of University committees and structures, as follows:

1. I will ask Provost Donovan to work with our faculty to examine their curricula for opportunities to engage students in the scholarship of diversity and inclusion.

1

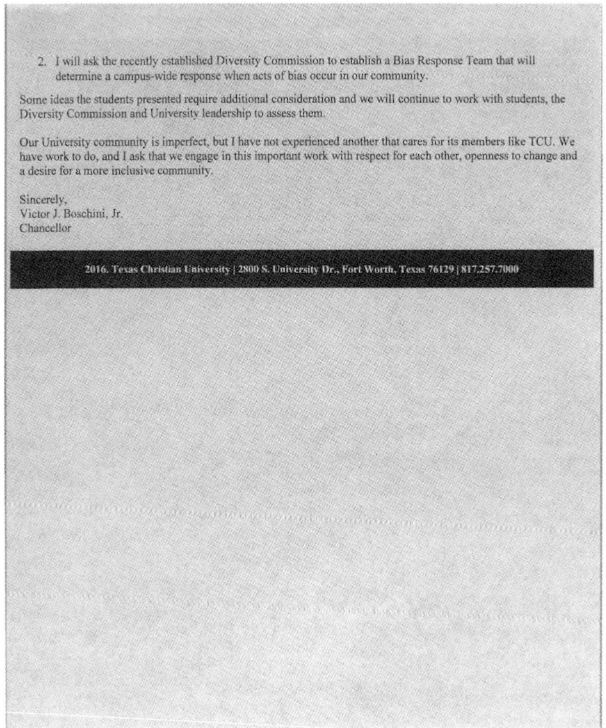

2. I will ask the recently established Diversity Commission to establish a Bias Response Team that will determine a campus-wide response when acts of bias occur in our community.

Some ideas the students presented require additional consideration and we will continue to work with students, the Diversity Commission and University leadership to assess them.

Our University community is imperfect, but I have not experienced another that cares for its members like TCU. We have work to do, and I ask that we engage in this important work with respect for each other, openness to change and a desire for a more inclusive community.

Sincerely,
Victor J. Boschini, Jr.
Chancellor

2016. Texas Christian University | 2800 S. University Dr., Fort Worth, Texas 76129 | 817.257.7000

Above
On October 18, 2016, Chancellor Victor Boschini responded directly to Black student concerns, which presaged the creation of TCU's Chief Inclusion Officer position and the Office of Diversity and Inclusion. *Courtesy of Minorities at TCU.*

While the full list of demands can be accessed in the Appendices, of note is the organizing students' critique not necessarily of the university's attempt to recognize and redress their diversity deficiencies, but of the *university community's response*, which arguably is endemic of the "light switch conundrum," or rather, how does an institution effectively foster fundamental, systemic change over time? The group described campus response to the Innovative Community Scholars Program that intentionally recruited talented local students by asserting: "With scholarships like Community Scholars, minority students from the area get the opportunity to attend TCU, but not without receiving denigrating stares from other students, derogatory comments, and low expectations from other peers."

This intervention by students actually resulted in several substantive changes, including the creation of a new administrative outfit entitled the Office of Diversity and Inclusion, with former TCU football player Dr. Darron E. Turner being installed as the Chief Inclusion Officer at the cabinet level.

Around the same time, a new major provided TCU students with additional opportunities to learn and understand the theory and lexicon behind race relations with the formation of Comparative Race and Ethnic Studies in the spring of 2017, a mere few months after the fall 2016 intervention.[23] A more complete list of their demands may be found in Appendix B.

2020: Recent but Related Histories

In January 2020, the TCU community once again had to reckon with Black student intervention. A federal civil rights lawsuit filed on behalf of "Jane Doe" alleged mistreatment at TCU based upon her Black race. She was joined by four other Black TCU students.[24] While many of the claims were dismissed, the case was ultimately settled out of court during mediation nearly two years later, in November 2021.[25]

This student intervention was similar to Ray Turner's 1974 attempt to force TCU to abide by federal antidiscrimination mechanisms by filing a discrimination lawsuit in US District court. This intervention differed in that the plaintiff's counsel decided to contextualize the present-day complaint against the backdrop of TCU's larger institutional memory. Thus, the complaint chronicled numerous instances from the student newspaper and yearbooks where students of color might indeed have had difficulty with TCU's predominately white institutional environment. Whether true or not, the allegations clearly struck a chord within the court of public opinion. Many students rallied around the plaintiffs, and several students leveraged social media as a means of publicly sharing unpleasant experiences on campus, discovering similar stories suggesting exclusion. Students organized into a coalition entitled Coalition for University Justice and Equality (CUJE) and issued their eighteen demands to administration (see Appendix C).[26]

Charting Change over Time

In considering the three student interventions profiled above, one key theme that emerges is how throughout time, it is students who have often taken the responsible lead in uncovering, understanding, and unburdening their *voices*—arguably, skills and abilities they agree to pay tuition to learn. While many parts contribute to the working machinery of a university, students are the lifeblood of any campus. Without students paying tuition, no university is possible. This provides students with considerable leverage. But with most students cycling off every four years or so, sustained organization is difficult, and potential power is diffused. Further, as young adults still learning and testing their own capacities for leadership and independence, it is not uncommon for students to feel powerless or to resign themselves to following directions handed down from executive leadership. In order to be effective, students have routinely sought creative ways to attract attention to leverage support for their causes.

It is no surprise, then, that in 2016, Black students cleverly thought to use a football game as a vehicle for attracting attention. Whenever oppressed groups of people are negotiating power with systems, Derrick Bell theorized that systems generally act in their own self-interest. Thus, whenever it appears that the system is operating on behalf of the oppressed, the question is whether the system is genuine and sincere with its efforts or whether there is some benefit extracted from the transaction in the name of interest convergence.

Suffice it to say, when TCU in 2017 responded to the 2016 student protests by creating an Office of Diversity and Inclusion, the question is whether TCU did so because it was the right thing to do, or did TCU agree to create said office because they were thrust into the public spotlight, were nationally embarrassed, and had to react in order to best preserve and control the narrative regarding how they operated? In any event, it was students who facilitated a dynamic whereby through introspection, university leadership was able to see that responding to student demands for equitable initiatives on its campus was not only the right thing to do, but also in TCU's best interest.

If students had not protested in 2016, when would TCU have decided that a new office would be necessary to better service its campus community? What is as amazing as it is alarming is to see that students were still asking for the same issues to be resolved forty years apart. Apparently the university had indeed *changed* over the years, yet different students have had remarkably similar experiences despite the passage of time.

No Protest, No Problem?

In recounting the social history of TCU, one might simply count on one hand the number of student protests, and be relatively assured that "there are no racial problems" on TCU's campus. But the absence of a reaction to a problem does not mean that there was no problem to navigate in the first place. Fewer protests or interventions on campus does not necessarily indicate fewer racial tensions. By our count, there are three student interventions led by Black American students at TCU: one in 1971, one in 2016, and one in 2020. That is not to say that there were no other times in TCU's history when Black students were aggrieved or upset and made their thoughts and ideas known publicly on campus, but in our research to date these are the three dates that stand apart as most historically significant. Perhaps latent tensions were not fully manifested on TCU's campus until there was a critical mass of Black students.

TCU's status as a Predominately White Institution (PWI) is often taken for granted by both sides. Many white students will feign or claim ignorance of racial issues, only because they live or have lived a lifestyle where they simply did not have to take stock of race, or more to the point, were never asked to think about it. Consider how this sustained ignorance only fuels many of the long-standing tensions existing on campus.

But at an institution of higher education, ignorance should be immediately and swiftly dealt with. The pursuit of knowledge and the insatiable thirst for better answers brings back into focus the rubric introduced in the introduction entitled the "3Es." With the 3Es, the premise is that most of the people in the world are good people, however when it comes to race, many people are afraid of saying and doing the wrong thing *and do say* or do the wrong thing. Such ignorance does not exist because they are an evil, frothing-at-the-mouth, card-carrying member of the Ku Klux Klan, but merely because they lack the 3Es—education, exposure, and experience—when it comes to establishing meaningful and substantive race relations on campus.

The 3Es is a succinct rubric to help readers recall that people simply do not know what they do not know. If the prevailing profile of TCU students is of young people mostly from upper-middle-class families who can afford the *not insignificant* tuition price tag, then what type of *preparatory* education these incoming students have had is a question that requires more attention. It is not uncommon for parents who have the means to emphasize college preparatory programs for their hopeful youth who wish to be accepted at a good university. If they have the means, some parents will pay handsome tuition for private high schools in order to have their children best prepared for college with rigor, mental discipline, and high test scores.

These independent schools, prolific throughout the country, are often, though not always, majority-white institutions themselves. While well-resourced, these schools are often deficient when it comes to diversity among high-ranking professional staff or faculty. In other words, we are not talking about the "cheerful" Black bus driver that picked up all the school-bound bodies or the "gregarious" cafeteria worker who extended pleasant greetings in the morning. Instead, we measure the quality of structural diversity by the diversity among those individuals who have the power and influence to shape policy decisions. All this to say that the very "ideal student" that TCU attracts may actually be systematically deficient when it comes to education about the Black American experience before they even arrive on campus.

Beyond formal education—learning facts and dates—exposure is the next level of understanding. Exposure can mean extended conversation or specific opportunities to deepen one's connection, whether through practicing new forms of communication or exploring new cuisines or learning about others through music. But beyond exposure is experience, arguably the most difficult but most meaningful step of the 3Es. For an experience requires that one relinquish control, immerse themselves in a live scenario that allows them to internalize what they know to be true. This is what so many students arguably miss—substantive opportunities to apply what they should be learning. For TCU to remain effective in its race relations generally, and with Black Americans specifically, it must remain willing to wrestle with the lack of education, exposure, and experience.

The Road to Reconciliation

In looking at the road ahead, it is entirely possible given the history of race relations thus far, there may be additional opportunities to dialogue and learn through future student interventions. Over what and when, we politely demur to predict; our business here is simply to study the past. However, much like the individual who packs an umbrella in case of rain, we now turn our attention to TCU initiatives that have the power and potential to institutionalize its habit of remembering the future, especially when it comes to acknowledging the role that Black history has played in TCU's history.

One example that honors TCU's Black past comes in a bubbling up of new portraits installed on campus to visually interrupt the apparent absence of institutionalized Black presence. A simple geographical inventory around campus will demonstrate that there is little to no diversity among all of the artistic structures on campus—whether it be a statue located outside on campus grounds or paintings seen within a campus building. A small volunteer group of TCU community members endeavored to add to the homogenous groupings of campus heroes by engaging in what is called the "Portrait Project," where the goal is to leverage publicly shared art to honor "trailblazers from TCU's past [that] can inspire students, faculty, and staff as we continue to work toward a more diverse and equitable campus."[27]

In April 2022 additional pieces were added to the canvas plane with the acquisition of two works of art by the Comanche/Kiowa artist, J. NiCole Hatfield (Nahmi-A-Piah). The names of the two works are *Based on Mrs. Jack Treetop-Standing Rock 1908* and *Based on Quanah Parker Kwahadi Band of Comanche* and were originally installed in The Harrison administration building.[28]

Perviously, in July 2020, the university created a Race and Reconciliation Initiative (RRI) to study TCU's relationship with slavery, racism, and the Confederacy.[29] While difficult to unequivocally or officially draw a straight line connecting the two in terms of interest convergence, the January 2020 lawsuit, coupled with the elevated tensions surrounding the initial arrival of the global COVID-19 pandemic in March 2020, followed by the incomprehensible murder of George Floyd in May 2020 and the resulting summer of sustained international social justice protests likely not seen since the 1960s—all likely were contributing factors in the university deciding to create its inaugural Race and Reconciliation Initiative in July of 2020. As this event occurred so close to the time of this publication, out of respect for preserving the authenticity of the original voices without making hasty commentary, the organized student demands are also provided in Appendix C, in their original form.

Answering the question posed by Janus at the doorway, "Which way do we wish to go?" there are three key institutional interventions fostered by the RRI to track over time. First, the initiative helped create an academically based, research-focused, and socially sanctioned space to talk about race within the university's institutional structure. The university ultimately committed to a five-year plan that provided an initial Survey Report in 2021, with a Summary Report slated for 2026 publication. Based upon *Operation: Triangulation,* the three key windows in time for specifically understanding TCU's relationship with race are: 1) *The Founding Years: TCU, Slavery, and the Confederacy, 1861–1891*; 2) *Transition to Integration, 1941–1971*; and 3) *Recent but Related Histories, 1998–2020.* Perhaps in response or in dialogue with the January 2020 student intervention, the first year focused upon African American narratives out of practical considerations for telling the story of slavery, racism, and the Confederacy effectively.

The initial window, "The Founding Years," spans the start of the Civil War to the start of the Jim Crow era. It appears that TCU's founding was a reaction to the decimation wrought by the Civil War, which continued in the wake of the war, but had little direct connection to either enslavement or the Confederacy. The subsequent window in time, "Transition to Integration," spans the start of World War II and Chancellor McGruder Ellis Sadler's tenure to the then high watermark when the first Black homecoming queen was crowned in 1970. This period includes the emergence of baseless fears and concerns over the institution's reluctant acceptance of a more diverse society that unfortunately cast a lingering shadow over subsequent attempts to embrace a less monochromatic existence in the twenty-first century. The last window in time, "Recent but Related Histories," begins with Chancellor Michael Ferrari's tenure and ends with the 2019–2020 academic year. Michael Ferrari is significant in that he represents the first non-Texan and first university leader not officially affiliated with the Disciples of Christ, the church denomination linked to the university's founders, a move that marked TCU's new outward look and expansion. More critically, within this window several needed areas of growth are identified by the Key Recommendations if TCU plans to deliver on its charge to past and potential graduates to "lead on."

The second institutional intervention occurred on April 21, 2021, when the TCU Board of Trustees unanimously agreed to approve the seven Key Recommendations offered by RRI at the conclusion of its first-year study, based upon recommendations from its seven subcommittees:[30]

■ *Slavery* We recommend that TCU develop and implement a comprehensive strategic plan to promote equity and inclusion in graduate and undergraduate student admissions, faculty and staff recruitment and retention, and the illumination of TCU's full history through curricula programs such as Frog Camp and the universal first-year course, University Life.

■ *Confederacy* We recommend providing more robust contextual information near the Clark Brothers statue, memorializing a more complete story of TCU, commemorating the efforts of underrepresented or marginalized groups who contributed to TCU's development, and highlighting racist attitudes and behaviors from earlier years as an educational step toward creating an anti-racist community.

■ *Segregation* We recommend the development and maintenance of an online digital depository specifically focused upon Race and Reconciliation, which all members of the TCU community are able to access to understand the collective histories that contribute to TCU's legacy.

■ *Desegregation* We recommend more consistently recognizing the contributions of our Black, Indigenous, and other alumni of color, more specifically through the ongoing funding, development, and maintenance of the RRI Oral History Project designed to capture key alumni experiences.

■ *Voice* We recommend the perpetual and continued observance of "TCU Reconciliation Day" as a means to maintain open forums of communication and expression on the topic of race and reconciliation while deliberately, intentionally, and strategically increasing access to existing TCU media channels (i.e., student-run television, print, and radio) to amplify multiple voices and perspectives on campus.

■ *Good Neighbor?* We recommend conducting a comprehensive inventory of all official vendors conducting business with TCU to qualitatively measure and assess equitable representation by diverse members of our business community.

■ *Repair* We recommend continuing this Race and Reconciliation Initiative beyond the initial one-year time frame originally set for this committee's investigation by continuing to make the modest investment in the human capital necessary to carry out the work of research and reconciliation as part and parcel of TCU's efforts to lead on.

The thrust of these recommendations was to institutionalize efforts aimed at equity under the same Office of Diversity and Inclusion created in 2017 after the 2016 student intervention—which would necessarily benefit Black students, faculty, and staff. Of note is the inclusion of an annual observance entitled "Reconciliation Day," usually to be observed the third Wednesday of every April, as a day for the TCU community "to come together so we can move forward together on the path toward reconciliation."[31]

In a third intervention, the university formally acknowledged that it is on the path toward publicly remembering, recognizing, and reconciling its relationship with early Black TCU contributors and employees, Charley and Kate Thorp.[32] This connection was only made possible through the institutionalization of organized research through RRI's Oral History Project, orchestrated by lead researcher and RRI Postdoctoral Fellow Dr. Sylviane Greensword and the university's support and commitment through collaborative library staff, organized student researchers, contributing History Department faculty, and of course, economic resources to compensate many, but not all of them, for their contributory labors.

How to Remember the Future?

How the university will continue to tell the Charley and Kate Thorp story remains to be seen. The future telling and

Above
The Harvard Business School "Glass House" faculty residence was renamed "Cash House" in honor of Dr. James I. Cash in 2020; TCU announced its plans for a Cash statue in 2021. *Courtesy of TCU Photo Collection.*

retelling of the truth represents a profound opportunity to rectify "Randolph's Lament," in that TCU's cofounder Randolph Clark himself recognized and praised Charley Thorp's indispensable service because he understood Charley's underappreciated intellect as a person able to deftly balance and juggle so many difficult tasks. Randolph's son, Joseph Lynn Clark, wrote, "When the Clarks opened the school in the Thorp building Charley was occasionally employed for janitorial service, as the school developed, gradually accepting wider responsibility for practically every detail, aside from academic activities, not specifically belonging to someone else."[33] This intellect, while not acknowledged, was absolutely appreciated when Clark observed, "There were three individuals . . . whose services to the school and to the people of the town entitle them to an exalted place in the annals of the Thorp Spring enterprise. They were John W. Kay, Charles Thorp and Kate Thorp. . . . In efficiency, dependability, and loyalty, they were superior in their respective spheres."[34]

Further, at Charley Thorp's funeral Randolph Clark appeared to observe with melancholy that "Charley was endowed with far more than ordinary intellect. With opportunity, he could have been the equal of Booker Washington in education, or a success in the business world. He practiced the Spirit of Christ in unselfish service to others."[35] We call this public rumination after the fact of Charley's death "Randolph's Lament." We also must pause to think of just where Charley could possibly have had an "opportunity" to succeed, perhaps through the benefit of a high-quality education offered by an institution like TCU. While we continue to ponder, we offer Randolph's words again who solemnly stated about Charley, "After emancipation he was told that he was free, but he never realized the freedom. If any difference it was harder work. He was not allowed to get an education. . . . Who is responsible for this waste?" While difficult to answer that question in the past, TCU with each new day has an opportunity to embrace the past—rather than erase it—and influence the future of incoming TCU students who can benefit from knowing and appreciating TCU's full history, which must necessarily include the Black experience.

Only through continued dialogue and dedicated study can the TCU community continue to wrestle with the 3Es, or lack of education, exposure, and experience. For with new information comes the opportunity for new insight. Consider, for example, the existing statue of TCU cofounders Addison and Randolph Clark placed, as of this printing, directly across from the former administration building, Sadler Hall, and near the entrance of TCU's Academic Commons. Perhaps before but especially during the summer of social justice and protest—during national media coverage of the George Floyd murder and local coverage of Atatiana Jefferson and Botham Jean's untimely deaths—the narrative that the Clark Brothers statue was a "Confederate Statue" began to gain steam. There was a larger national conversation about dismantling and taking down Confederate statues that also crested as a direct result of such public protest.[36]

Through research and dialogue, TCU was able to shift the narrative and share that contrary to popular belief, the Brothers Clark statue is not a *Confederate statue* in the strict sense. In contrast to the 1993 Clark Brothers statue, more than 1,500 Confederate statues and memorials were erected in the years following the failed Reconstruction period, with the bulk being erected between 1900 and 1940. The statue of the two brothers walking together without any Confederate regalia or insignia does not on its face undergird the "Lost Cause" interpretation of the Civil War, which presents the Civil War from a perspective most sympathetic to the Confederate cause. Typically, such statues are adorned with symbolic ornamentation indisputably demonstrating that they are affiliated with the Confederacy.

Thus, the Brothers Clark statue neither explicitly nor expressly makes any direct connection to the Confederacy, and presumptively was erected with the intention of honoring and recognizing Addison and Randolph Clark as TCU's founders. However, this is not to deny that the Clark Brothers share *Confederate ties*. For we do know is that in 1862 Addison Clark formally enlisted in the Confederate army in Grayson County, and was mustered in Collin County, as a Second Lieutenant, Company D, Sixteenth Texas Cavalry.[37] Randolph joined Addison for a short period towards the war's end, but not as a formally enrolled soldier. Randolph Clark's memoirs in the book *Reminiscences* indicate that the brothers felt compelled—though not conscripted—to pick up arms and join the cause as a matter of duty to local defense. Be that as it may, as with most human portraits, this picture remains complex as their legacies are simultaneously tied to an ignominious fight for enslavement as well as a noble struggle for intellectual freedom.

It is interesting to consider how these statues might be analyzed through the lens of Black perspective. Statues are by design discursive constructs that keep alive ongoing historical debates: "[statue] designers shape mute materials to evoke people, events, ideas, and places from the past to shape the emotions and experiences of audiences in the present."[38] Thus, when considering that statues can serve as informative historical markers that "give meaning to life by providing communities and groups with a way to communicate their traditions and beliefs from generation to generation," one question to consider is what does it mean or symbolize if there is a life-sized statue of TCU's mascot, SuperFrog on campus, but as of this printing, no permanent Black presence in the form of a statue.[39]

That omission was recently corrected. TCU Athletic Director Jeremiah Donati announced publicly at the inaugural Reconciliation Day on April 21, 2021, that the university would erect a statue of Black TCU trailblazer Dr. James Cash. This announcement is significant in that statues "comprise a unique cultural heritage that gives form and focus to shared values and experiences," and therefore existing statues on TCU's campus of sports icons like Dutch Meyer, Dave O'Brien, or entrepreneurial titans like Charles Tandy collectively represent success to those who erected statues in their honor.[40] Now Dr. James Cash will forever stand among these statues of white males as a TCU icon, or at the very least, a person important to the university's past history and present identity moving forward in time.

Time will also tell how TCU will continue to adapt and overcome future manifestations of racial discrimination, as anti-Black racism has shifted over time, as well.[41] In the Jim Crow period of the 1950s, racism was much more overt and offensive. The closer to the present we get, the more we see that racism becomes more subtle and sophisticated. In more recent times more people acknowledge and discuss racism, but it is much harder to spot, identify, and eliminate rather than merely mitigate.

Hence, another ongoing challenge facing TCU and its future with Black staff, students, faculty, and alumni is whether the university is interested in truly changing its trajectory versus altering whatever is necessary to maintain the status quo. As the tradition and habit of racial exclusivity had been practiced by TCU for so long (i.e., racial segregation up until January 23, 1964), it is now difficult to parse out what is custom and culture from what is fundamentally and philosophically racially problematic and in need of change. Thus, even as TCU says all the right things about wanting to embrace change for the future, there is still significant historical momentum to overcome.

We offer this book as one of many additional perspectives that may help hew out that which is true about the Black experience at TCU over time. When TCU cofounder Randolph Clark rhetorically asks "Who is responsible for this waste?" about Charley Thorp, a Black man whom he distinctly recognized as another human being who "was endowed with far more than ordinary intellect," we believe this book may offer insight into an answer.[42] Perhaps Randolph Clark was clever to implicate himself in posing the rhetorical question about how society and institutions can move forward, fostering substantive change within society. But with the scholarship contained within this manuscript, we offer an answer that looks to understand the past as the key to unlocking the art of the possible in the near and distant future. We can observe from "Randolph's Lament," its logical limitations and feel liberated to "lead on" in our present window of time. For it would be a travesty to be blind to solutions "hidden in plain sight" as TCU endeavors to proceed down the path to progress.

Perhaps there is hope for Black students and others if the path to racial progress also pursues reconciliation on the way. With "Randolph's Lament," inexplicably he did not see that he himself had not only the power to co-create an institution of higher learning that serviced both men and women, but also capable, competent, and creative Black men and women like Charley and Kate Thorp. When it comes to recognizing and reconciling its relationship with Black students, staff, alumni, and faculty, opportunity beckons with each new day for TCU to eliminate the need for any conscientious member of its community to have to rhetorically ask sometime hence, "Who is responsible for this waste?"

APPENDIX A

1971 Demands

Where Is Rights Proposal? (See Page 6)

The Skiff

Texas Christian University • • • • Fort Worth, Texas 76129

Volume 69, Number 32
Friday, February 5 1971

Walkout Spurs Black Outcry

By JOHNNY LIVENGOOD
GREG BURDEN
and GEORGE STONE

Voluntary withdrawal of four black athletes from the University's grid squad Thursday triggered a chain of demands by black students generally.

The four players are Larry Dibbles, Hodges Mitchell, Raymond Rhodes, and Ervin Garnett. They officially removed themselves from the team Wednesday.

Underlying the statement released at a 9 a.m. press conference was the charge of racist attitudes among general and athletic administrations of the Univeristy.

In a meeting Wednesday night at Clark Dormitory blacks, led by Eddie Miles and SAAC president Franklin Callaway, determined now was the time for action in fighting institutionalized racism as well as writing the demands for the press conference the next morning. The students discussed inadequacies of the recruiting systems for blacks and a black studies program. After the decisions were made their previous nervousness changed to a calm strength coming from their commitment. During the writing of the press release, they joked about Coach Jim Pittman, Dr. J.M. Moudy, and the possibilities of being thrown out of school for their actions.

General Denial

First, they denied that the black athletes left, as Pittman claimed, because of inadequate social life and that the reasons are based on the policy changes and dress codes.

Second, they charged discrimination against Jennifer Giddings, 1970 Homecoming Queen. The blacks charge she was purposely excluded from Cotton - Bowl activities in which she was entitled to participate. A formal public apology, to be printed in the 1971 edition of the Horned Frog on an entire page across from the Queen's picture, was demanded.

Because of the unique problems related to blackness the students also demanded that a black minister and black psychologist be hired to handle these problems and that more black professors be hired for more relevant teaching. They feel the exposure would also be educational for the white students as well.

A full investigation of the denial of the enrollment of Jimmie Leach was also demanded. Because they feel that Leach was denied under questionable circumstances they want to determine if discrimination has taken

(Continued on Page 8)

AT THURSDAY'S Press Conference Frank Callaway, Larry Dibbles, Jennifer Giddings, and Eddie Miles answered reporter's questions.

Pages 121-122
While we do not have an original copy of the students' requests, this February 5, 1971, article captures their sentiments closer to that window in time. *Courtesy of TCU Photo Collection.*

Demand List Presented To Press

(Continued from Page 1)

place and that Ray Turner, president of the TCU campus NAACP, receive all the facts of the case.

No Revolution

They concluded that they are not revolutionaries and are not trying to change the basic structure of TCU, but are trying to make it a more effective educational institution for black students. They feel if they are to be effective members of their communities they must demand relevant courses.

In Thursday morning's press conference several spokesmen representing the black students in general read the prepared statement and asnwered questions from the press.

The spokesmen were Frank Callaway of SAAC, Jennifer Giddings, 1970 Homecoming Queen, Larry Dibbles, and Eddie Miles.

Callaway read a portion of the statement relating to Dibbles and then let Dibbles make a statement of his own. Dibbles said said that "lack of adequate social life" was not his reason for leaving.

He said that his reasons for leaving were precipitated by the change in the staff and the change in rules.

New Rules

"My reason for leaving is the new rules, not because of the social life. The social life is getting better and I'd like to stay, but Coach Pittman has his rules and I have mine."

HODGES MITCHELL

Callaway then read the portion of his statement relating to Jennifer Giddings not being invited to the Cotton Bowl parade.

Miss Giddings said, "I am disappointed to know that the students selected me to represent them but I was denied this opportunity on Jan. 1. I know that some people would say "Well, that would happen anyway" but sometimes you think a little differently when you are black."

Eddie Miles then read the completion of the statement, listing the complaints and demands.

In the questioning that followed, Dibbles said there had been no harrassment from the white players.

Dibbles also stated that he had not yet decided where to transfer, that the four players may or may not go to Florida State as Coach Pittman had said.

Plans Not Known

As for the basketball players, Dibbles said he did not know their plans.

Dibbles cited his and Rhodes' denial of food at the training tables as a precipitating factor. He also said that one time Rhodes' plate was taken from him at the training table as he prepared to eat.

Dibbles said he could not change his mind and return. "It would create an air of dissension on the team, and that is not good for a winning team." He said Pittman had asked him to stay.

He said the other three players were not present because they did not want to jeopardize their chances at getting into another school. Dibbles said he considered the incident important enough to speak out.

The spokesmen said they considered the new rules related to racism because only one white athlete had a moustache, while most of the blacks did. Callaway said the moustache issue goes deeper than it seems since blacks consider it a way of expressing manhood and militancy.

Uniform Rules

In relation to the demands for more black professors and staff members, Callaway said TCU has only two-and-a-half black faculty members: one in nursing, one in Upward Bound, and one in an unspecified field.

Callaway said the blacks are not trying to change the rules and that the rules should be uniform for both white and black players, and called for an investigation.

Miss Giddings underscored the fact that she is a transfer student and not familiar with TCU rules and traditions and said she is concerned because she was not contacted at all.

Mike Usnick, student body president, then made a statement. He said that for the last two years invitations to the Cotton Bowl game had been sent for the student body president, the cheerleaders, and the TCU sweetheart. This year's sweetheart was Angela Ambrose.

Eddie Miles summed up the black student's feelings: "We will take whatever means are necessary, and you can take that any way you want."

Speculation

The athletes' action, coming soon after the assumption of the head coaching duties by Jim Pittman, aroused speculation that racial issues or dissatisfaction with dress and appearance codes recently introduced by Pittman may have been involved in the decision.

Pittman, who was previously the head coach at Tulane, returned from a recruiting mission in West Texas Tuesday and met with the players on Wednesday.

He said that in his discussion with the players, "They expressed no dissatisfaction" with him or the changes that he has instituted.

According to Pittman, the athletes told him their dissatisfaction stemmed from the lack of adequate social life for them, and that Florida State is in an area more suited to their needs.

LARRY DIBBLES

Only One

Pittman also said that the only one of the four who felt the effects of the new appearance code was Dibbles, who was not allowed to eat at the athletes' training table because of his moustache.

The new appearance code calls for all football players to be clean-shaven, to wear shoes, socks, and a belt, and to have reasonbaly short hair.

The players, Pittman, said, expressed no displeasure with the code at the time of their meeting, saying that they felt it was necessary to apply it to blacks as well as whites.

At the end of the meeting Pittman said, that the players "shook my hand and wished me luck."

At present, the dress code applies only to the football team, but it has been suggested that it be made applicable to all athletes.

Athletic director Abe Martin said the suggestion has been made.

"One of the coaches, I can't remember which one, did say that he thinks all of them (the coaches) ought to get together on this thing, but there's nothing official yet," Martin said.

Martin met with Mitchell, Rhodes and Garnett Wednesday and said the athletes had told him the same things they had said to Pittman, that their reason for leaving was the unsatisfactory social life at TCU.

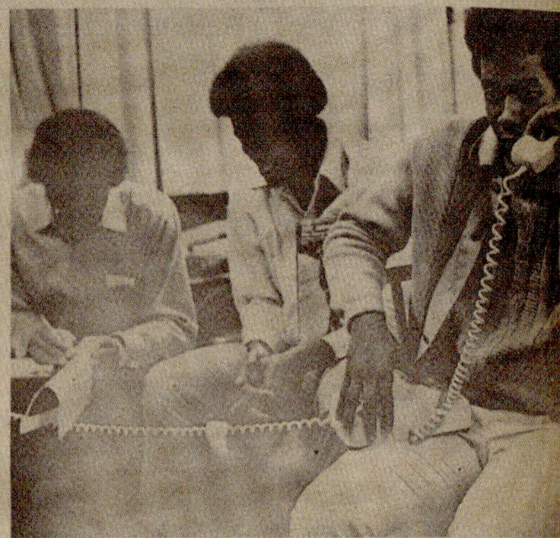

AT WEDNESDAY night's meeting Eddie Miles, Eli Madison, and Frank Callaway work on the black student statement.

Swimmers Working Hard Hours

One of the least publicized of TCU's athletic teams is probably one of the most dedicated.

The TCU Swimming Squad arrives at 6:15 a.m. almost every day and works out in the University pool until nearly 8:00 a.m.

Swimming coach John Brewton

APPENDIX B

2016 List of Demands

To Whom It May Concern:

When one decides on an institution of higher education they have two options: a student can go where they are most comfortable or dive into a world where they never imagined being and hope for the best. As a minority student, being comfortable means attending a school where almost everyone looks like you, an HBCU. We as students of color are at a constant disadvantage and at TCU we should not be. With scholarships like Community Scholars, minority students from the area get the opportunity to attend TCU, but not without receiving denigrating stares from other students, derogatory comments, and low expectations from other peers. Feeling a sense of alienation along with trying to maintain a high grade point average and remain involved on campus creates unnecessary burdens that can hurt students in the long run. To encourage the inclusiveness of our campus and to change attitudes towards minorities on this campus, we have a thorough list of demands that we want to see implemented.

Students of all colors have recognized the disadvantages that certain groups have experienced on this so called, "inclusive" campus and frankly we are tired of it. The mission of TCU is "To educate individuals to think and act as ethical leaders and responsible citizens in the global community," but how is this enforced? Students and faculty go around campus spewing micro-aggressions and expecting students of color to pretend that what has been done is acceptable. Being that this is 2016, change is long overdue.

We are prepared to provide more information and work with administration directly on the implementation of these demands. With an open line of communication, resolutions can and will be made. It is our duty as students to recognize our feelings toward the powers that be and work to implement change. We have put lots of thought into the demands and are passionate about change, we can only hope that you, and fellow members of administration will be just as open to the change as we are.

The demands listed below are in no particular order. If we do not hear something regarding our demands within 20 days, various forms of escalation will take place until some if not all of our demands are met.

Signed,

Black Students and Allies of TCU

Pages 123-125
In October 2016, "Black Students and Allies of TCU" sent a letter to the chancellor outlining their concerns and demands at the time.
Courtesy of RRI Box file.

Mission Statement:

It is our goal to elevate the people of color on Texas Christian University's campus by promoting empathy through cultural education, and creating truly ethical leaders in the global community by ensuring that black people are fairly represented and heard by administration.

What we want to accomplish:

We have started by compiling a list of demands crafted with careful consideration based on concerns voiced on TCU's campus and campuses around the nation. However, that is just the beginning. Through these demands as well as creating a video message that finally voices the many (often ignored or unheard) grievances that people of color have on TCU's campus, we plan on shifting the issue of race from "dialogue" to tangible action. We will stop at nothing to ensure that the cultural presence of black people on this campus is acknowledged and appreciated. Most of all we seek to educate this campus of the cultural origin and struggles that make black people who they are--and actively work to shift people's ignorance to awareness.

Executive Summary

1. We demand that TCU revise the Code of Conduct to reflect a zero-tolerance policy for racially insensitive and hateful speech. This will include developing and implementing protocol that will appropriately handle instances of hate speech as well as hate crimes involving TCU students. To do this we propose that a student led Diversity/Inclusion/Accountability board be created to focus on all issues of racial insensitivity on campus. The board will focus on initiating campus-wide conversation on diversity and inclusion on TCU's campus as well as holding students, faculty and staff accountable for insensitivity.

2. We demand that TCU increase faculty of color by at least 10%, in addition the retention rate these faculty members will remain above 75%. (to reflect the population of Texas)

3. We demand that all TCU faculty, staff, and students attend a sensitivity training with a trained professional during orientation that focuses not only on racial and anti-Semitic intolerance but also micro-aggressions in order to maintain diversity and inclusion.

4. We demand accurate annual reports that reflect TCU's progress in terms of increasing diversity, not solely based on locations but also race in incoming classes as well as the diversity of all faculty and staff.

5. We demand a spark of meaningful dialogue- administrators and student media outlets must use existing communication channels to start, continue, and deepen our discussion of racism and ethnocentrism through conversations during orientation and throughout the core curriculum. In the core curriculum, focusing on the Cultural Awareness as being exclusively for the awareness of world cultures and people.

6. We demand a 100 million dollar endowment to further support minority students, and make TCU a more fiscally feasible option through non-athletic scholarships offered to low-income high schools not included within the realm of Community Scholars, and the creation of a multicultural center that is for students and by students.

7. We demand that a department of diverse studies are created along with an Ethnic Studies course that will be a core curriculum requirement for all students. We also demand a rigorous reevaluation of the courses that currently fulfill the core curriculum's diversity requirement, led by a board comprised of faculty of color who would be compensated for this service.

8. We demand that TCU create a Greek-life diversity task force to implementing a mandatory cultural sensitivity training, with a trained professional, for all students considering Greek life.

9. We demand housing for members of both the Multicultural Greek Council and National Pan-Hellenic Council, as they are a vital part of diversity on this campus.

10. We demand the establishment an Asian American studies major and a Native American studies major, because they are representative of people both in the state of Texas and beyond.

11. We demand a university-funded speaker series, that focuses on diversity and how we can better implement and celebrate it on campus.

12. We demand that TCU hire a Chief Officer of Diversity and Inclusion in charge of overseeing the curriculums and projects set forth in this document.

13. We demand that the flag be lowered when people of color around the nation are murdered by people who are supposed to protect and serve.

14. We demand that the students involved in the implementation of these demands, and the faculty and staff supporting them, do not suffer negative repercussions as they engage in this process of systematic and cultural change.

APPENDIX C

2020 List of Demands

Dear Chancellor Boschini, Dr. Dahlberg, and Texas Christian University Board of Trustees,

As a collective of Texas Christian University (TCU) undergraduate and graduate students from various historically marginalized backgrounds, we are deeply concerned with the allegations against the institution that were raised in the recent lawsuits put forth by "Jane Doe #1" and former TCU faculty member, Dr. Silda Nikaj. Both cases highlight the deep history of unchecked overt and systemic racism that has run rampant at this institution since its founding. As leaders of this university, we call on you to make substantive changes across TCU that will work to transform the campus climate, advance equity, and realize justice through TCU's meaningful atonement for its white supremacist, patriarchal, classist and ableist past and present. We put forth these demands with the hope that you all will immediately act in good faith. This administration has until **Wednesday, February 12, 2020** to publicly respond and commit in writing to our demands. Should our demands not be met, our peers will continue to pressure the university via the legal system and we will continue to exercise our right to protest.

1. WE DEMAND THE IMMEDIATE TERMINATION OF Dr. DIANE SNOW. In her capacity as Dean of the John V. Roach Honors College, Dr. Snow is listed as one of the primary TCU employees that helped create a hostile learning environment for Jane Doe #1. Dr. Snow has been accused of conspiracy, unlawful detainment, assault, retaliation and fraud within the legal case. Additionally, it is alleged that Dr. Snow was intoxicated and disorderly in front of TCU students and abandoned students while serving as a chaperone on an out of state trip. Both of the latter offenses are in clear violation of TCU's Faculty and Staff Handbook and campus policy. Given Dr. Snow's heinous acts, it is apparent that she is unfit to serve as a TCU leader, let alone a member of the faculty.

2. WE DEMAND THE IMMEDIATE DEMOTION AND REPLACEMENT OF Dr. Darron Turner. As Chief Inclusion Officer and Title IX Coordinator, Dr. Darron Turner has been tasked with ensuring TCU complies with various federal laws—Equal Employment Opportunity, Title IX, The Age Discrimination Act, etc.— that aim to protect the rights of the most marginalized. This office has a history of mishandling and neglecting various complaints and cases that has not been addressed nor remedied, even under the leadership of Dr. Turner. A position of this magnitude requires a person with extensive legal knowledge and competence in order to accurately and appropriately address the needs of the TCU community. This position would be better suited for someone with an education law and/or civil rights background.

WE PUT FORTH THAT Dr. Turner's POSITION AND OFFICE BE RESTRUCTURED. We propose that Dr. Turner's current office in addition to the Office of Compliance led by Chief University Compliance Officer, Andrea Nordmann, be merged and converted into a full-service Office of Investigations and Civil Rights Compliance overseen by a Chief Civil Rights Officer accompanied by three new Directors of Title IX, Equal Employment Opportunity, and Affirmative Action. Furthermore, the Office of Diversity and Inclusion will be renamed the Office of Diversity, EQUITY, and Inclusion and led by a Chief DEI Officer and three new Directors of Student Access and Success, Faculty Access and Success, and Staff Access and Success. In addition to these staff, the office will also include 4 ombudspersons: 2 student representatives, 1 staff representative, and 1 faculty

Pages 127-134
In January 2020, "Coalition for University Justice & Equity" sent a letter to the chancellor outlining their concerns and demands at the time. *Courtesy of RRI Box file.*

representative. These departments should be audited annually by an external investigative firm to ensure that the department runs effectively and appropriately. These audits should be published and accessible to the entire TCU community. We demand that all new hires for these appointments be made through an external nationwide search and that no internal hire is approved. We also demand that both a historically marginalized graduate and undergraduate student be appointed to the search committee for each position and that they each have a vote.

3. WE DEMAND THE IMMEDIATE INVESTIGATION AND REMOVAL OF Drs. Russel Mack, Robert Garnett and Frederick Gooding. With these faculty members also being named in Jane Doe #1's lawsuit we believe that it is important that both faculty members be removed from all university instruction and service work until the university's external investigation has been completed. It is problematic to continue to allow faculty that have been accused of conspiracy and discrimination to continue to teach. The allegations made by Jane Doe #1 with regards to having her grade manipulated as a form of retaliation is concerning. These faculty members have broken student trust. Moreover, they potentially jeopardize the university's accreditation and credibility. If either faculty member is being considered for a promotion and/or tenure, we ask that those decisions are not made until the university concludes its external investigation and Jane Doe #1's lawsuit is resolved.

4. WE DEMAND THE IMMEDIATE DISSOLUTION OF THE JOHN V. ROACH HONORS COLLEGE. While just over ten years old, the Honors College has thrived as a highly selective space for what are often perceived as TCU's "brightest." However, many of us have witnessed this space (and its resources) be used to further exclusion, inequities, and racism. The college is overwhelmingly a white space, with few opportunities for historically marginalized students. It should be noted that the college recently updated its Admissions Policy and Diversity, Equity, and Inclusion efforts JUST this past Fall, per their own website. The allegations that Jane Doe #1 lays out are not surprising. The college has been given dedicated space, faculty, housing, and often disproportionately more resources than other departments. Students from the Honors College are able to receive a unique experience at TCU that is not afforded to all, even those that often meet the college's admissions criteria. Moreover, the few historically marginalized students that are in the space are often antagonized by their white peers and professors simply because of their presence. It is for these reasons that we strongly believe that the college should be dissolved.

WE PUT FORTH THAT THE JOHN V. ROACH HONORS COLLEGE BE DISSOLVED AND MADE INTO A PROGRAM. There are many peer and aspirant institutions where Honors students are enrolled in a program NOT a college with the types of privileges and excess that have been afforded to ours. So, such a move would not be unheard of. All Honors faculty should be relocated to departments reflective of the disciplines they currently teach at the College. Given the creation of the new School of Interdisciplinary Studies, we view this School as a potential site to house the Honors program. We also demand that all Honors College program and staff funding, office and classroom space, housing, and unused tenure lines be reallocated to departments and programs that are best positioned to tackle DEI—the Department of Comparative Race and Ethnic Studies, Women and Gender Studies, the Africana/African American Studies Program, and the Latinx Studies Program. We demand that Honors housing be converted to accommodate themed-living learning communities for Black, Latinx, Asian American and Pacific Islander, Native American/Indigenous, and LGBTQ students.

5. WE DEMAND A PUBLIC WRITTEN COMMITMENT FROM THE TCU BOARD OF TRUSTEES, CHANCELLOR VICTOR BOSCHINI, AND VICE CHANCELLOR KATHYRN CAVINS-TULL TO BUILD A CROSS-CULTURAL STUDENT CENTER WITHIN THE NEXT THREE ACADEMIC YEARS. For far too long have students at TCU not been privy to the many resources, spaces, programming, and support that are accessible at most universities, including a center dedicated to the recruitment, retention, support, and visibility of students of color and LGBTQ students. We have been told time and time again that we have to wait for space. A new administrative building and additional football stadium skyboxes were both seen as priorities while providing historically marginalized students with a space remains on the backburner. This is unacceptable and we demand a new multi-floor building on this campus!

WE PUT FORTH THAT THE NEW CROSS-CULTURAL STUDENT CENTER BE IN DEVELOPMENT AND NEAR COMPLETION WITHIN THE NEXT THREE ACADEMIC YEARS. This building should be on par with all university buildings with regards to staffing, technology, and funding. This space should include a recruitment and retention office dedicated to working with historically marginalized students. This space should include a library filled with books and media reflective of our diverse histories and scholarship. This space should be provided funding to develop identity-relevant programming for students, like Native American Heritage Month, Black History Month, Asian Pacific Heritage Month, Latinx Heritage Month, Pride Month and other identity-relevant celebrations. This space should include a Gender Resource Office. This space should include ample study and lounge space, and be decorated to reflect our various cultures. This space should include conference rooms that will allow marginalized students to hold meetings and gather for social, academic, and/or professional planning. This space should also include a tutoring/writing center staffed with tutors and educators that reflect the cultural backgrounds of the students the building aims to serve. This space should also have office space for additional mental health counselors of color. This space should include gender-neutral bathrooms that are easily accessible. This space should also include campus restaurants that reflect the various cultural cuisines of Black, Latinx, Asian American and Pacific Islander, Native American/Indigenous students. These restaurants should also accommodate various dietary needs and restrictions such as plant-based diets, gluten-free diets, and religious diets. These eateries should be included within existing TCU meal plan options, accept both campus cash and meal swipes, and offer late night service. During the development of this center, we demand that students are actively included in the process. We demand that various student representatives from historically marginalized backgrounds be appointed to the taskforce assigned to complete the project. We demand that this new cross-cultural student center is funded by a separate endowment, NOT by university general funds that can be reallocated or defunded; only increased.

WE ALSO PUT FORTH THAT THE NEW CROSS-CULTURAL STUDENT CENTER BE COMPRISED OF SEPARATE OFFICES FOR EACH REFLECTED IDENTITY (i.e. Black, Latinx, Asian American and Pacific Islander, Native American/Indigenous, Women, and LGBTQ). Each office should be staffed with its own qualified Director, Assistant Director, and at least three non-student support staff. We demand that all new hires for these appointments be made through an external nationwide search and that no internal hire is approved. We also demand that both a historically marginalized graduate and undergraduate student be appointed to the search committee for each position and that they each have a vote. These personnel would be in charge of planning and executing culturally-relevant programming for students.

6. WE DEMAND THAT THE NEW CROSS-CULTURAL STUDENT CENTER BE NAMED THE FRED ROUSE STUDENT COMMUNITY CENTER TO COMMEMORATE HIS LIFE AND PUBLICLY ACKNOWLEDGE THE VIOLENT LYNCHING IN WHICH TCU FACULTY AND STUDENTS PARTOOK AND SUPPORTED IN 1921.

WE ALSO DEMAND THAT THE FOUNDER'S STATUES BE REMOVED AND REPLACED WITH A PLAQUE THAT EXPLICITLY ACKNOWLEDGES THEIR PARTICIPATION AS CONFEDERATE SOLDIERS IN THE AMERICAN CIVIL WAR. THEIR PARTICIPATION IN THE CONFEDERACY SHOULD ALSO BE MENTIONED IN EVERY OTHER PUBLIC AND WRITTEN HISTORICAL ACKNOWLEDGEMENT AND COMMEMORATION OF THE FOUNDERS, Addison and Randolph Clark.

If TCU is truly committed to "examining and understanding" its racist history as stated in response to the recent lawsuit concerning Jane Doe #1, the university must begin with explicitly and publicly acknowledging the racism, classism, and sexism upon which it was founded and has continued to thrive. Likewise, the university must actively commit to dismantling such structures that continue to plague this campus and inhibit the full realization of its mission statement. "Ethical leaders" cannot only "think" about ways to resolve such issues, they must also "act". "Responsible citizens" cannot only serve those who think and look like themselves, they must extend service to the entire "global community".

7. WE DEMAND THAT THE UNIVERSITY IMPLEMENT ZERO-TOLERANCE HARSH SANCTIONING AGAINST HATE SPEECH AND PROPAGANDA (e.g. slurs, symbols, manifestos, flyers etc.) USED OR SPREAD BY MEMBERS OF THE TCU COMMUNITY (i.e. students, faculty, and staff). Those who are found guilty of committing or engaging in such actions will be subject to suspension for their first offense and expulsion for any offense thereafter. This sanctioning will be added to the Student Code of Conduct and publicly announced to the campus community by administration.

8. WE DEMAND THAT THE UNIVERSITY IMMEDIATELY ERECT A BEST PRACTICES TASK FORCE FOR NON-BINARY AND TRANS STUDENTS. This task force will be comprised of staff members representative of the following departments: housing and residence life, Greek life, campus life, the Rec center, the health center, and the counseling center led by a professional or expert within non-binary and/or trans activism or Queer studies. This expert will also serve as a personal consultant for students.

WE ALSO PUT FORTH THAT THE UNIVERSITY MAKES PUBLIC STATEMENT THAT EXPLICITLY AFFIRM AND SUPPORT LGBTQ STUDENTS IN RESPONSE TO PUBLIC HOMOPHOBIC AND TRANSPHOBIC SPEECH, PROPAGANDA, AND/OR ACTIONS.

9. WE DEMAND A PUBLIC WRITTEN COMMITMENT FROM CHANCELLOR VICTOR BOSHINI AND PROVOST/VICE CHANCELLOR TERESA DAHLBERG TO INCREASE FACULTY DIVERSITY VIA CLUSTER HIRES ACROSS THE UNIVERSITY AND ADDITIONAL TENURE TRACK LINES PROVIDED TO CRES AND WGST. TCU's faculty membership is overwhelmingly white and male. Many of TCU's faculty are also not teaching or researching in cutting-edge fields or new areas of study. We need to work to transform and diversify the faculty. We put forth that the university actively recruit ten scholars during the 2020-2021 academic year via a cluster hire. Candidates for the cluster hire should be expected to have expertise in an Ethnic Studies area—African American Studies, Chicanx/Latinx Studies, Asian American and Pacific Islander Studies, Native American Studies—or Women and Gender Studies (prioritizing transnational feminism, Black feminism, Native American feminism, Asian American feminism, Queer Studies, and Trans Studies) and a traditional field like, History, English, Biology, Political Science, Journalism, or Business. With this cluster hire, TCU would then be able to bring in qualified and diverse faculty with a critical race and/or gender background to teach in traditional departments. These hires should be made at the Assistant, Associate, and Full Professor rank.

We also put forth that CRES and WGST be allocated at least one tenure/tenure track line (at the rank of Assistant, Associate, and Full Professor) for the next five academic years to adequately grow the departments and to put them on parity with existing departments. More faculty in the aforementioned departments will result in increased course offerings that will certainly satisfy the DEI core requirement.

10. WE DEMAND IMMEDIATE TRANSPARENCY AND AN ANNUAL REPORTING OF RECEIVED TITLE IX AND OTHER CIVIL RIGHTS COMPLAINTS.

11. WE DEMAND THE IMMEDIATE PUBLICATION OF THE FINDINGS FROM ALL CAMPUS CLIMATE SURVEYS. We also demand that a campus-wide climate survey be conducted every three to five years and the results are shared with the TCU community, including alumni.

12. WE DEMAND THAT THE UNIVERSITY IMMEDIATELY CREATE AND PUBLISH A CAMPUS MAP THAT EXPLICITLY DISPLAYS ACCESSIBILITY POINTS AND

SERVICES ON CAMPUS. THIS MAP SHOULD ALSO INCLUDE INFORMATION ABOUT RESOURCES AND SERVICES FOR PEOPLE WITH DISABILITIES.

WE ALSO PUT FORTH THAT THE UNIVERSITY OFFER HYBRID COURSES THAT WILL ACCOMMODATE THE NEEDS OF NON-TRADITIONAL STUDENTS AND STUDENTS WITH DISABILITIES.

13. WE DEMAND INCREASED FINANCIAL SUPPORT OF HISTORICALLY MARGINALIZED AND VULNERABLE STUDENTS. Given the high cost to attend TCU, many people from historically marginalized communities and even middle-income families are not able to even consider the institution as an option for higher education. TCU is able to maintain the dismal racial demographics that it has because of the inflated cost of tuition and fees, which continues to rise every year. For this reason, we demand that the university dramatically increase the staffing, programming, and scholarship budgets for the Community Scholars and STEM Scholars programs. Additionally, we demand that the university aggressively invest in merit/academic scholarships specifically for students from historically marginalized communities that exist outside of the current Community Scholars and STEM Scholars programs. As the cost of attendance continuously rises, gift aid should also increase to accommodate the ever-growing population of marginalized, financially disadvantaged, and even middle-class families who cannot afford the institution.

We also demand that the university increase funding for some of the most vulnerable students on campus—graduate students. There are currently graduate students on campus that are making well below a livable wage while being threatened if they take on any other forms of employment. This is shameful and must be fixed immediately. Graduate students are deserving of living stipends that match or are similar to what other graduate students in the region and state earn. Graduate funding packages must also include summer funding and opportunities for conference travel and research funds.

14. WE DEMAND THAT THE DEI-CORE REQUIREMENT BE OVERSEEN BY THE SCHOOL OF INTERDISCIPLINARY STUDIES, SPECIFICALLY CRES AND WGST FACULTY. We strongly believe that faculty in these departments are best suited to assess and roll-out DEI courses across the campus as they possess the necessary skills (in being able to work with diverse groups), knowledge and expertise, and backgrounds. Any attempts at having faculty from other departments with minimal experience in teaching specifically about race, gender, class, ability, etc. is insufficient and, as Jane Doe #1 notes, fraud. Moreover, we do not believe that faculty can simply be trained to teach about diversity, equity, inclusion, and justice. Thus, any attempt at offering faculty in other departments training is also insufficient. We don't simply offer training in Chemistry for faculty in other departments to teach Chemistry; the same should not be done in this case.

15. WE DEMAND THAT THE TCU BOARD OF TRUSTEES COMMITS IN WRITING TO EXPANDING THE BOARD BY TWO SEATS WITH VOTING POWER FOR A

HISTORICALLY MARGINALIZED GRADUATE AND UNDERGRADUATE STUDENT REPRESENTATIVE.

16. WE DEMAND THAT FIRST-YEAR EXPERIENCE PROGRAMS BECOME INCLUSIVE AND PRIORITIZE THE EXPERIENCES AND NEEDS OF HISTORICALLY MARGINALIZED STUDENTS. Students from historically marginalized backgrounds, both within and especially outside of scholarship programs and athletic communities, have a unique transition period and tend to be at a higher-risk of experiencing isolation and disconnection from the TCU community. In an effort to directly combat this issue and strengthen the retention of these students, we demand that funding be allocated to create culturally and identity relevant programming and curriculum that is specific and sensitive to the unique experiences of marginalized students and their entrance into the university. This programming should include opportunities for historically marginalized students to find community among one another, meet faculty/staff from similar backgrounds and who share similar identities, and learn about campus resources specific to their communities and/or experiences.

17. WE DEMAND THAT HIGH-PROFILE CAMPUS ENTERTAINMENT EVENTS HOSTED BY THE END AND THE CREW REFLECT THE INTERESTS AND CULTURES OF EVERY HISTORICALLY MARGINALIZED COMMUNITY (i.e. Black, Latinx, Asian American and Pacific Islander, Native American/Indigenous, and LGBTQ) BE BROUGHT TO CAMPUS BY THE END OF EVERY ACADEMIC YEAR. This includes, but is not limited to, vocal and instrumental artists, comedians, public figures and celebrities.

18. WE DEMAND A MORE DEMOCRATIC AND INCLUSIVE STUDENT GOVERNING SYSTEM. The current Student Government Association (SGA) is explicitly representative of TCU's systemic exclusion of marginalized students. Every fabric of this association, especially its election system, disproportionately privileges IFC and Panhellenic recruits who have access to larger populations of students. This association's illusion of democracy directly supports and perpetuates nepotism and the erasure of marginalized voices and power.

Therefore, we demand that class representative elections be moved to the end of fall semester. This will allow students to adequately become acquainted with all candidates and provide more students the opportunity to learn about SGA and the opportunity to serve their class as a representative. Moreover, the number of class representatives should be increased to one representative per 500 students for every class. Additionally, a supplemental endowment fund comparable to the budget of the SGA budget must be created to automatically fund TCU organizations for and by students of color, LGBTQ and other marginalized identities each and every academic year. These funds cannot be reallocated or decreased; only increased.

While we expect to be met with concerns around where funding will come from to meet these demands, we call on you as leaders to engage this as an equity-driven project. By this we mean that it is high time that TCU aggressively allocate and invest in areas (as listed above) that have either been intentionally underfunded or have barely received funding. This also means that areas that have been privileged should be in part divested from. We provided an example of reallocating the funds, resources, and space from the John V. Roach Honors College to grow CRES and WGST. The budgets of athletics, TCU Police, TCU Student Government Association, Fraternity & Greek Life, and major campus events like the annual Christmas Tree Lighting, and money frivolously spent on fireworks, travel, food and campus swag should all be reduced to offset costs that may be incurred to meet our demands and vision for a more diverse, equitable, and inclusive campus.

Sincerely,

Coalition for University Justice & Equity (CUJE)

APPENDIX D

TCU's Race and Reconciliation Initiative Committee Members

Academic Year 2020 – 2021

COMMITTEE MEMBERS

Tosin Alao, '23
RRI Undergraduate Student Representative

Sue Anderson, EdD
RRI Committee Member, College of Education

Jean Marie Brown, MA
RRI Committee Member, Journalism

Katie Conzonire, '21
RRI Archival Crew Member

Leslie Ekpe, MA, MBA
RRI Graduate Student Representative

Alan Gallay, PhD
RRI Committee Member, History

Frederick Gooding Jr., PhD
RRI Chair, John V. Roach Honors College

Sylviane Greensword, PhD
RRI Postdoctoral Fellow, Director of RRI Oral History Project

Lynn Hampton, PhD
RRI Committee Member, John V. Roach Honors College

Clifford Harrell II, EdD
RRI Committee Member, Athletics

Alex Hidalgo, PhD
RRI Committee Member, History Trustee

J. Bryan King, MBA
RRI Committee Member, Board of Trustees

Scott Kurashige, PhD
RRI Committee Member, Comparative Race & Ethnic Studies

Jacque Lambiase, PhD
RRI Committee Member, Strategic Communications

Lauren Laphen, '21
RRI Archival Crew Member

Adam McKinney, MFA
RRI Committee Member, Dance

Trung Nguyen, EdD
RRI Committee Member, Interim Assistant Vice Chancellor for Student Affairs

Marcellis Perkins, BA
RRI Graduate Research Assistant

Marsha Ramsay
RRI Administrative Support, Vice Chancellor of Academic Affairs

Sarah Robbins, PhD
RRI Committee Member, English

Nancy Ruiz, MA, '07
RRI Committee Member, TCU Alumni Association

Briana Salas, BA
RRI Archival Crew Member

Mary Taylor Williams, '20
RRI Archival Crew Member

Uma Tiwari, '22
RRI Oral History Project Intern

EX OFFICIO MEMBERS

Holly Ellman, BS
Marketing & Communication

Mary Saffell, MLS
Mary Couts Burnett Library

Claire Sanders, PhD
History

Karen Steele, PhD
English and Office of the Provost

Tracy Syler-Jones, MBA
Marketing & Communication

Aisha Torrey-Sawyer
Interim Chief Diversity Officer

Academic Year 2021 – 2022

COMMITTEE MEMBERS

Haylee Chiariello
Undergraduate Student Representative

Sean Atkinson, PhD
Committee Member, College of Fine Arts

Kenneth Chapman, PhD
Committee Member, Neeley School of Business

Amy Ceniceros
Graduate Research Assistant

Leslie Epke, MA, MBA
Graduate Student Representative

Alan Gallay, PhD
Committee Member, History

Frederick Gooding Jr., PhD
Chair, John V. Roach Honors College

Sylviane Greensword, PhD
Postdoctoral Fellow, Director of
RRI Oral History Project

Lynn Hampton, PhD
RRI Committee Member, John V. Roach Honors College

Clifford E. Harrell II, EdD
RRI Committee Member, Athletics

Alex Hidalgo, PhD
RRI Committee Member, History

J. Bryan King, MBA
RRI Committee Member, TCU Board of Trustees

Brandy Quinn, PhD
RRI Committee Member, College of Education

Callie Strelow
RRI Committee Member, Undergraduate Student
Representative

Lauren Laphen
RRI Archival Crew Member

Adam W. McKinney, MFA
RRI Committee Member, Dance

Trung Nguyen, EdD
Committee Member, Interim Assistant Vice Chancellor for Student Affairs

Marcellis Perkins, MEd
Graduate Research Assistant

Sheila Williams
Administrative Support, Office of the Provost

Rebecca Sharpless, PhD
Committee Member, History

Nancy Ruiz '07
Committee Member, TCU Alumni Association

Briana Salas
Archival Crew Member

Uma Tiwari
RRI Oral History Project Intern

Gregg Cantrell, PhD
Committee Member, AddRan College

Ronald Burriss II, PhD
Archival Crew Member

EX OFFICIO MEMBERS

Holly Ellman
Marketing & Communication

Mary Saffell, MLS
Mary Couts Burnett Library

Claire Sanders, PhD
History

Karen Steele, PhD
English and Office of the Provost

Tracy Syler-Jones, MBA
Marketing & Communication

Aisha Torrey-Sawyer, MEd
Interim Chief Diversity Officer

APPENDIX E

Thorp Family Tree

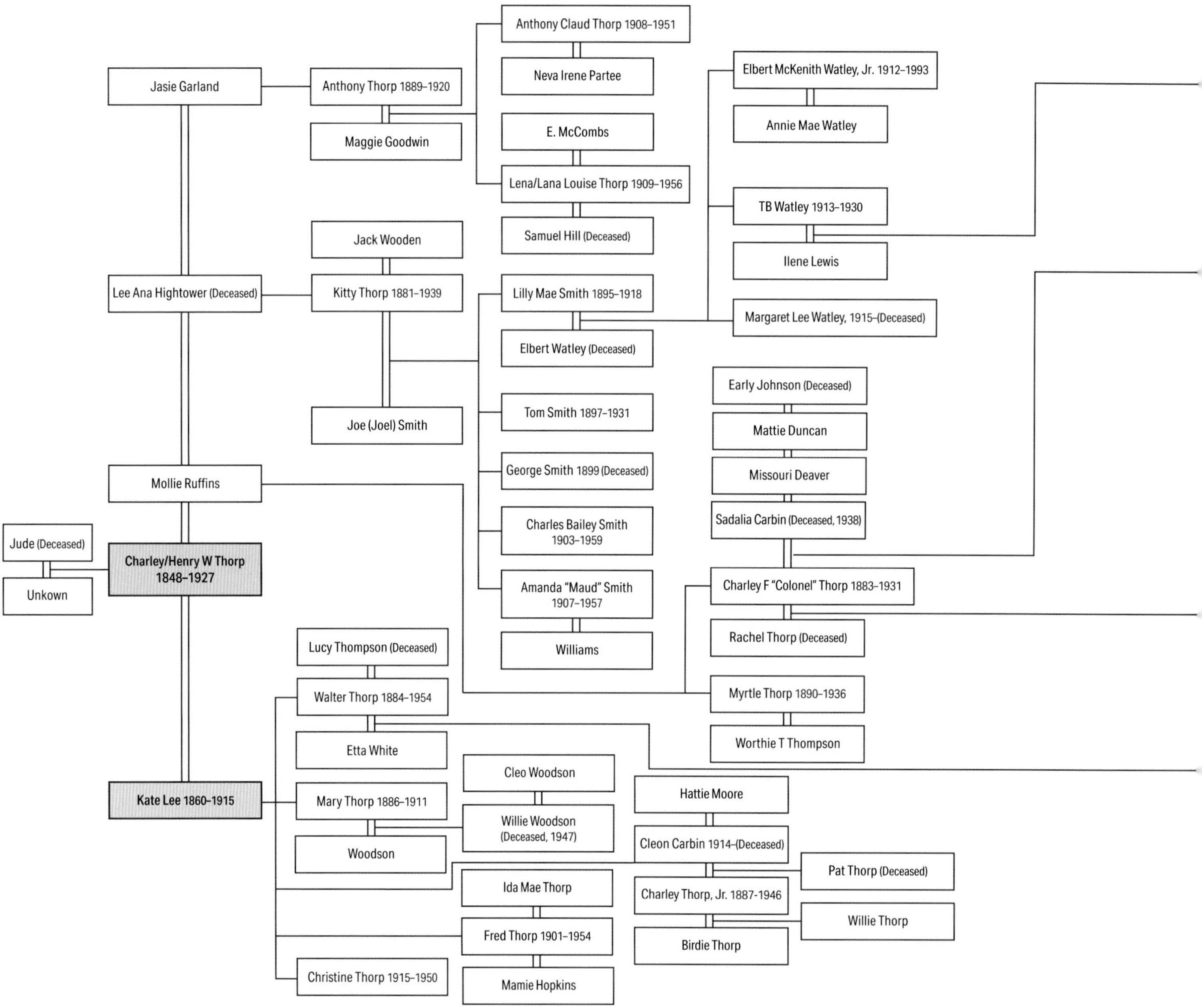

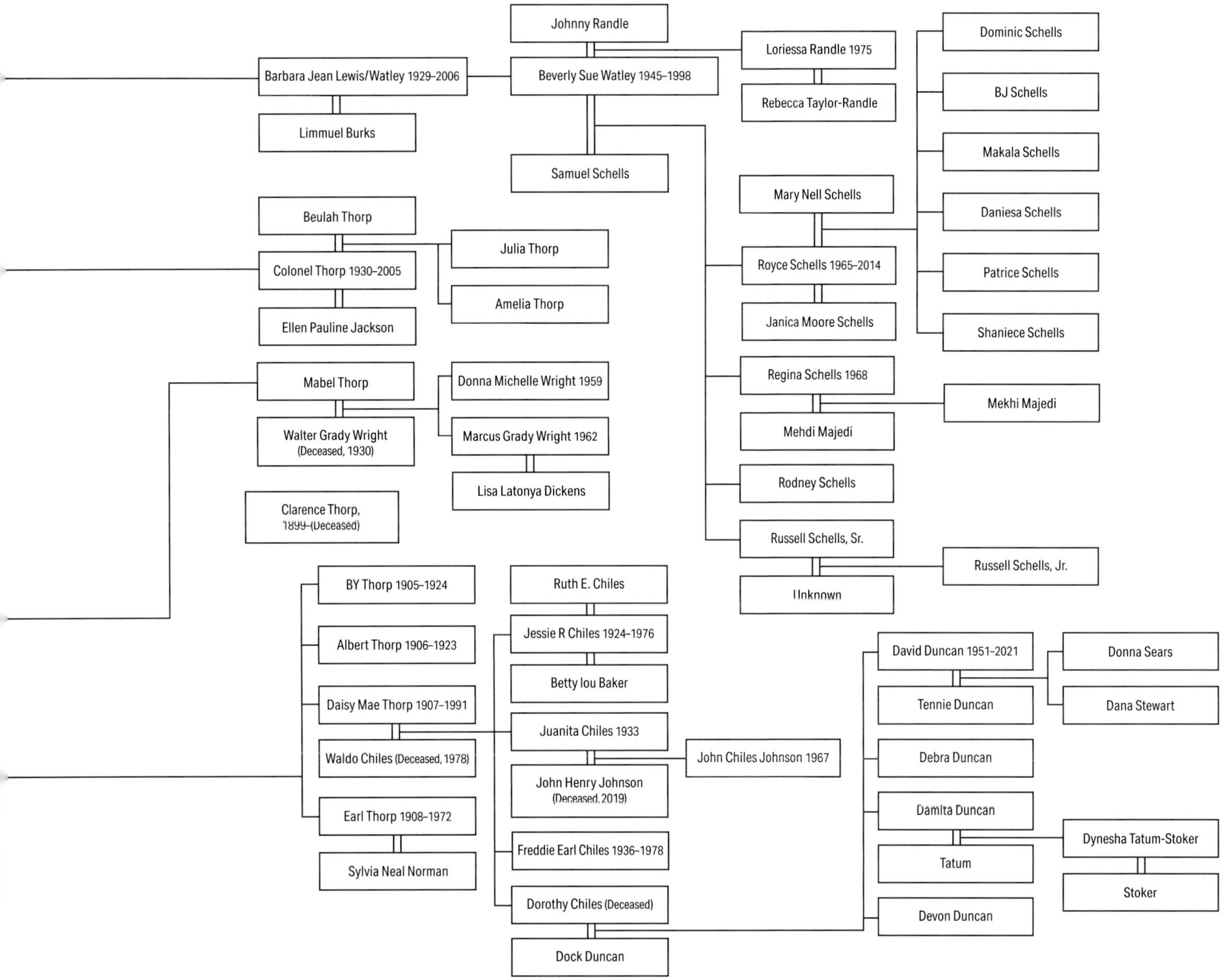
Johnny Randle
Barbara Jean Lewis/Watley 1929–2006
Beverly Sue Watley 1945–1998
Loriessa Randle 1975
Rebecca Taylor-Randle
Limmuel Burks
Samuel Schells
Dominic Schells
BJ Schells
Makala Schells
Daniesa Schells
Patrice Schells
Shaniece Schells
Mary Nell Schells
Royce Schells 1965–2014
Janica Moore Schells
Beulah Thorp
Colonel Thorp 1930–2005
Ellen Pauline Jackson
Julia Thorp
Amelia Thorp
Mabel Thorp
Walter Grady Wright
(Deceased, 1930)
Donna Michelle Wright 1959
Marcus Grady Wright 1962
Lisa Latonya Dickens
Regina Schells 1968
Mehdi Majedi
Mekhi Majedi
Rodney Schells
Russell Schells, Sr.
Unknown
Russell Schells, Jr.
Clarence Thorp,
1899–(Deceased)
BY Thorp 1905–1924
Albert Thorp 1906–1923
Daisy Mae Thorp 1907–1991
Waldo Chiles (Deceased, 1978)
Earl Thorp 1908–1972
Sylvia Neal Norman
Ruth E. Chiles
Jessie R Chiles 1924–1976
Betty lou Baker
Juanita Chiles 1933
John Henry Johnson
(Deceased, 2019)
John Chiles Johnson 1967
Freddie Earl Chiles 1936–1978
Dorothy Chiles (Deceased)
Dock Duncan
David Duncan 1951–2021
Tennie Duncan
Donna Sears
Dana Stewart
Debra Duncan
Damita Duncan
Tatum
Dynesha Tatum-Stoker
Stoker
Devon Duncan

APPENDIX F

Key Jarvis Dates Timeline

TCU and Jarvis Connected History until 1968

1904 – Led by Mrs. Mary Alphin, The Negro Disciples of Christ in Texas begin to plan for a school that would service Black youth. The financial goal of raising $1,000 from The Negro Disciples of Christ in Texas was met, which prompted The Christian Women's Board of Missions to contribute $10,000.

1910 – The Jarvis family deeds 456 acres of land in Hawkins, Texas, to establish a college that will be a part of the Disciples of Christ church.

1930s – "They all call me 'Mother Jarvis and I am very proud of my dusky children.'" Jarvis College has a series of campus fires that puts the institution into financial debt.

1963 (November 22) – TCU students begin to write to the *Skiff* to raise awareness and money for Jarvis's financial troubles. "You see if Jarvis college dissolves, there will be a surplus of intelligent Christian Negro students in the Southwest. And where will these forlorn souls exert pressure for admission? 'There you go, you have it, at TCU. Now we have a common cause to rally around. Help support Jarvis College! Give now, buy bonds. After all most of us are opposed to the opinion of the Supreme Court about separate facilities being inherently unequal. We all know that Jarvis College has practically everything it needs to be equal—a dorm, a few class rooms, perhaps a student center and maybe even a library. But in one small area they are a bit deficient: money. Now, not only to prove to that silly Supreme Court that they can be equal but to preserve a light campus hue at TCU, let's all contribute.'" – Jon S. Notezal

1963 (December 9) – Chairman of TCU Student Congress, Mike Walsh, writes a letter to TCU faculty and staff asking to financially support Jarvis Christian College, which is currently on the brink of closure due to an acquired debt of $450,000. If this debt is not cleared, Jarvis will officially close.

1964 (January 23) – TCU desegregates and decides to increase tuition and academic requirements.

1964 (March 17) – "Nothing like what is proposed is now being done anywhere in the U.S." TCU forms an official partnership with Jarvis Christian, which becomes formally affiliated with TCU under a joint board. TCU assumes all academic responsibilities, including determining curriculum, faculty, and granting degrees. Ultimately, this partnership was aimed to allow for Jarvis to become a branch, college, or school of TCU.

1965 (July 17) – Revised and updated Memorandum of Understanding between Texas Christian University and Jarvis Christian College.

1965 – The Olin Library on Jarvis's campus is funded and opened by way of the Olin Foundation.

1967 (February 10) – "Slave Auction Due for Campus Chest." TCU students engage in fundraising efforts to aid Jarvis's accreditation.

1968 – Jarvis and TCU create an exchange program where students from both schools attend the other school for a week.

1968 – Negro Literature classes are being taught at TCU by Jarvis professors.

APPENDIX G

Key Black Dates Timeline

Black Fort Worth & TCU Timeline

1865

- April 9, 1865 – Civil War ends
- December 18, 1865 – Thirteenth Amendment ratified and proclaimed as part of Constitution abolishing enslavement

1869

- TCU cofounders Addison and Randolph Clark operated the **Male and Female Seminary**, a children's preparatory school in Fort Worth, Texas, with just thirteen students

1873

- Addison and Randolph Clark formally began **Add-Ran Male and Female College** in Thorp Spring, TX

1889

- After new charter establishing affiliation with Disciples of Christ, institution renamed **Add-Ran Christian University**
- Como Lake in nearby Arlington Heights neighborhood created, originally envisioned as a lake resort

1895

- Add-Ran Christian University moved to Waco, Texas

1896

- *Plessy v. Ferguson* Supreme Court decision legalizes Jim Crow "separate, but equal" segregation

1902

- Add-Ran Christian University becomes **Texas Christian University** (TCU); school colors: "purple for royalty, white for a clean game"

1904

- **Negro Industrial & Mechanical College** moves to Fort Worth area

1910

- TCU moves to Fort Worth from Waco after March 23, 1910, fire destroyed Waco campus; city of Fort Worth offered fifty acres, $200K (@ $5.8M in 2022) and promise of streetcar service
- Nearby Lake Como is a thriving residential area

1916

- Seventeen-year-old Black male Jessie Washington was lynched at Waco town square
- The Ku Klux Klan publicly led a Halloween parade on horseback in full regalia directly behind Fort Worth Mayor E. T. Tyra

1921

- December 6, 1921 – Black male Fred Rouse was lynched from the "hanging tree" on Northeast Twelfth Street in Fort Worth; Rouse crossed a picket line of white meatpacking laborers

1922

- Fort Worth Klan had grown to one of the nation's strongest chapters; Dr. Hiram Wesley Evans of Dallas and Brown Harwood of Fort Worth were elected to the national organization's top two offices

1923

- The *Dallas Morning News* on September 20 reported the "first Ku Klux Klan funeral parade ever held" in honor of Fort Worth city finance commissioner W. B. Townsend

1924

- The Fort Worth Klan fielded a baseball team in the Major City League, with games held at Sycamore Park
- May 19, 1924 – cornerstone laid for Ku Klux Klan Lodge no. 101 at 1012 North Main Street in Fort Worth; the Klavern contained a two thousand seat auditorium
- October 24, 1924 – "Ku Klux Klan Day" at State Fair of Texas in Dallas

1926

- Klavern listed on detailed map by the Sanborn Map Company

1929

- Great Depression begins

1930

- Sherman Riots occur over George Hughes's lynching in Sherman, Texas

1942

- Black military students taking some TCU evening college classes off campus

1945

- September 2, 1945 – World War II ends
- June 6, 1950 – Heman Sweatt, postal worker, is first Black student admitted to University of Texas Law School
- July 5, 1950 – William "Gooseneck Bill" McDonald passes away. McDonald was a Black entrepreneur who opened the state's first Black-owned bank on Ninth Street in downtown Fort Worth and is believed to be the first Black millionaire in Texas

1952

- Brite College of the Bible accepts Black students

1953

- Lawrence & Ava Peters purchase a Fort Worth home at 109 Judkins Street, becoming the first Black family to cross Riverside's neighborhood racial threshold east of downtown; they endured significant harassment
- November 2, 1953 – Peters's car was bombed and destroyed

1954

- *Brown v. Board of Education* Supreme Court decision desegregates schools nationally "with all deliberate speed"
- Black teachers take TCU education classes at the Gay Street Elementary School off campus

1955

- Maury Wills becomes the first Black player of local Fort Worth Cats baseball team, the top farm team of Brooklyn Dodgers; seven years later he stole 104 bases and was named the National League MVP

1956

- August 30, 1956 – Texas Governor Allan Shivers dispatched Texas Rangers to prevent school integration in nearby Mansfield
- September 1, 1956 – after saving for twelve years to escape the Rock Island Bottoms neighborhood, Black couple Macie and Lloyd Austin moved into the Riverside neighborhood at 209 Judkins Street; a mob of more than two hundred surrounded their home to protest, complete with effigy of Lloyd Austin hanging from a maple tree near the curb with a wooden stake sticking out of its chest with "blood" running down its shirt

1958

- June 19, 1958 – Juneteenth was the only day when Blacks "were allowed" to swim in the Forest Park public pool; officials would drain the pool the following day

1959

- October 22, 1959 – Brite College of the Bible student Vada Felder invites and hosts civil rights activist Dr. Martin Luther King Jr. in Fort Worth to speak at the Majestic Theater; due to Jim Crow segregation, Dr. King stayed the night at Ms. Felder's home

1960

- TCU students protest for additional Sunday library hours

1961

- Lake Como, a historically Black neighborhood on the west side, was separated from the more prosperous Ridglea neighborhood by a wall dubbed the "Como Wall," that ran for ten blocks along the west side of Bryant Irvin Road

1962

- TCU Harris College of Nursing admits Allene Jones and she becomes one of first three full-time undergraduate TCU students

1964

- January 23, 1964 – TCU declared "That from this day henceforth students be enrolled at TCU without reference to race, creed or nationality, and that the Board of Trustees trust the administration to carry out this responsibility"
- The same January 23, 1964, memo, also explains that in addition to tuition increasing, "our admissions requirements and course requirements are being raised increasingly, and very few negro students could qualify for admission"
- May 22, 1964 – TCU Board of Trustees approved a five-year formal affiliation between TCU and Jarvis
- August 1964 – five Black students fully enroll at TCU, but all leave before the conclusion of the first year

1965

- August 1965 – fourteen Black students enroll on TCU's main campus

1966

- Dr. James Cash integrates the Southwest Conference as the first Black student athlete at TCU

1968

- Dr. Edward Guinn becomes the first Black official elected to Fort Worth City Council
- Allene Jones becomes TCU's first Black professor; she specialized in clinical psychiatric nursing

1969

- Ronnie Hurdle becomes first black cheerleader at TCU
- TCU hosts its first fully integrated class of undergraduates

1970

- Jennifer Giddings elected first Black TCU Homecoming Queen

1971

- TCU approves its first Black fraternity/sorority
- TCU experiences its first Black student intervention (i.e., "protest"), led by football players

1972

- First sign of a Black Studies minor first introduced at TCU, although it did not last

1974

- Margie Major, who grew up in Lake Como, became the first Black guidance counselor at nearby Paschal High School

1981

- Tyrone Wilson becomes one of the first Black students to join and integrate the Lambda Chi Alpha fraternity at TCU

1990

- Colonial Country Club, the golf course closest in proximity to TCU, first racially integrated

1999

- TCU Black Alumni Alliance first formed

2016

- Second major Black student intervention occurs

2017

- TCU's first Chief Inclusion Officer named and installed (TCU alum and former student athlete, Dr. Darron Turner) in response to 2016 Black student intervention
- Comparative Race and Ethnic Studies Department formed

2018

- September 6, 2018 – Unarmed Black male Botham Jean shot dead in his own residence in Dallas

2019

- October 12, 2019 – Unarmed Black female Atatiana Jefferson shot dead in her own residence in Fort Worth

2020

- January 2020 – third major Black student intervention
- March 2020 – coronavirus disease (i.e., COVID-19) declared a global pandemic
- August 2020 – TCU's Race & Reconciliation Initiative to study TCU's relationship with slavery, racism, and the Confederacy formed in earnest

Notes

Introduction

1. Black interiority can be understood as "the inner life" of Black people that is infinitely more complex than the "beastly simplicity promoted by Thomas Dixon's popular Klan literatures" of Black people. Black interiority instead presumes Black protagonists have considerably more agency in "thinking, choices and fate" which demonstrate "psychological complexities in the Black subject." Christopher Freeburg, *Black Aesthetics and the Interior Life* (Charlottesville, VA: University of Virginia Press, 2017), 10.
2. "As a predominantly white institution, TCU has a white population that comprises 68.1 percent of the student body." Kendall Walbrun, "Beyond the Numbers: The Experiential Effects of Stereotype Threat on Students of Color at TCU," *Boller Review*, 2019, file:///Users/fgooding/Downloads/112-1-129-1-10-20200306.pdf. NB: The *Boller Review* is a "TCU Journal of Undergraduate Research and Creativity."
3. Taylor Boser, "Pillars Added to Worth Hills Give Representation to One Greek Council," *TCU360*, September 7, 2018, https://tcu360.com/2018/09/07/pillars-added-to-worth-hills-give-representation-to-one-greek-council/.
4. As of publication, TCU was tied for #89. "Texas Christian University," *U.S. News and World Report,* n.d., accessed September 12, 2022, https://www.usnews.com/best-colleges/tcu-3636.
5. 2022–2023 Total Fall and Spring Estimated Direct Cost (which includes tuition and fees, room and board) = $69,130 annually at time of publication, June 2022. "Cost Estimate," *TCU Undergraduate Admissions*, n.d., accessed May 17, 2022, https://admissions.tcu.edu/afford/cost-estimate.php.
6. For instance, Black male TCU alum Larry Dickson suggests that he made a calculation to deal with the racism assumed to be part of the TCU environment based upon his ability to leverage a TCU education for personal gain (i.e., employment). Said Dickson, "I think what I had in mind was that TCU, the stature of TCU would be good for my resume. In other words, it would be something that I could use once I got out of school to get a good job, and support myself, and my family. So, that was that was one expectation, but other than that, there was very low expectation of anything that would change racially." See "Interview with Larry Dickson," TCU's Race & Reconciliation Initiative Oral History Project, September 13, 2021, accessed June 6, 2022, https://repository.tcu.edu/handle/116099117/52684.
7. "Formal instruction in Texas before the Civil War was provided by private schools, colleges and academies." Due to a failed Reconstructionist policy that backtracked on brief egalitarian innovations to address the social ravages of enslavement for two and a half centuries prior, "a school law enacted in 1873, under a new political regime with Southern sentiments, overturned the earlier state-wide experiment in public free education," thereby making higher education quite difficult to access at the time. Jerome A. Moore, *Texas Christian University: A Hundred Years of History* (Fort Worth, TX: TCU Press, 1974), 13.
8. Randolph Clark, *Reminiscences: Biographical and Historical* (Wichita Falls, TX: Lee Clark, Publisher, 1919), 45.
9. "The school was free of community distractions, such as the Clarks feared in Fort Worth when the school was there." Joseph Lynn Clark, *Thank God We Made It! A Family Affair with Education* (Austin, TX: University of Texas Press, 1969), 363. NB: Joseph Lynn Clark is the son of TCU cofounder, Randolph Clark.
10. See also, Clark, *Reminiscences,* 57; and Colby D. Hall, *History of Texas Christian University* (Fort Worth, TX: TCU Press, 2014), 30.

11. "Add-Ran Christian University Charter," Mary Couts Burnett University Library, TCU Digital Repository, Special Collections, TCU Archives and Historical Materials, Vertical Files, n.d., accessed June 6, 2022, https://repository.tcu.edu/handle/116099117/11132.

12. See generally, Robert T. Boyd, *Indians, Fire, and the Land in the Pacific Northwest* (Corvallis, OR: Oregon State University Press, 1999).

13. Evan Watson, "Athletic Renovations Add to Texas Construction University," *TCU360*, November 30, 2015, accessed June 6, 2022, https://www.tcu360.com/2015/11/athletic-renovations-add-to-texas-construction-university/.

14. TCU also received a "relocation bonus" of $200,000. Marcia Melton, "How TCU Came to Fort Worth," *TCU Magazine*, Spring 2016, accessed June 6, 2022, https://magazine.tcu.edu/spring-2016/tcu-came-fort-worth/; see also, Hall, *History*, 136, which cites board of trustee minutes from November 29, 1910.

15. Trisha Spence, "The TCU Endowment," *TCU Magazine*, Fall 2021, accessed June 6, 2022, https://magazine.tcu.edu/fall-2021/university-endowment/.

16. Found under the subheading, "Preparing Global Citizens." "Quick Facts," *TCU*, n.d., accessed May 17, 2022, https://www.tcu.edu/about/quick-facts.php.

17. The Fact Books of TCU, published annually back to 1980 at the following website, report the race and ethnicity of students each year. See generally, "Facts & Data," *TCU Institutional Research*, n.d., accessed May 17, 2022, http://www.ir.tcu.edu/factbooks.asp.

18. Sarah Smith, "About 70 Percent of TCU Students Are White. Here's How the University Is Addressing Diversity," *Fort Worth Star-Telegram,* April 12, 2018, accessed May 17, 2022, https://www.star-telegram.com/news/local/education/article207914819.html.

19. Marc Parry, "Despite Obstacles, Black Colleges Are Pipelines to the Middle Class, Study Finds. Here's Its List of the Best," *Chronicle of Higher Education,* September 30, 2019, accessed May 17, 2022, https://www.chronicle.com/article/despite-obstacles-black-colleges-are-pipelines-to-the-middle-class-study-finds-heres-its-list-of-the-best/.

20. "Some Colleges Have More Students from the Top 1 Percent than the Bottom 60. Find Yours," *New York Times,* January 18, 2017, accessed May 17, 2022, https://www.nytimes.com/interactive/2017/01/18/upshot/some-colleges have-more-students-from-the-top-1-percent-than-the-bottom-60.html.

21. "Mission & History," n.d., accessed June 6, 2022, *TCU,* https://www.tcu.edu/about/mission-history.php.

22. See generally, Palca Shibale, "Guest Essay: Why I'm Tired of Explaining Racism to People," *Seattle Times,* June 20, 2016, accessed May 18, 2022, https://www.seattletimes.com/seattle-news/why-im-tired-of-explaining-racism-to-people/.

23. Frederick W. Gooding Jr., *American Dream Deferred: Black Federal Workers in Washington, DC, 1941-1981* (Pittsburgh, PA: University of Pittsburgh Press, 2018), 102.

24. The *Horned Frog* Yearbook, 1905, 27. See also chapter two, note #6, *infra.*

25. Christopher Bergland, "The Neuroscience of Recalling Old Memories," *Psychology Today,* July 3, 2015, https://www.psychologytoday.com/us/blog/the-athletes-way/201507/the-neuroscience-recalling-old-memories.

26. "Clipping: Obituary for Joseph Lynn Clark," Date Unknown; University of North Texas Libraries, *The Portal to Texas History*, accessed May 17, 2022, https://texashistory.unt.edu/ark:/67531/metapth907731/; crediting Private Collection of T. B. Willis. See also, "Clark, Joseph Lynn (1881–1969)," *Texas State Historical Association,* 1976, accessed June 6, 2022, https://www.tshaonline.org/handbook/entries/clark-joseph-lynn.

27. "Race & Reconciliation Initiative First Year Survey Report," *TCU,* April 21, 2021, 4, accessed May 17, 2022, https://www.tcu.edu/race-reconciliation-initiative/files/rri-first-year-survey-report.pdf.

28. See Freeburg, *Black Aesthetics and the Interior Life, infra.*

29. Leonard Sanders, *How Fort Worth Became the Texasmost City, 1849 - 1920* (Fort Worth, TX: TCU Press, 1973), 36.

30. William H. Watkins, *The White Architects of Black Education: Ideology and Power in America, 1865–1954* (New York, NY: Teachers College Press, 2001), 6.

31. [Flyer for Ku Klux Klan Day], pamphlet, 1923, University of North Texas Libraries, *The Portal to Texas History*, accessed May 17, 2022, https://texashistory.unt.edu/ark:/67531/metapth31223/m1/1/:; crediting Star of the Republic Museum.

32. Minyvonne Burke and The Associated Press, "Texas Senate Passes Bill that Removes Requirement to Teach Ku Klux Klan as 'Morally Wrong,'" *NBC News*, July 21, 2021, accessed May 17, 2022, https://www.nbcnews.com/politics/politics-news/texas-senate-passes-bill-removes-requirement-teach-ku-klux-klan-n1274610.

33. Miranda Suarez, "100 Years after His Death, A Man Lynched in Fort Worth Gets His First-Ever Memorial," *KERA News*, December 6, 2021, accessed May 17, 2022, https://www.keranews.org/arts-culture/2021-12-06/a-century-after-his-death-a-man-lynched-in-fort-worth-gets-his-first-ever-memorial.

34. "Ku Klux Klan," *Southern Poverty Law Center,* n.d., accessed June 22, 2022, https://www.splcenter.org/fighting-hate/extremist-files/ideology/ku-klux-klan.

35. Ty Cashion, *The New Frontier: A Contemporary History of Fort Worth & Tarrant County* (San Antonio, TX: Historical Publishing Network, 2006), 66.

36. See generally, "and there were rumors that Mayor E.R. Cockrell was a member," Richard F. Selcer and Kevin S. Foster, *Written in Blood The History of Fort Worth's Fallen Lawmen* (Denton, TX: University of North Texas Press, 2011), 212; "Mayor E.R. Cockrell and other city officials were also members," Victoria L. Buenger, Walter L. Buenger, *Texas Merchant Marvin Leonard and Fort Worth* (College Station, TX: Texas A&M Press, 2008), 63.

37. Lupe Zapata, "Historic KKK Building in Fort Worth Purchased with the Purpose of Healing," *Spectrum News 1*, February 15, 2022, accessed May 17, 2022, https://spectrumlocalnews.com/tx/dallas-fort-worth/news/2022/02/09/historic-kkk-building-in-fort-worth-purchased.

38. Jill Ament & Caroline Covington, "Poverty Is Central to Fort Worth Zip Code's Lowest Life Expectancy in State," *Texas Standard,* September 27, 2020, accessed May 17, 2022, https://www.keranews.org/texas-news/2020-09-27/poverty-is-central-to-fort-worth-zip-codes-lowest-life-expectancy-in-state.

39. Marcia Melton, "Stop Six: A Brief History of a Fort Worth Community," *TCU Magazine*, Spring 2016, accessed May 17, 2022, https://magazine.tcu.edu/spring-2016/stop-six-history-fort-worth-community/#:~:text=The%20East%20Fort%20Worth%20neighborhood,and%20the%20old%20Interurban%20Train.&text=Stop%20Six%20acquired%20its%20name,Fort%20Worth%2DDallas%20Interurban%20Train.

40. Hollace Ava Weiner, "Last Chance for a Swim? Fort Worth's Forest Park Pool to Be Demolished, Replaced," *Fort Worth Star-Telegram*, September 4, 2021, accessed May 17, 2022, https://www.star-telegram.com/news/local/fort-worth/article253944488.html.

41. Kevin Olsen, "Clear Waters and A Green Gas: A History of Chlorine as a Swimming Pool Sanitizer in the United States," *Bulletin for the History of Chemistry* 32, no. 2 (2007), accessed May 17, 2022, http://acshist.scs.illinois.edu/bulletin_open_access/v32-2/v32-2%20p129-140.pdf.

42. “Prestigious Country Club Admits First Black Members,” *UPI,* April 27, 1991, accessed May 17, 2022, https://www.upi.com/Archives/1991/04/27/Prestigious-country-club-admits-first-Black-members/6456672724800/.

43. Candi Bolden, *Fort Worth Star-Telegram,* May 6, 2021, accessed May 17, 2022, https://www.star-telegram.com/news/local/fort-worth/article249859563.html.

44. “[The Klan] now have a membership of 100,000 here in Texas, composed of the very best white citizens of the State. ... They have nothing against the honest, hardworking negro so long as he remains in his place.” Bud Kennedy, “When Easter in Fort Worth celebrated both Jesus and the KKK: It wasn’t that long ago,” *Fort Worth Star-Telegram*, April 12, 2022, accessed May 17, 2022, https://www.star-telegram.com/opinion/bud-kennedy/article260288810.html.

45. “Confederacy Cultural Memory Artifacts with Analysis,” *TCU Race & Reconciliation Initiative*, April 16, 2021, accessed May 17, 2022, https://www.tcu.edu/race-reconciliation-initiative/conversations/posts/confederacy-cultural-memory-artifacts.php.

46. “If you aren’t exposed to this information earlier..you might start to think differently as a result,” Megan Cardona, “Fort Worth Green Book Exhibit Focuses Jim Crow Era Traveling through a Local Lens,” *Fort Worth Star-Telegram*, February 11, 2022, accessed June 6, 2022, https://www.star-telegram.com/news/local/article257986973.html.

47. This article appears on page one, or the front page. “Southwestern Too! Another Addition to Varsity’s Long List of Victims,” the *Skiff* 7, no. 11 (November 18, 1908), accessed September 11, 2022, https://repository.tcu.edu/handle/116099117/12679.

48. The article appears on page one, or the front page. “Annual Shirley Program,” the *Skiff* 9, no. 36 (May 25, 1911), accessed September 11, 2022, https://repository.tcu.edu/handle/116099117/12765.

49. “Next to our room, are a couple of the ‘Japs,’ down the third door, are two Chinese and then comes a ‘Philipino,’ and finally at the end of the hall, a lone ‘black as the ace of spaces’ scholarly looking negro. And just here let me say, you don’t know how it does get next to this Texas boy, to see those ’thick-lip’ Africans sitting ‘jam-up’ side by side with the whites, in every street car, elevated and subway.” The article appears on pages 2-3. “Roy G. Tomlinson ‘12 Writes to Old Friends,” the *Skiff* 12, no. 7 (October 31, 1913), accessed September 11, 2022, https://repository.tcu.edu/handle/116099117/12876.

50. “The Doll House, under the direction of Annie McClendon and Mrs. A. M. Hill, chief dolls, enjoyed a splendid patronage through the evening, while even the ‘Hit the Negro Baby’ stand was not without its circle of Customers.” The article appears on page four. “Pep Carnival Funds to Furnish Goode Hall Parlors,” The *Skiff* 13, no. 9 (November 6, 1914), accessed September 11, 2022, https://repository.tcu.edu/handle/116099117/12916.

51. See also “New York Puts Ban on ‘African Dodger,’” *Chicago Defender,* April 24, 1915; “300,000 at Coney, 3,000 Sport in Surf,” *New York Times*, May 22, 1922. See generally, Dan MacGuill, “Was a Violently Racist Carnival Game Once Popular in America?” *Snopes*, February 26, 2018, accessed September 11, 2022, https://www.snopes.com/fact-check/racist-carnival-game/.

52. This article appears on page three. “Big Circus and Side Shows at the Pep Carnival, Nov. 6, Also Minstrels and Animals,” the *Skiff* 13, no. 8 (October 30, 1914), accessed September 11, 2022, https://repository.tcu.edu/handle/116099117/12915.

53. This article appears on page two. “A Little Ventilation Please,” the *Skiff* 13, no. 7 (January 1, 1915), accessed September 11, 2022, https://repository.tcu.edu/handle/116099117/12924.

54. “Clubs,” the *Horned Frog* 11 (1915), 101, accessed September 11, 2022, https://repository.tcu.edu/handle/116099117/11041.

55. This article appears on page four. "When Seniors Lost Their Dignity," the *Skiff* 17, no. 5 (October 12, 1918), accessed September 11, 2022, https://repository.tcu.edu/handle/116099117/13063.

56. This article appears on page four. "Consider the Woodpecker," the *Skiff* 19, no. 21, (February 25, 1921), 4, accessed September 11, 2022, https://repository.tcu.edu/handle/116099117/13146.

57. "African Golf," the *Skiff* 22, no. 5 (October 16, 1923), 2, accessed September 11, 2022, https://repository.tcu.edu/handle/116099117/13227.

58. This article appears on page one, or the front page. "Can You Solve These," the *Skiff* 22, no. 17 (January 29, 1924), accessed September 11, 2022, https://repository.tcu.edu/handle/116099117/13239.

59. See generally, Diane Lewis, "Anthropology and Colonialism," *Current Anthropology* 14, no. 5 (1973): 581–602, http://www.jstor.org/stable/2741037.

60. Christopher M. Span and Brenda N. Sanya, "Education and the African Diaspora," in John L. Rury, Eileen H. Tamura (eds.), *The Oxford Handbook of the History of Education* (Oxford, UK: Oxford University Press, 2019), 402.

61. "The 1619 Project," Nicole Hannah Jones, n.d., accessed June 6, 2022, https://1619education.org/?gclid=CjwKCA-jwy_aUBhACEiwA2IHHQD5-GHzt38ECKU8UiQBocDx6vXVQgrtI43QQalk_EXb8K2SS7SAHmRoCIAcQAvD_BwE.

62. The Emancipation Proclamation did not eliminate enslavement since enslavement was still legal in northern states such as Maryland and Delaware at the time. This fact rudely interrupts the blanket narrative that with the signing of the Emancipation Proclamation Lincoln "freed all the slaves" with the mere stroke of a pen. See Miranda S. Spivack, "The Not-quite-free State: Maryland Dragged Its Feet on Emancipation During Civil War," *Washington Post,* September 13, 2013, accessed June 6, 2022, https://www.washingtonpost.com/local/md-politics/the-not-quite-free-state-maryland-dragged-its-feet-on-emancipation-during-civil-war/2013/09/13/a34d35de-fec7-11e2-bd97-676ec24f1f3f_story.html.

63. See generally, Trevor Burnard, *Mastery, Tyranny, and Desire: Thomas Thistlewood and His Slaves in the Anglo-Jamaican World* (Chapel Hill, NC: University of North Carolina Press, 2004).

64. Frederick Gooding Jr., *Introduction to African American Studies: A Critical Reader* (Dubuque, IA: Kendall Hunt Publishing Company, 2016), 4.

65. For more about TCU Black voices, see TCU's Race & Reconciliation Initiative Oral History Project, https://repository.tcu.edu/handle/116099117/52684.

66. Jeffrey B. Perry, ed., *A Hubert Harrison Reader* (Middletown, CT: Wesleyan University Press, 2001), 282.

67. While many hands make the load light, in particular the co-authors wish to shout out the contributory research efforts of the following (mostly) TCU History Department students and professors whose labors for TCU's Race & Reconciliation Initiative helped inspire many of the factual finds analyzed through the Black lens in this book: Sue Anderson, Ronald "Bird" Burriss, Gregg Cantrell, Katie Conzonire, Leslie Ekpe, Alan Gallay, Clifford Harrell II, Lauren Laphen, Sarah Robbins, Briana Salas, Claire Sanders, Rebecca Sharpless, Karen Steele. Uma Tiwari, and Mary Taylor Williams.

Chapter 1

1. Melinda Jo Ray, *Limestone Legacies* (Granbury, TX: Blue Topaz Publications, 2020). NB: General Morehouse is the same namesake of Morehouse College in Atlanta, Georgia—alma mater of Dr. Martin Luther King Jr. who visited Fort Worth on account of an invitation by Brite Divinity Student Vada Phillips Felder in 1959.

2. Barbara Thorp Wilkins, "High Hopes & Human Frailties," *Granbury! Magazine*, Summer 1986.

3. "Promissory Note," Joseph Lynn Clark Papers, Box 36, Folder 1, Special Collections, Mary Couts Burnett Library, Texas Christian University.

4. "Joseph Addison Clark to Sons 1865-1865," March 20, 1865, Joseph Lynn Clark Papers, Group 156, Series II, Box 41, Special Collections, Mary Couts Burnett Library, Texas Christian University.

5. Randolph Clark, *Reminiscences: Biographical and Historical* (Wichita Falls, TX: Lee Clark, 1919), 25.

6. Ronald D. Burriss II, *A Higher Calling: The Lives of Addison and Randolph Clark,* 2014, Doctoral dissertation, Texas Christian University, 81

7. Randolph Clark, "Memoir of sorts," Letters, Poems, Clippings of Randolph Clark 1919-1932, 10/15/1932, Joseph Lynn Clark Papers, Group 156, Series II, Box 39, Folders 84-7, Special Collections, Mary Couts Burnett Library, Texas Christian University.

8. Clark, "Memoir of sorts."

9. "Letter from Joseph Addison Clark to Addison and Randolph Clark," March 1, 1868, Joseph Lynn Clark Papers, Box 41.

10. "Letter to Addison and Randolph Clark," March 8, 1868, Joseph Lynn Clark Papers, Group 156, Series II, Box 41, Special Collections, Mary Couts Burnett Library, Texas Christian University.

11. Addison Clark, "The Youth must Be Educated," n.d., Clark Family Materials, https://repository.tcu.edu/handle/116099117/42604; Burriss II, *A Higher Calling*.

12. Clark, *Reminiscences*, 29.

13. Colby Hall, *History of Texas Christian University: A College of the Cattle Frontier*, 1947, 28. NB: On page 36 of *Reminiscences*, it is stated that Addison got a state teaching certificate and sought permission to teach in Tarrant County. But because of the oath, he never sought a public school job. This seemed to send them in the private school direction from the beginning. Because they were devoutly religious they founded a religious school, not a public one. They also both had teaching jobs in the Fort Worth area; see Joseph Lynn Clark, *Thank God We Made It! A Family Affair with Education* (Austin, TX: University of Texas Press, 1969), 300.

14. NB: early catalogs never explicitly state that the institution was whites only. However, racial segregation was already so readily accepted in Texas that perhaps TCU officials did not need to state their segregationist principles explicitly—it was just a given that Black people would simply not apply to TCU for intellectual admission.

15. Melinda Jo Ray, *Limestone Legacies* (Grandbury, TX: Blue Topaz Publications, 2020).

16. Texas Department of State Health Services. Texas Death Certificates, 1903–1982, iArchives, Orem, Utah, Original data: Texas Department of State Health Services, Texas.

17. Family History Library, 2009, Year: 1870; Census Place: Hood, Texas; Roll: M593_1592, Page: 29A, Image: 61, Family History Library Film: 553091.

18. Mary Estelle Gott Salterelli, *Historic Hood County: An Illustrated History* (San Antonio, TX: HPN Books, 2009).

19. The Church of Jesus Christ of Latter-day Saints, n.d., 1880 United States Federal Census, Year: 1880, Census Place: Precinct 6, Hood, Texas, Roll: 1311, Page: 35B, Enumeration District: 143.

20. The Church of Jesus Christ of Latter-day Saints, n.d., 1880 United States Federal Census, Year: 1880, Census Place: Precinct 6, Hood, Texas, Roll: 1311, Page: 35B, Enumeration District: 143; Ancestry.com, 1920 United States Federal Census, Year: 1920, Census Place: Justice Precinct 6, Hood, Texas, Roll: T625_1819, Page: 1A, Enumeration District: 30.

21. Clark, *Thank God We Made It!*, 361.

22. Clark, *Thank God We Made It!*, 264.

23. Clark, *Thank God We Made It!*, 364.

24. 1870 United States Federal Census, Year: 1870, Census Place: Bonham, Fannin, Texas, Roll: M593_1584, Page: 164B.

25. 1870 United States Federal Census.

26. Clark, *Thank God We Made It!*, 361.

27. *Granbury News* (Granbury, Texas), March 8, 1894, 5; *Granbury News* (Granbury, Texas), June 7, 1894, 8.

28. Clark, *Thank God We Made It!*, 362.

29. Lillian Warner-Green, "Interview with Lillian Warner-Green," Interview by Sylviane Greensword and Marcellis Perkins, Race and Reconciliation Initiative Oral History Project, Texas Christian University, https://repository.tcu.edu/handle/116099117/52346.

30. Randolph Clark, "Charles Thorp," *Christian Courier*, 1927.

31. Charley was arrested in 1883 for theft, and his case was dismissed in 1885 (*Hood County Court Fee Book*, 65, Granbury Depot); a warrant for his arrest was issued in 1897, but there is no evidence of a conviction or time served (*1896-1898 Warrants of Arrest*, Granbury Depot); he was again arrested in 1909 for an unknown charged, but released by order of the County Court (1908-1912 Hood County criminal fee book, 1908-1912, case 2362-2786, Granbury Depot).

32. Charley appears on the Hood County taxpayer list from 1877 to 1909, even though he had already moved to Dallas, Texas, by 1900.

33. Charley appears on the Hood County taxpayer list from 1877 to 1909, even though he had already moved to Dallas, Texas, by 1900.

34. 1920 United States Federal Census, Year: 1920, Census Place: Justice Precinct 6, Hood, Texas, Roll: T625_1819, Page: 1A, Enumeration District: 30.

35. "TCU These 50 Years 1923," June 5, 1923, Box 122, Group 156, Series III, Folder "TCU These 50 Years 1923," Joseph Lynn Clark Papers, Special Collections, Mary Couts Burnett Library, Texas Christian University.

36. Photo - AddRan College at Thorp Springs, TX, n.d. Box 1, Mattie Cooper Harlin Collection, Photograph of AddRan College with Mattie Harlin, Special Collections, Mary Couts Burnett Library, Texas Christian University.

37. Mattie Cooper Harlin Diary, March 29, 1890, 32.

38. *The Student*, August 7, 1880, Joseph Lynn Clark Papers, Box 116, Folder 1, TCU Mary Couts Burnett Library, Archives and Special Collections.

39. Ben Bean, the *Student* 1, no. 19 (August 7, 1880). Granbury Depot.

40. The *Skiff* is a different publication than the aforementioned Thorp Spring campus publication, *The Student*. The first issue of the *Skiff* was published in fall 1902 in Waco, years after the move from Thorp Spring. The founding of the *Skiff* is detailed in Hall, *History of Texas Christian University*, 117.

41. The *Skiff*, "Ku Klux Klan Revived," May 5, 1919.

42. Student Life Scrapbook 1919-1924, Newspaper Clipping, Box 30, Record Unit 8, TCU Scrapbook Collection, Special Collections, Mary Couts Burnett Library, Texas Christian University.

43. Edward Carl Tomlinson Scrapbook: Newspaper Clipping, 1913-1916, Box 25, Record Unit 8, TCU Scrapbook Collection, Special Collections, Mary Couts Burnett Library, Texas Christian University. The clipping originated from the *Fort Worth Star-Telegram,* March 29, 1914.
44. *1900 United States Federal Census* [database on-line], Provo, UT, USA: Ancestry.com Operations Inc, 2004.
45. Judge Davis notes pg. 6A, n.d. Granbury Depot; *Waco, Texas, City Directory*, 1900, 96.
46. Unknown author, 1903, Primary Department class, TCU Photo Collection 2505, TCU Special Collections, https://repository.tcu.edu/handle/116099117/2644, Add-Ran College catalogue, 1876-1877, TCU Special Collections. https://repository.tcu.edu/handle/116099117/41568.
47. Annual Report of the President of Texas Christian University to the State Convention of the Christian Church, May 1930, 38, https://repository.tcu.edu/handle/116099117/7075.
48. "Aerial view includes Clark Field behind Library," 1930, Digital Repository, Mary Couts Burnett Library, Texas Christian University, https://repository.tcu.edu/handle/116099117/2798; "TCU Contour Map, 1927," 1927, Asset Management and Technical Services, Texas Christian University.

Chapter 2

1. Texas Christian University, "Our Campus," TCU, n.d, https://www.tcu.edu/about/our-campus.php.
2. Board of Education, 347 U.S. 483 (1954).
3. James Moudy, "Statement by Moudy on Race," June 7, 1963, NB: In 1963 then Vice Chancellor Moudy spoke in favor of integration to the board of trustees. He addressed fears about integration that included interracial dating but dismissed that fear, basically saying that the white TCU students had been raised to avoid interracial marriage. That was a racist viewpoint but he did favor integration of the university. His full statement can be read here: https://repository.tcu.edu/handle/116099117/21231.
4. Nyshicka Jordan and Kelly Morris, "Color Contrast," *IMAGE* 31, no. 3 (March 2004), https://repository.tcu.edu/handle/116099117/21240.
5. Jordan and Morris, "Color Contrast."
6. See for example, the *Horned Frog*, 1915, 25; the *Horned Frog*, 1943.
7. Joseph Lynn Clark, *Thank God We Made It!*, 1st ed. (Austin: University of Texas, 1969), 364.
8. "Negroes Attending TCU," the *Skiff* 50, no. 7 (November 2, 1951), https://repository.tcu.edu/handle/116099117/14454.
9. "Lack of Enrollment Ends Negro Classes," the *Skiff*, February 14, 1954, https://repository.tcu.edu/handle/116099117/14525.
10. "3 Negroes Attending Seminary," the *Skiff*, September 9, 1952, https://exhibits.tcu.edu/items/show/320.
11. Rick Waters, "Allene Jones'63, among first Black students at TCU and first black professor, passes away after rich career in nursing and teaching," *TCU Magazine*, June 30, 2015, magazine.tcu.edu.
12. Sylvia Carrizales, "Through the Halls," the *Skiff,* n.d., http://www.skiff.tcu.edu/skiffweb021501/life.html.
13. "NAACP Ties Hurt Rushee," the *Skiff* 68, no 2 (September 9, 1969), https://repository.tcu.edu/handle/116099117/15268.

14. "NAACP Ties Hurt Rushee."
15. Keith Clark, "Black Student Denied a Fraternity," the *Skiff*, September 9, 1976.
16. "TCU Petition Hits Racism," *Fort Worth Star-Telegram*, March 6, 1980.
17. "Racism: Actions Speak Louder than Words," the *Skiff* 78, no.68 (April 25, 1980), https://repository.tcu.edu/handle/116099117/45461.
18. "Black TCU Student Joins White Fraternity," *Fort Worth Star-Telegram*, February 12, 1981," TCU Library Exhibits, accessed September 14, 2022, https://exhibits.tcu.edu/items/show/316.
19. Mike Edwards, "Now for a Last Word," the *Skiff* 69, no. 27 (December 12, 1969), https://repository.tcu.edu/handle/116099117/15293.
20. Marsha Webb, "Chairperson 'Gamble's' with New Ideas," the *Skiff* 73, no. 48 (November 26, 1974), https://repository.tcu.edu/handle/116099117/15735.
21. Brandon Kitchin, "Celebrating Black Leadership at TCU," *TCU Magazine,* February 24, 2022, https://magazine.tcu.edu/latest-news/lets-do-more-honoring-black-leadership-at-tcu/.
22. Kirk Williams, "Group to Advance Afro-Culture," the *Skiff* 67, no. 46 (April 22, 1969), https://repository.tcu.edu/handle/116099117/15256.
23. Proffer, Elizabeth, Letter to TCU Faculty and Staff, "Letter & Black Student Information Guide," November 27, 1979.
24. "Black Student Information Guide," November 27, 1979, 15, https://repository.tcu.edu/handle/116099117/21238.
25. "Black Student Information Guide," November 27, 1979, 15, https://repository.tcu.edu/handle/116099117/21238.
26. Rick Waters, "Allene Jones '63 1933-2015," *TCU Magazine*, Summer 2015, https://magazine.tcu.edu/summer-2015/allene-jones-631933-2015/.
27. David Van Meter, "Diveristy Amid All Our Differenes are opportunities to Work Together," Spring 1999, *TCU Magazine,* http://www.magarchive.tcu.edu/articles/1999-01-F04.asp?issueid=199901.
28. "Community Scholars," Texas Christian University, n.d, https://communityscholars.tcu.edu/.
29. "Tracy Syler-Jones," CASE, 2022, https://www.case.org/awards/district-iv-awards/2022/tracy-syler-jones.

Chapter 3

1. "Trustees Drop Racial Barriers," the *Skiff*, February 4, 1964, TCU Library Exhibits, accessed May 11, 2022, https://exhibits.tcu.edu/items/show/322.
2. "Graduates and Underclassmen, Book III," the *Horned Frog* 12 (1916): 61, accessed September 11, 2022, https://repository.tcu.edu/handle/116099117/11042.
3. "Graduates and Underclassmen, Book III," the *Horned Frog* 11 (1915): 31, accessed September 11, 2022, https://repository.tcu.edu/handle/116099117/11041.
4. See generally, Kelly McWilliams, "The Day I Passed for White," *Time*, November 19, 2021, accessed May 18, 2022, https://time.com/6116209/passing-for-white/.
5. "Mission & History," n.d., *TCU,* accessed June 6, 2022, https://www.tcu.edu/about/mission-history.php.

6. Richard F. Selcer, *A History of Fort Worth in Black and White: 165 Years of African-American Life* (Denton, TX: University of North Texas Press, 2016), 472; See also the *TCU Skiff,* March 20, 1935.
7. Marcia Melton, "An Argument Worth Having," *TCU Magazine,* Spring 2015, https://magazine.tcu.edu/spring-2015/an-argument-worth-having/.
8. "Negroes Attending TCU, Sadler Says," the *Skiff*, November 2, 1951, *TCU Library Exhibits*, accessed May 18, 2022, https://exhibits.tcu.edu/items/show/317.
9. See generally, T. B. Craddock, "Patriotism: The Price Paid by the African American Soldier," *Journal of Veterans Studies* 7, no. 3 (2021): 23–37, http://doi.org/10.21061/jvs.v7i3.260.
10. Matthew Delmont, "Why African-American Soldiers Saw World War II as a Two-Front Battle," *Smithsonian Magazine,* August 24, 2017, accessed June 6, 2022, https://www.smithsonianmag.com/history/why-african-american-soldiers-saw-world-war-ii-two-front-battle-180964616/.
11. Matthew Taub, "'Are We Not American Soldiers?' When the U.S. Military Treated German POWs Better Than Black Troops," *Time,* July 28, 2020, accessed May 17, 2022, https://time.com/5872361/wwii-german-pows-civil-rights/.
12. "Negroes Attending TCU, Sadler Says," the *Skiff*, November 2, 1951, TCU Library Exhibits, accessed May 18, 2022, https://exhibits.tcu.edu/items/show/317.
13. "Trustees Open Brite College to Negroes," *Fort Worth Star-Telegram*, September 7, 1952, *TCU Library Exhibits*, accessed May 11, 2022, https://exhibits.tcu.edu/items/show/318.
14. "Accreditation and Change: From Brite College of the Bible to Brite Divinity School, 1939-1963" in Mark G. Toulouse, Jeffrey Williams, and Dyan M. Dietz, eds., *Institutional Change in Theological Education: A History of Brite Divinity School* (Fort Worth, TX: TCU Press, 2011), 104.
15. This article appears on page one, or the front page. "Brite to Admit Negro Students," the *Skiff* 51, no. 1 (January 29, 1924), accessed September 11, 2022, https://repository.tcu.edu/handle/116099117/14477.
16. "3 Negroes attending seminary," the *Skiff*, September 26, 1952, TCU Library Exhibits, accessed May 11, 2022, https://exhibits.tcu.edu/items/show/320.
17. "Accreditation and Change," 103.
18. "3 Negroes attending seminary."
19. "Lack of Enrollment Ends Negro Classes," the *Skiff*, February 14, 1954, TCU Library Exhibits, accessed May 11, 2022, https://exhibits.tcu.edu/items/show/315.
20. "Negroes Attending TCU, Sadler Says."
21. Sandy A. Wall, "Teacher Relates Blacks' Rise," the *Skiff* 75, no. 62 (February 15, 1977): 2, accessed September 11, 2022, https://repository.tcu.edu/handle/116099117/15949.
22. "4 Negroes to Enroll," the *Skiff,* September 18, 1962, TCU Library Exhibits, accessed May 11, 2022, https://exhibits.tcu.edu/items/show/314.
23. "4 Negroes to Enroll."
24. Sarah Bahari, "Trailblazer in Nursing: Allene Parks Jones '63," *Harris College Quarterly Newsletter*, Winter 2011, January 23, 2012, accessed September 11, 2022, https://magazine.tcu.edu/winter-2011/trailblazer-in-nursing-allene-parks-jones-63/.

25. "Dodgers: Vin Scully Reveals Why Players Wear 42 on Jackie Robinson Day," *Sports Illustrated,* April 16, 2022, accessed May 18, 2022, https://www.si.com/mlb/dodgers/news/dodgers-vin-scully-reveals-why-players-wear-42-on-jackie-robinson-day.

26. "Harris College Desegregates as 6,200 Register in the Round," the *Skiff* 61, no. 2 (September 25, 1962), accessed May 11, 2022, https://repository.tcu.edu/handle/116099117/14873.

27. Nyshicka Jordan and Kelly Morris, "Color Contrast: Taking A Look At 40 Years of Integration and the Road That Brought Us Here," *IMAGE* 31, no. 11–19 (March 2004): 18.

28. Jordan and Morris, "Color Contrast."

29. "Trustees Drop Racial Barriers," the *Skiff*, February 4, 1964, TCU Library Exhibits, accessed May 11, 2022, https://exhibits.tcu.edu/items/show/322.

30. Jordan and Morris, "Color Contrast." N.B.: Mr. Wassenich also submitted a statement to the archives located here: https://repository.tcu.edu/handle/116099117/21243. His story begins on page 16.

31. "Celebrating Black Leadership at TCU," *TCU Magazine*, February 24, 2022, accessed June 6, 2022, https://magazine.tcu.edu/latest-news/lets-do-more-honoring-black-leadership-at-tcu/. N.B.: the same year Ms. Leslie Ekpe was elected as TCU's first Black Graduate Student Senate president.

32. Jordan and Morris, "Color Contrast," 15.

33. Jordan and Morris, "Color Contrast," 15.

34. "Former SMU football player recounts trials of integration," *TCU 360*, September 21, 2007, accessed May 17, 2022, https://www.tcu360.com/story/former-smu-football-player-recounts-trials-of-integration-12289341/.

35. The introduction to the 1939 movie *Gone with the Wind* includes the following text shown onscreen: "There was a land of Cavaliers and cotton fields called the Old South . . . Here in this patrician world the age of Chivalry took its last bow . . . Here was the last ever seen of Knights and their Ladies Fair, of Master and of Slave . . . Look for it only in books, for it is no more than a dream remembered, a Civilization gone with the wind." Frederick Gooding Jr., *Black Oscars: From Mammy to Minny, What the Academy Awards Tell Us about African Americans* (Lanham, MD: Rowman & Littlefield, 2020), 35.

36. Jordan and Morris, "Color Contrast," 18.

37. Margaret Downing, "100 Years White, Only 9 Black," the *Skiff,* January 18, 1973, 8, accessed September 11, 2022, https://repository.tcu.edu/handle/116099117/21237.

38. "Most Pleas Were Reasonable, Eruption Reveals Differences," the *Skiff*, February 9, 1971, TCU Library Exhibits, accessed May 11, 2022, https://exhibits.tcu.edu/items/show/302.

39. Robert Bobbins, "Forums Votes to Invite Klansman," the *Skiff*, November 5, 1974, 1; Robert Robbins, "Speaker Panel OK's Duke's Visit," the *Skiff,* November 8, 1974, 1.

40. "Klan Speaker Canceled," the *Skiff* 73, no. 41 (November 13, 1974), accessed September 11, 2022, https://repository.tcu.edu/handle/116099117/15728.

41. Jordan and Morris, "Color Contrast," 15.

42. See generally, "TCU Hosts Last Witness to Emmett Till Kidnapping," Deborah Ferguson, *NBCDFW*, February 23, 2022, accessed May 18, 2022, https://www.nbcdfw.com/news/local/tcu-hosts-last-witness-to-emmett-till-kidnapping/2897685/; "A Conversation on Race & Education in the 21st Century," *TCU Event Details*, n.d., accessed May 18, 2022, https://chancellor.tcu.edu/initiatives/center-for-connection-culture/speakers/.

43. Kara Rogge, "Black TCU Student Joins White Fraternity," *Fort Worth Star-Telegram*, February 12, 1981, TCU Library Exhibits, accessed May 11, 2022, https://exhibits.tcu.edu/items/show/316, accessed May 17, 2022.

44. Yvonne Webb and Kristie Aylett, "Activity No Game to Some," the *Skiff*, April 7, 1988, 1.

45. Lucy Calvert, "Awareness Starts in Class," *TCU Daily Skiff*, April 20, 1998, 1.

46. Jason Crane, "Black Males Discuss Rights during Forum," the *Skiff*, February 11, 1999.

47. Crane, "Black Males Discuss Rights during Forum."

48. See generally, Vinson Cunningham, "The Argument of 'Afropessimism,'" *The New Yorker*, July 13, 2020, accessed May 17, 2022, https://www.newyorker.com/magazine/2020/07/20/the-argument-of-afropessimism.

49. "LXA Sells Slaves, CAA Gets Profits," *Daily Skiff* 70, no. 33 (October 26, 1971), accessed May 17, 2022, https://repository.tcu.edu/bitstream/handle/116099117/15409/19711026.pdf?sequence=1.

50. "Minutes from the Special Meeting of the Board of Trustees on January 23, 1964 Discussing the University's Stance on Integration," January 23, 1964, TCU Special Collections Minorities at TCU, accessed May 17, 2022, https://repository.tcu.edu/bitstream/handle/116099117/21232/1964-01-23_Trustee_Minutes.pdf?sequence=1&isAllowed=y.

51. For instance, TCU alum Larry Dickson shares that he had an older brother who attempted to seek admission into TCU in the early 1960s unsuccessfully. Dickson elaborates by stating, "Well, at that time, I really didn't know what grounds he was refused, but we all assumed it was based on race. And so, when that happened to our family, quite naturally being a younger brother, I had no intention of coming to TCU after that happened." Dickson is mindful that his brother's attempt was before TCU officially integrated, but still offered, "Because I was four years younger than he, I was never told what the official quote on quote reason was. We all knew he tried to get in and he did not get in. And so, the assumption was that it was based on race, but I can't verify that." See "Interview with Larry Dickson," TCU's Race & Reconciliation Initiative Oral History Project, September, 13, 2021, accessed June 6, 2022, https://repository.tcu.edu/handle/116099117/52684.

52. Photocopy of Trustee Minutes, "Minutes from a Special Meeting of the TCU Board of Trustees, January 23, 1964," TCU Mary Couts Burnett, Library Special Collections, accessed September 12, 2022, https://repository.tcu.edu/handle/116099117/21232https://repository.tcu.edu/handle/116099117/21232.

53. "Negroes Attending TCU, Sadler Says," *TCU Skiff*, November 2, 1951," TCU Library Exhibits, accessed May 11, 2022, https://exhibits.tcu.edu/items/show/289.

54. "Negroes Attending TCU, Sadler Says."

55. "There is no reason what-so-ever for negroes to attend T.C.U. as long as they have schools that can offer the same courses," Letter to Betty Wilkes Pederson, dated December 26, 1951, Records of M. E. Sadler, "Biography, correspondence & press releases," File Box 9, 1950-1965, Mary Couts Burnett Library, Special Collections/TCU Archives, Fort Worth, TX.

56. Tim Madigan conducted an award-winning seven-part journalistic deep dive into the anti-black history of Fort Worth. Tim Madigan, "Showdown on Judkins Street," *Fort Worth Star-Telegram,* October 6, 2002, 16-17A.

57. "Immature Segregationists," the *Skiff* 59, no. 13 (November 4, 1960).

58. Bud Kennedy, "Memories Fading of MLK's Fort Worth Visit, but Landmarks Remain," *Fort Worth Star-Telegram,* January 15, 2022, accessed May 18, 2022, https://www.star-telegram.com/opinion/bud-kennedy/article7231049.html.

59. "Accreditation and Change: From Brite College of the Bible to Brite Divinity School, 1939-1963," in Mark G. Toulouse, Jeffrey Williams, and Dyan M. Dietz, eds., *Institutional Change in Theological Education: A History of Brite Divinity School* (Fort Worth, TX: TCU Press, 2011), 104.

60. The *Skiff* 59, no. 37 (March 10, 1961).

61. Jordan and Morris, "Color Contrast," 15–16.

62. "Photocopy of statement by Moudy on Race," TCU Digital Repository, Special Collections/TCU Archives and Historical Materials/Minorities at TCU, June 7, 1963, accessed May 18, 2022, https://repository.tcu.edu/handle/116099117/21231.

63. Jordan and Morris, "Color Contrast," 16.

64. Jordan and Morris, "Color Contrast," 18.

65. Jordan and Morris, "Color Contrast," 16.

66. "Basic Classification Description," *Carnegie Classification of Institutions of Higher Education*, n.d., accessed May 18, 2022, https://carnegieclassifications.iu.edu/classification_descriptions/basic.php.

67. "Rice University Between Decisions: from Co-Education to Integration (1957-1970)," *Woodson Research Center*, Fondren Library, Rice University, n.d., accessed May 18, 2022, https://digitalprojects.rice.edu/wrc/between-decisions/exhibits/show/between-decisions/race.

68. "Rice University Between Decisions."

69. "Rice University Between Decisions."

70. Jerome A. Moore, *Texas Christian University: A Hundred Years of History* (Fort Worth, TX: TCU Press, 1974), 212.

Chapter 4

1. Marcia Melton, "An Argument Worth Having," *TCU Magazine*, Spring 2015, https://magazine.tcu.edu/spring-2015/an-argument-worth-having/.

2. Melton, "An Argument Worth Having." The Wiley debate team returned to TCU in 1936; see also https://repository.tcu.edu/handle/116099117/19750.

3. Andrew Chavez, "Former SMU Football player Recounts Trials of Integration," *TCU Skiff* 105, no. 19 (September 21, 2007), https://repository.tcu.edu/handle/116099117/45922.

4. "Meet Four Men Who Broke The NFL's Color Line: How It Happened," NFPLA, accessed September 1, 2022, https://nflpa.com/posts/meet-the-four-men-who-broke-the-nfl-s-color-line.

5. Chavez, "Former SMU Football player Recounts Trials of Integration."

6. Greg Burden, Johnny Livengood, and George Stone, "Walkout Spurs Black Outcry," the *Skiff*, February 5, 1971, https://repository.tcu.edu/handle/116099117/15353.

7. "Mission & History," Texas Christian University, accessed September 13, 2022, www.tcu.edu/about/mission-history.

8. "James Cash's No. 54 jersey to be retired at Air Force game Saturday," *TCU 360* Staff, January 26, 2011, https://tcu360.com/2011/01/26/james-cash-s-no-54-jersey-to-be-retired-at-air-force-game-saturday-12448527/#:~:text=54%20jersey%20retired%20on%20Jan,ever%20walk%20on%20our%20campus.

9. "Dr. James Cash to be Honored with TCU Campus Monument," *GoFrogs.com*, April, 21, 2021, https://gofrogs.com/news/2021/4/21/mens-basketball-dr-james-cash-to-be-honored-with-tcu-campus-monument.aspx.

10. Will Holden, "Forget Me Not: Linzy Cole Quietly Revolutionized TCU Football," The MTN, February 12, 2012, http://www.themtn.tv/02/10/12/Forget-Me-Not-Linzy-Cole-Quietly-Revolut/landing.html?blockID=649042&feedID=2984.

11. Holden, "Forget Me Not."
12. Holden, "Forget Me Not."
13. Holden, "Forget Me Not."
14. Rachel Stowe Master, "Attorney Ron Hurdle Broke Barriers at TCU," *TCU Magazine*, Winter 2021, https://magazine.tcu.edu/winter-2021/ron-hurdle-cheerleader-attorney/.
15. Master, "Attorney Ron Hurdle Broke Barriers at TCU."
16. Burden, Livengood, and Stone, "Walkout Spurs Black Outcry."
17. Burden, Livengood, and Stone, "Walkout Spurs Black Outcry."
18. "African American firsts at TCU," *TCU Magazine*: Mem'ries Sweet Blog, February 18, 2009, http://thetcumagazine.blogspot.com/2009/02/african-american-firsts-at-tcu.html.
19. Education Amendments Act of 1972, 20 U.S.C. §§1681 - 1688 (2018).
20. TCU Women's Basketball Fact Book Archives 2021-2022, Texas Christian University Athletics, https://gofrogs.com/sports/2021/10/13/wbb-fact-books.aspx?id=4050.
21. Block T Association, Hall of Fame Class of 2003, accessed September 10, 2022, https://blockt.tcu.edu/hall-of-fame-2/.
22. Burden, Livengood, and Stone, "Walkout Spurs Black Outcry."
23. Texas Christian University, the *Horned Frog*, Fort Worth, Texas: 1993, 148, TCU Special Collections.
24. "Shell Dailey," IMG Academy, accessed September 13, 2022, https://www.imgacademy.com/people/shell-dailey.
25. Mike Jones, "Robinson to take over TCU's women's basketball program," *Fort Worth Star-Telegram*, April 13, 1993.
26. Chris Kelley, "Athletic Recruiter Resigns," the *Skiff*, March 28, 1980.
27. "Kim Johnson," TCU Athletics, Texas Christian University Athletics, accessed September 13, 2022, https://gofrogs.com/staff-directory/kim-johnson/176.
28. "Dougherty fired after posting 75-108 record in six seasons at TCU," *Associated Press,* March 16, 2008, https://www.espn.com/mens-college-basketball/news/story?id=3297296.
29. "Former Head Basketball Coach Neil Dougherty Dies at age 50," *TCU 360*, July 8, 2011
30. Rick Waters, "First Person Basketball Coach Trent Johnson," Winter 2012, https://magazine.tcu.edu/winter-2012/first-person-basketball-coach-trent-johnson/.
31. "Trent Johnson," SRCBB, accessed September 10, 2022, sports-reference.com/cbb.
32. "Darrly Anderson," TCU Athletics, accessed September 13, 2022, https://gofrogs.com/sports/womens-cross-country/roster/coaches/darryl-anderson/456.
33. "Darrly Anderson."
34. "Eric Bell," TCU Athletics, accessed September 13, 2022, https://gofrogs.com/sports/womens-soccer/roster/coaches/eric-bell/986.
35. "Eric Bell."

Chapter 5

1. Larry Dickson, "Oral History Interview with Larry Dickson," 2021, Interview by Sylviane Greensword, Race and Reconciliation Initiative Oral History Project, Texas Christian University, https://repository.tcu.edu/handle/116099117/52346.
2. Ron Hurdle, "Oral History Interview with Ron Hurdle," 2021, Interview by Sylviane Greensword, Race and Reconciliation Initiative Oral History Project, Texas Christian University, https://repository.tcu.edu/handle/116099117/52346.
3. Tasha Ronnette Coble Ginn, *A Historical Study of I. M. Terrell High School: Its Legacy and Implications for Improved Education of Black Students* (Order No. 28493915). Doctoral Dissertation, Texas Christian University, 2021, http://library.tcu.edu/PURL/EZproxy_link.asp?/login?url=https://www.proquest.com/dissertations-theses/historical-study-i-m-terrell-high-school-legacy/docview/2571036533/se-2.
4. Marian Brooks Bryant, "Oral History Interview Marian Brooks Bryant," 2021, Interview by Sylviane Greensword, Race and Reconciliation Initiative Oral History Project, Texas Christian University, https://repository.tcu.edu/handle/116099117/52346.
5. The *Skiff*, September 21, 2007.
6. Harvard Business School, "A Campus Built on Philanthropy," https://www.hbs.edu/about/campus-and-culture/campus-built-on-philanthropy/Pages/cash-house.aspx.
7. James Cash, "Oral History Interview with James Cash," 2021, Interview by Sylviane Greensword and Frederick Gooding Jr., Race and Reconciliation Initiative Oral History Project, Texas Christian University, https://repository.tcu.edu/handle/116099117/52346.
8. The *Skiff*, February 15, 1977.
9. https://www.tcu360.com/2021/04/historical-findings-plans-for-action-announced-at-tcus-first-reconciliation-day/.
10. Leon Reed Jr., "Interview with Leon Reed, Jr.," 2021, Interview by Sylviane Greensword, Race and Reconciliation Initiative Oral History Project, Texas Christian University, https://repository.tcu.edu/handle/116099117/52346.
11. "Oral History Interview with Leon Reed, Jr.," 2022, Interview by Sylviane Greensword, Race and Reconciliation Initiative Oral History Project, Texas Christian University, https://repository.tcu.edu/handle/116099117/52346."
12. "Oral History Interview with Leon Reed, Jr."
13. Zuberi Williams, "Oral History Interview with Zuberi Williams," 2022, Interview by Sylviane Greensword, Race and Reconciliation Initiative Oral History Project, Texas Christian University, https://repository.tcu.edu/handle/116099117/52346.
14. "New alumni alliance formed: Group to unite African-American graduates," the *Skiff*, November 19, 1999, http://www.skiff.tcu.edu/SkiffWeb111999/News.html.
15. Sarah Bahari, "Trailblazer in Nursing: Allene Parks Jones '63," *TCU Magazine*, 2011, https://magazine.tcu.edu/winter-2011/trailblazer-in-nursing-allene-parks-jones-63/
16. Rick Waters, "Allene Jones '63 1933-2015," *TCU Magazine*, 2015, https://magazine.tcu.edu/summer-2015/allene-jones-631933-2015/.
17. "Alumna Paints Tribute to TCU's First African-American Faculty Member," Bob Schieffer College of Communication Strategic Communication News, April 1, 2019, https://schieffercollege.tcu.edu/stratcomm/news/alumna-paints-tribute-to-tcus-first-african-american-faculty-member/.

18. The *Skiff*, February 5, 1971.
19. "Oral History Interview with Jennifer Giddings Brooks," 2021, Interview by Sylviane Greensword, Race and Reconciliation Initiative Oral History Project, Texas Christian University, https://repository.tcu.edu/handle/116099117/52346.
20. Jennifer Giddings Brooks. *Six outstanding contemporary African-American female educators: A biographical study*. Doctoral Dissertation, Texas Woman's University, 1993.
21. "Center for Public Education & Community Engagement," Texas Christian University College of Education, https://coe.tcu.edu/research-outreach/center-for-public-education/index.php.
22. Ronald Parker, "Oral History Interview with Ronald Parker," 2022, Interview by Sylviane Greensword, Race and Reconciliation Initiative Oral History Project, Texas Christian University, https://repository.tcu.edu/handle/116099117/52346.
23. Darron Turner, "Interview with Dr. Darron Turner," Interview by Christie Shields, The TCU Oral History Project, https://tcu.digication.com/the_tcu_oral_history_project/Darron_Turner.
24. "Alumni Give Back through Black Alliance," the *Skiff*, February 21, 2001, https://skiff.tcu.edu/SkiffWeb022101/alumni.html.
25. Zoranna Jones, "Oral History Interview with Zoranna Jones," 2021, Interview by Sylviane Greensword, Race and Reconciliation Initiative Oral History Project, Texas Christian University, https://repository.tcu.edu/handle/116099117/52684.
26. Zoranna Jones, "Oral History Interview with Zoranna Jones."

Chapter 6

1. The *Skiff*, December 6, 1963, https://repository.tcu.edu/handle/116099117/14951.
2. "Race and Reconciliation Initiative Oral History Project," Texas Christian University, https://repository.tcu.edu/handle/116099117/52346.
3. NB: One of the entering five students, Marian Brooks Bryant, was valedictorian for local Fort Worth high school I. M. Terrell in 1964.
4. Marian Brooks Bryant, "Oral History Interview with Marian Brooks Bryant," 2021, Interview by Sylviane Greensword, Race and Reconciliation Initiative Oral History Project, Texas Christian University, https://repository.tcu.edu/handle/116099117/52346.
5. Marian Brooks Bryant, "Oral History Interview with Marian Brooks Bryant."
6. "Through the Halls," the *Skiff*, February 15, 2001, http://www.skiff.tcu.edu/skiffweb021501/life.html."
7. The *Skiff*, February 15, 2001.
8. "Answer in Sight for Black Woes?" the *Skiff*, February 9, 1971
9. "Black Minor Passed for Next Fall," the *Skiff*, April 2, 1971, accessed September 11, 2022, https://repository.tcu.edu/handle/116099117/15369; "Black Studies Seen Optimistically," the *Skiff*, May 7, 1971, accessed September 11, 2022, https://repository.tcu.edu/handle/116099117/15376; "Some Black Students Still Not Satisfied," the *Skiff*, September 8, 1971, accessed September 11, 2022, https://repository.tcu.edu/handle/116099117/15382.
10. "TCU Charged with Race Bias," the *Skiff*, April 2, 1971, accessed September 11, 2022, https://repository.tcu.edu/handle/116099117/15687.

11. "Spokesman Ray Turner Explains NAACP Complaints," the *Horned Frog*, 1974, p. 13.
12. "HEW to Investigate Race Bias," the *Skiff,* May 2, 1974, https://repository.tcu.edu/bitstream/handle/116099117/15691/19740502.pdf?sequence=1&isAllowed=y; "HEW report caught in 'backlog'," The *Skiff*, March 12, 1976.
13. William E. Tucker, "Letter to John Mark Williams, Tau Chi Upsilon," 1980.
14. John Mark Williams, "Oral History Interview with members of Tau Chi Upsilon," 2021, Interview by Sylviane Greensword, Race and Reconciliation Initiative Oral History Project, Texas Christian University, https://repository.tcu.edu/handle/116099117/52684.
15. The *Skiff* 67, no. 46, https://repository.tcu.edu/handle/116099117/15256; The *Horned Frog* (1970): 141, https://repository.tcu.edu/handle/116099117/11096.
16. "Activity No Game to Some," the *Skiff*, April 7, 1988, https://repository.tcu.edu/bitstream/handle/116099117/16992/19880407.pdf?sequence=1&isAllowed=y.
17. The *Skiff*, April 7, 1988, https://repository.tcu.edu/handle/116099117/16992m.
18. Linda Moore, "Oral History Interview with Linda Moore," 2021, Interview by Sylviane Greensword, Race and Reconciliation Initiative Oral History Project, Texas Christian University, https://repository.tcu.edu/handle/116099117/52684.
19. L. Michelle Smith, "Oral History Interview with L. Michelle Smith," 2022, Interview by Sylviane Greensword, Race and Reconciliation Initiative Oral History Project, Texas Christian University, https://repository.tcu.edu/handle/116099117/52684.
20. L. Michelle Smith, LinkedIn post, https://www.linkedin.com/posts/lmichellesmith_leadership-mlkday-theblackchurch-activity-6888922084236439552-jvl6.
21. The *Skiff*, February 10, 1998.
22. Leon Reed, "Oral History Interview with Leon Reed," 2021, Interview by Sylviane Greensword, Race and Reconciliation Initiative Oral History Project, Texas Christian University, https://repository.tcu.edu/handle/116099117/52684.
23. "Black Males Discuss Rights During Forum," the *Skiff*, February 11, 1999.
24. "Students Denounce Area Violence," the *Skiff*, February 1, 1999, https://repository.tcu.edu/handle/116099117/18112.
25. Tamera Hyatte, "Organizers of Protests Release List of Demands," *TCU 360*, October 18, 2016, https://www.tcu360.com/2016/10/the-organizers-of-the-protests-release-list-of-demands/#:~:text=These%20include%20online%20sensitivity%20training,hate%20speech%20and%20micro%2Daggressions.
26. Shanel Alexander, "Oral History Interview with Shanel Alexander," 2021, Interview by Sylviane Greensword, Race and Reconciliation Initiative Oral History Project, Texas Christian University, https://repository.tcu.edu/handle/116099117/52684.
27. Emily Laff, "Oral History Interview with Emily Laff," 2021, Interview by Sylviane Greensword, Race and Reconciliation Initiative Oral History Project, Texas Christian University, https://repository.tcu.edu/handle/116099117/52684.
28. "Students collaborate with faculty on African-American studies minor," *TCU 360*, October 6, 2015, https://www.tcu360.com/2015/10/students-collaborate-with-faculty-on-african-american-studies-minor/; Claire Sanders, "Interview with Claire Sanders" 2022, Interview by Sylviane Greensword, Race and Reconciliation Initiative Oral History Project, Texas Christian University, https://repository.tcu.edu/handle/116099117/52684.

Chapter 7

1. Glossary for Understanding the Dismantling Structural Racism/Promoting Racial Equity Analysis, s.v. "Structural Racism (noun)," accessed September 13, 2022.
2. Marice Ritcher, "Fort Worth still growing fast but can't claim 12th largest city ranking," *Fort Worth Business Press*, June 1, 2022, https://fortworthbusiness.com/business/13-again-fort-worth-still-growing-but-slips-from-12th-largest-city-ranking/.
3. "The Establishment of Fort Worth," Welcome to the City of Fort Worth, accessed September 13, 2022, https://www.fortworthtexas.gov/about/history.
4. Doualy Xaykaothao, "He Wanted to Be a Peacekeeper: Bronze Statue Honors Man Who Founded Fort Worth," *KERA News*, June 6, 2014, https://www.keranews.org/texas-news/2014-06-06/he-wanted-to-be-a-peacekeeper-bronze-statue-honors-man-who-founded-fort-worth.
5. Richard F. Selcer, *A History of Fort Worth in Black and White: 165 Years of African-American Life* (Denton, TX: University of North Texas Press), 19.
6. Olivia B. Waxman, "'Alarmingly Similar,' What the Chaos Around Lincoln's First Inauguration Can Tell Us About Today," *TIME*, January 15, 2021.
7. Vicki Betts, "Marshall Texas Republican," *By Title*, 2016, https://scholarworks.uttyler.edu/cw_newstitles/66/.
8. Donald Reynolds, "Texas Troubles," *Texas State Historical Association*, November 1, 1995, https://www.tshaonline.org/handbook/entries/texas-troubles.
9. Reynolds, "Texas Troubles."
10. Reynolds, "Texas Troubles."
11. "No Man's Land Will be Made Holocaust by Police," *Fort Worth Star-Telegram* 35, no. 65 (March 29, 1915), 12.
12. Selcer, *A History of Fort Worth in Black and White*, 86
13. Reby Cary, "We've Come This Far: A 2007 Retrospective on Blacks in Fort Worth and Tarrant County," Self-published, n.d.
14. Deah Berry Mitchell, "Fort Worth History: William 'Gooseneck Bill' McDonald," Visit Fort Worth, October 15, 2020, https://www.fortworth.com/blog/post/fort-worth-history-william-gooseneck-mcdonald/.
15. "The Story of William 'Gooseneck' McDonald," Tarrant County Black Historical and Genealogical Society, 2021, https://www.youtube.com/watch?v=GHqr4SBQ5Vw.
16. "The Story of William 'Gooseneck' McDonald."
17. "In Market: When Fort Worth was Green Booked," *Fort Worth Business Press*, March 8, 2019, https://fortworthbusiness.com/opinion/in-market-when-fort-worth-was-green-booked/.
18. "In Market: When Fort Worth Was Green Booked."
19. Cary, "We've Come This Far," 34.
20. Cary, "We've Come This Far," 55.
21. Selcer, *A History of Fort Worth in Black and White*, 173.
22. Selcer, *A History of Fort Worth in Black and White*, 55.

23. Selcer, *A History of Fort Worth in Black and White*, 55.
24. Selcer, *A History of Fort Worth in Black and White*, 62.
25. Gayle Henson, "Isaiah Milligan Terrell," Texas State Historical Association, May 1, 2007, https://www.tshaonline.org/handbook/entries/terrell-isaiah-milligan-im.
26. Selcer, *A History of Fort Worth in Black and White*, 163.
27. Selcer, *A History of Fort Worth in Black and White*, 163.
28. "Negro Industrial Building Complete," *Fort Worth Star-Telegram* 26, no. 165 (June 28, 1908).
29. Selcer, *A History of Fort Worth in Black and White*, 163.
30. Selcer, *A History of Fort Worth in Black and White*, 165.
31. Kitty Barry, "Jarvis Institute Is Memorial to Loved and Faithful Slaves," *Fort Worth Star-Telegram* 31, no. 52 (March 8, 1913).
32. Selcer, *A History of Fort Worth in Black and White*, 162.
33. Colby Hall, *History of Texas Christian University: A College of the Cattle Frontier* (Fort Worth, TX: TCU Press, 1947). NB: Jarvis was also the first president of the board of trustees appointed in 1889, Hall, *History of Texas Christian University*, 31, and board of trustee meeting minutes, Sept 27, 1889. Jarvis is listed as a "board of director" in an early catalog, but once the Disciples took over the school in 1889, the ruling body of the school was formalized as the Board of Trustees. Also of note, Ida Jarvis Van Zandt was the first female trustee of TCU, appointed in 1929.
34. "Negroes Attending TCU, Sadler Says," *TCU Skiff*, November 2, 1951, TCU Library Exhibits, accessed September 14, 2022, https://exhibits.tcu.edu/items/show/289.
35. "Lack of Enrollment Ends Negro Classes," the *Skiff*, February 14, 1954, https://repository.tcu.edu/handle/116099117/14525.
36. "Lack of Enrollment Ends Negro Classes."
37. "Lack of Enrollment Ends Negro Classes."
38. Mike Walsh, Letter to Faculty and Staff, Fort Worth, Texas, December 9, 1963, TCU Special Collections.
39. "Students Rejecting Plea," the *Skiff* 61, no. 19 (November 22, 1963).
40. "Minutes from a Special Meeting of the TCU Board of Trustees, January 23, 1964," TCU Library Exhibits, accessed September 14, 2022, https://exhibits.tcu.edu/items/show/292.
41. "Minutes from a Special Meeting of the TCU Board of Trustees, January 23, 1964."
42. "Minutes from a Special Meeting of the TCU Board of Trustees, March 17, 1964."

Chapter 8

1. Callan Davenport, "Who was Janus, the Roman god of beginnings and endings?" *The Conversation,* December 31, 2017, https://theconversation.com/who-was-janus-the-roman-god-of-beginnings-and-endings-86853, accessed May 17, 2022.
2. Joshua Bote, "'A riot is the language of the unheard': MLK's powerful quote resonates amid George Floyd protests," *USA Today,* May 29, 2020, accessed May 18, 2022, https://www.usatoday.com/story/news/nation/2020/05/29/minneapolis-protest-martin-luther-king-quote-riot-george-floyd/5282486002/.

3. Marcia Melton, "Protesting the Library in the 1960s," *TCU Magazine*, Winter 2016, accessed September 11, 2022, https://magazine.tcu.edu/winter-2016/protesting-the-library-in-the-1960s/.
4. Joe William Trotter Jr., *Workers on Arrival: Black Labor in the Making of America* (Oakland, CA: University of California Press, 2019), 109.
5. "Revolt," the *Horned Frog* 59, (1963): 66-69, accessed September 11, 2022, https://repository.tcu.edu/handle/116099117/11089.
6. "Walkout Spurs Black Outcry," the *Skiff*, February 5, 1971, TCU Library Exhibits, accessed May 17, 2022, https://exhibits.tcu.edu/items/show/309.
7. "Welcome Jim Pittman and Staff," the *Horned Frog* 67, (1971): 102, accessed September 11, 2022, https://repository.tcu.edu/handle/116099117/11097.
8. "Most Pleas Were Reasonable, Eruption Reveals Differences," the *Skiff,* February 9, 1971, *TCU Library Exhibits*, accessed May 17, 2022, https://exhibits.tcu.edu/items/show/302.
9. "Most Pleas Were Reasonable, Eruption Reveals Differences."
10. "Welcome Jim Pittman and Staff," the *Horned Frog* 67, (1971): 102, accessed September 11, 2022, https://repository.tcu.edu/handle/116099117/11097.
11. Rich Doty, "Spokesman Ray Turner Explains NAACP Complaints," *IMAGE* 2, no. 2 (1974): 13-16, accessed September 11, 2022, https://repository.tcu.edu/handle/116099117/21334. NB: Published twice a semester, *IMAGE* was a periodical that welcomed "submission of articles, letters, short stories, poetry and photographs from TCU students, faculty or administrators." *IMAGE* was a distinct publication from the yearbook. When TCU did not have a yearbook published in 1974, these periodical publications of *IMAGE* were an experimental stand in.
12. Doty, "Spokesman Ray Turner," 13.
13. Doty, "Spokesman Ray Turner," 14.
14. Doty, "Spokesman Ray Turner," 14.
15. Doty, "Spokesman Ray Turner," 16.
16. Kelly Huang and Valeria Olivares, "Why Are So Few Black Professors Tenured? Texas Has Made Little Progress Despite Promises of Change," *Dallas Morning News,* July 15, 2021, accessed May 18, 2022, https://www.dallasnews.com/news/education/2021/07/15/why-are-so-few-black-professors-tenured-texas-has-made-little-progress-despite-promises-of-change/.
17. Quantalane Henry, "Discrimination No Barrier for Bell," *etCetera,* September 28, 1981, 2, https://repository.tcu.edu/handle/116099117/16312.
18. Lisa Deeley, "TCU Charged with Race Bias: EEOC to Investigate Claim," the *Skiff* 72, no. 99 (April 25, 1974), accessed September 11, 2022, https://repository.tcu.edu/handle/116099117/15687.
19. "In its first year of existence, the EEOC received over two hundred complaints a week and had a backlog of three thousand cases—although none directly involved federal actors or agencies. Furthermore, only five conciliators were on staff to render decisions. By August 1968, the average case took sixteen months to complete. By 1969, the backlog had grown to nearly two years." Frederick Gooding Jr., *American Dream Deferred: Black Federal Workers in Washington, DC, 1941-1981* (Pittsburgh, PA: University of Pittsburgh Press, 2018), 131.

20. Lisa Deeley Smith, "HEW Report Caught in 'Backlog': No Results Yet from 2-Year Investigation," *Daily Skiff* 74, no. 79 (March 12, 1976), accessed September 11, 2022, https://repository.tcu.edu/handle/116099117/15871.

21. Tamera Hyatte, "Organizers of Protests Release List of Demands," *TCU360,* October 18, 2016, accessed May 17, 2022, https://www.tcu360.com/2016/10/the-organizers-of-the-protests-release-list-of-demands/.

22. Hunter Hampton, "Losing Our Religion: Texas's College Football Identity Crisis," *Texas Monthly,* August 17, 2021, accessed May 18, 2022, https://www.texasmonthly.com/arts-entertainment/texas-college-football-religion/.

23. Brandon Kitchin, "'More than a Major. A Movement,'" *TCU360,* January 25, 2018, accessed May 17, 2022, https://www.tcu360.com/2018/01/more-than-a-major-a-movement/.

24. Kaley Johnson, "TCU Student's Lawsuit Says Faculty 'Dehumanized' Her, School Ignored Reports of Racism," *Fort Worth Star-Telegram,* January 27, 2020, accessed May 18, 2022, https://www.star-telegram.com/news/local/education/article239541988.html.

25. J. D. Pells, "Settlement Reached between TCU and Former Students, Alumni in Lawsuit," *TCU360,* November 4, 2021, accessed May 17, 2022, https://www.tcu360.com/2021/11/settlement-reached-in-lawsuit-between-former-tcu-students-faculty/.

26. Hannah Patterson, "WGST Feature Story: Student Social Justice Group, CUJE, Awaits Campus Change after Demands," *TCU School of Interdisciplinary Studies, SIS News*, n.d., accessed June 6, 2022, https://sis.tcu.edu/wgst-feature-story-student-social-justice-group-cuje-awaits-campus-change-after-demands/.

27. "TCU Diverse History Project," *TCU Women & Gender Studies*, n.d., accessed May 18, 2022, https://sis.tcu.edu/wgst/initiatives/tcu-diverse-history-project/.

28. "Artwork Creates Space to Learn, Partner with NAIP," *TCU News,* April 19, 2022, accessed May 18, 2022, https://www.tcu.edu/news/2022/artwork-creates-space-to-learn-partner-with-naip.php.

29. See "About," *TCU Race & Reconciliation Initiative,* n.d., accessed September 11, 2022, https://www.tcu.edu/race-reconciliation-initiative/about/index.php.

30. "Race & Reconciliation First Year Survey Report, April 21, 2021," *TCU Race & Reconciliation Initiative*, April 21, 2021, accessed May 18, 2022, https://www.tcu.edu/race-reconciliation-initiative/files/rri-first-year-survey-report.pdf, 28.

31. "Past, Present and Future TCU's Race & Reconciliation Initiative Shares and Celebrates Progress at Second Annual Reconciliation Day," *Texas Christian University in Campus Life*, April 25, 2022, accessed May 18, 2022, https://stories.tcu.edu/past-present-and-future.

32. Mariana Rivas, "'We're Not Going to Sugarcoat This': Students, Faculty Grapple with TCU's Racist Past," *Fort Worth Star-Telegram*, April 21, 2022, accessed May 18, 2022, https://www.star-telegram.com/news/local/crossroads-lab/article260606962.html.

33. Joseph Lynn Clark, *Thank God We Made It! A Family Affair with Education* (Austin, TX: University of Texas Press, 1969), 361.

34. Clark, *Thank God We Made It!*, 359.

35. Clark, *Thank God We Made It!*, 364; also see Randolph Clark, "Charley Thorp," *Christian Courier,* September 1927.

36. "Not a single statue honored a Black person's legacy until 1974. That has had very real repercussions," *Fast Company,* February 17, 2022, accessed May 18, 2022, https://www.fastcompany.com/90722199/not-a-single-statue-honored-a-black-persons-legacy-until-1974-that-has-had-very-real-repercussions.

37. "Race & Reconciliation First Year Survey Report, April 21, 2021," *TCU Race & Reconciliation Initiative*, April 21, 2021, 12, accessed May 18, 2022, https://www.tcu.edu/race-reconciliation-initiative/files/rri-first-year-survey-report.pdf.

38. Quentin Stevens and Karen A. Franck, *Memorials as Spaces of Engagement: Design, Use and Meaning* (New York, NY: Routledge, 2016), 139.

39. Donald Martin Reynolds, *Monuments and Masterpieces: Histories and Views of Public Sculpture in New York City* (New York, NY: Macmillan Publishing Company, 1988), xi.

40. Carol Morris Little, *A Comprehensive Guide to Outdoor Sculpture in Texas* (Austin, TX: University of Texas Press, 1996), 1.

41. Audra D. S. Burch and Luke Vander Ploeg, "Buffalo Shooting Highlights Rise of Hate Crimes against Black Americans," *New York Times,* May 17, 2022, accessed May 18, 2022, https://www.nytimes.com/2022/05/16/us/hate-crimes-black-african-americans.html.

42. Randolph Clark, "Charley Thorp," *Christian Courier,* September 1927.

Index

About the Authors

Frederick W. Gooding Jr. is an associate history professor and the inaugural holder of the Dr. Ronald E. Moore Endowed Professor of the Humanities at Texas Christian University. "Dr. G," as he is affectionately known, also served as inaugural chair of TCU's Race & Reconciliation Initiative from 2020–2022.

Sylviane Ngandu-Kalenga Greensword has a PhD in geography and anthropology from Louisiana State University. She is a postdoctoral fellow at TCU's Race and Reconciliation Initiative, where she directs archival research and oral history. Her work centers on ethnic identity and cultural performance in the African Diaspora.

Marcellis R. Perkins is a Virginia native and a current doctoral student at TCU in Fort Worth, Texas, where he also completed his master's. Before TCU, Perkins graduated from The College of the Holy Cross where he earned a BA in sociology with a minor in philosophy.